Gift of

The John W. Bowman Family
in memory of
TIMOTHY DILLON BOWMAN

Antitrust Law

Richard A. Posner

Antitrust Law
An Economic Perspective

The University of Chicago Press
Chicago and London

The University of Chicago Press, Chicago 60637
The University of Chicago Press, Ltd., London

© 1976 by The University of Chicago
All rights reserved. Published 1976
Printed in the United States of America

Library of Congress Cataloging in Publication Data
Posner, Richard A.
   Antitrust law, an economic perspective.

   Includes bibliographical references and index.
   1. Antitrust law—United States.   1.   Title.
KF1649.P66   343'.73'072   76-598
ISBN 0-226-67557-2

RICHARD A. POSNER is professor of law at the
University of Chicago Law School. He is the author
of *Economic Analysis of Law* and *Antitrust: Cases,
Economic Notes, and Other Materials*, and of
numerous articles in scholarly journals.

Contents

Preface

This book had its genesis in a series of articles, written over the past seven years, dealing with various problems in the legal and economic analysis of antitrust policy. Implicit in these articles, I have come to realize, is a thorough dissatisfaction with the existing state of antitrust and a reasonably detailed blueprint for its overhaul.

During the period in which these articles were appearing, the antitrust laws were achieving a level of prominence in public discussion such as they had not known since the days of Thurman Arnold in the early 1940s. The ITT "scandal," the filing by the Justice Department of well-publicized actions designed to break up IBM and AT&T, the explosion of private antitrust actions exemplified by the judgment (later reversed) of almost $300 million that Telex obtained against IBM, the growing tendency to attribute economic problems—recession, inflation, high gasoline prices, or whatever—to the conspiratorial machinations of Big Business, and the recent amendment to the Sherman Act making violation of the act a felony punishable by up to three years imprisonment and (in the case of corporate defendants) a $1 million fine—all have served to rivet the nation's attention on antitrust policy. But more than notoriety is involved. The reach of antitrust policy has broadened and its thrust has deepened, and in the process confusion about both its aims and methods has grown. The conventional tools of antitrust analysis have not stood up well under the pressures of rapid expansion of the role and importance of antitrust enforcement.

It seems timely, therefore, to try to place a distinctive approach to antitrust before a somewhat larger audience than the readership of the scholarly journals in which my articles on antitrust have appeared. I thought at first that the articles could be reprinted with few changes, but a rereading has convinced me that a collection of the unrevised articles would contain too much detail, too much repetition, and too many gaps to sustain a coherent argument. What I have done instead is to take portions of some of the articles and revise them, rearrange them, and combine them with new material in order to create what I hope is a cohesive book.

Chapters 1–4 are new, although chapter 2 ("The Costs of Monopoly") draws on ideas developed more fully in an article published recently in the *Journal of Political Economy*,[1] and chapter 4 ("Price Fixing and the Oligopoly Problem") draws heavily on my previous writings on the subject.[2] Chapter 5 ("Breaking Up Large Firms") is a revised version of a previously published article on the subject,[3] with the addition of heretofore unpublished empirical results. Chapter 6 ("Horizontal Mergers, Potential Competition, and Market Definition") reprints with some revisions two parts of a recent *Columbia Law Review* article;[4] the section on market definition is new.[5] Chapter 7 ("Collusion: Two Problems of Characterization") combines a revision of another part of the *Columbia Law Review* article[6] with a previously unpublished analysis of the Supreme Court's decisions dealing with the exchange of information among competitors. Chapter 8 ("Exclusionary Practices, Real and Imagined") is a substantially revised and expanded version of a similarly titled article.[7] Chapters 9 and 10 are entirely new, and the Appendix largely so.[8]

1. Richard A. Posner, "The Social Costs of Monopoly and Regulation," 83 *J. Pol. Econ.* 807 (1975).

2. See Richard A. Posner, "Oligopoly and the Antitrust Laws: A Suggested Approach," 21 *Stan. L. Rev.* 1562, 1563–87 (1969); "A Program for the Antitrust Division," 38 *U. Chi. L. Rev.* 500, 514–22 (1971); *Antitrust: Cases, Economic Notes, and Other Materials* 128–35 (1974).

3. "Problems of a Policy of Deconcentration," in *Industrial Concentration: The New Learning* 393–400 (Harvey J. Goldschmid, H. Michael Mann, & J. Fred Weston eds. 1974). In slightly different form this piece appears in my *Antitrust: Cases, Economic Notes, and Other Materials*, supra note 2, at 520–25.

4. "Antitrust Policy and the Supreme Court: An Analysis of the Restricted Distribution, Horizontal Merger and Potential Competition Decisions," 75 *Colum. L. Rev.* 282, 299–325 (1975).

5. However, it incorporates with minor revisions pp. 1598–1601 of my *Stanford Law Review* article, supra note 2.

6. Note 4 supra at 283–99.

7. "Exclusionary Practices and the Antitrust Laws," 41 *U. Chi. L. Rev.* 506 (1974).

8. However, the Appendix borrows a few pages from my *Journal of Political Economy* article, supra note 1.

For permission to reprint portions of my published writings, I am grateful to the following: "Oligopoly and the Antitrust Laws: A Suggested Approach," *Stanford Law Review* (copyright © 1969, Board of Trustees, Leland Stanford Junior University) 21 (1969): 1562–87, 1598–1601; "Antitrust Policy and the Supreme Court: An Analysis of the Restricted Distribution, Horizontal Merger and Potential Competition Decisions," *Columbia Law Review* (copyright © 1975, Directors of the Columbia Law Review Association, Inc.) 75 (1975): 282–327; "A Program for the Antitrust Division," *University of Chicago Law Review* 38 (1971): 514–22; "Exclusionary Practices and the Antitrust Laws," *University of Chicago Law Review* 41 (1974): 506–35; *Industrial Concentration: The New Learning*, Little, Brown & Co., 1974, pp. 393–400; *Antitrust: Cases, Economic Notes, and Other Materials*, copyright © 1974, West Publishing Co., 1974, pp. 128–35, 520–25; "The Social Costs of Monopoly and Regulation," *Journal of Political Economy* (copyright © 1975, University of Chicago Press) 83 (1975): 812–20.

The fundamental approach of the book can be described simply. It is to develop the implications for antitrust policy of the assumption that the proper purpose of the antitrust laws is to promote competition, as that term is understood in economics. This assumption is defended in chapter 2 and elsewhere throughout the book. In many cases the implications turn out to be startling ones. They lead me to propose fundamental changes in the antitrust principles governing collusion, mergers, exchanges of information among competitors, restrictions on competition in the distribution of products, monopolization, boycotts, and other traditional areas of antitrust doctrine. Since I believe that economics is relevant to the administration as well as the substance of antitrust policy, I am led also to propose fundamental changes in the criminal and other remedies by which we seek to obtain compliance with the rules of antitrust law.

The application of economics to antitrust law is of course not new, and much of the ground traversed in the following pages has been covered by other scholars before me. What I have tried to do in this book is to explain, extend, and in places revise the economic approach to antitrust law. Although the presentation throughout the text is nontechnical, the appendix at the end of the book contains a slightly more technical treatment of a few of the salient features of the theory of monopoly.

Although many topics are covered, the book is far from a treatise on the antitrust laws. It does not touch all of the bases of what has become an enormous field of law, nor does it exhaust the analysis even of those topics that are discussed. The discussion is limited to what seem to me to be the major problems in the antitrust field, and in dealing with them I have attempted to go to their heart and have ruthlessly ignored the peripheral areas. However, some topics are discussed in greater detail than others, and in this respect the book reveals its origin in a series of articles written for different audiences and occasions. At least one major contemporary problem in antitrust is almost completely ignored in the book—that of establishing the boundary between the antitrust laws and the other laws, including patent, labor, public-utility and common-carrier laws, as well as the First Amendment, that arguably exempt certain activities from the coverage of the antitrust laws. A proper treatment of the antitrust exemptions would require a detailed analysis of the purpose and scope of the laws argued to establish the exemption, and such an analysis would, I believe, carry author and reader too far away from the central concerns of this book. Finally, there is only incidental discussion of the Robinson-Patman Act, a major antitrust statute.

My ideas on antitrust have been greatly influenced over the years by Aaron Director and George J. Stigler. I want to take this opportunity once again to acknowledge my intellectual debts to them while absolving them from responsibility for my conclusions and recommendations, with which they may disagree. I also want to thank Kenneth W. Dam, Harold Demsetz, William M. Landes, Bernard D. Meltzer, George L. Priest, and Donald F. Turner for their helpful comments on portions of the manuscript, and the Law and Economics Program of the University of Chicago Law School for defraying the costs of typing, cite-checking, and research assistance.

I The Law and Economics of Antitrust

1   Introduction

To the layman a "law" is a rule written down in a book somewhere. The lawyer, however, realizes that the matter is frequently a good deal more complex. There are federal antitrust statutes, and they are quite brief and readable compared to the Internal Revenue Code. But their operative terms—"restraint of trade," "substantially to lessen competition," "monopolize"— are opaque; and the congressional debates and reports that preceded their enactment, and other relevant historical materials, only dimly illuminate the intended meaning of the key terms. The courts have spent many years interpreting, or perhaps more accurately supplying, their meaning, but the course of judicial interpretation has been so marked by contradiction and ambiguity as to leave the law in an exceedingly uncertain and fluid state. What is more, the rules of law as they are articulated and as they are applied to alter behavior are often, as is true in this instance, two quite different things. The rules in practice, as distinct from the theory, are critically affected by sanctions, by procedures, and by the policies and incentives of enforcers. Thus the situation in antitrust law is fluid and uncertain and is frequently in conflict with the legal theory, such as it is.

The antitrust field is in need of a thorough rethinking of both its substantive and administrative aspects, and the essential intellectual tool for this process of rethinking, I believe—besides simple logic and common sense, which are scarce commodities in this as in most fields—is the science of economics. The basic concern of the antitrust laws is with monopoly, which for many years economists have been studying intensively, free of the entanglements of precedents and legalism that prevent lawyers from rethinking a field of law from the ground up. The work of the economists provides at least a starting point for analysis. Since, unfortunately, they are not unanimous on the essential points of the theory of monopoly, a necessary first step is to thread one's way through the doctrinal controversies that have surrounded and continue to afflict the development of the theory. I will spare the reader the details of these controversies and will say simply that chapter 2 presents a version of the economic theory of monopoly that seems, to me at least, to represent its common core. Legal policy-makers should focus on the core, rather than try to pick and choose among the warring factions in the science. But that is not always possible, and I am well aware that the economic views presented in this book are in places highly controversial.

Chapter 2 argues that economic theory provides a firm basis for the belief that monopoly pricing, which results when firms create an artificial scarcity of their product and thereby drive price above its level under competition, is inefficient. Since efficiency is an important, although not the only, social value, this conclusion establishes a prima facie case for having an antitrust policy. It also implies the limitations of that policy: to the extent that efficiency is the goal of antitrust enforcement there is no justification for carrying enforcement into areas where competition is less efficient than monopoly because the costs of monopoly pricing are outweighed by the economies of centralizing production in one or a very few firms. Nor is there justification for using the antitrust laws to attain goals unrelated or antithetical to efficiency, such as promoting a society of small tradespeople.

Of course it does not necessarily follow that, because efficiency is an important social goal, it should be the only goal of antitrust law. But chapter 2 argues that it should be, because the only competing goal suggested with any frequency or conviction—the protection of small business—whatever its intrinsic merit cannot be attained within the framework of antitrust principles and procedures. The small businessman is, in general, helped rather than hurt by monopoly, so unless the antitrust laws are stood completely on their head they are an inapt vehicle (compared, say, to tax preferences) for assisting small business.

Having established that the goal of antitrust law should be to promote efficiency in the economic sense, I next proceed to develop the implications for the law of adopting this view of its purpose. The focus is on price-fixing agreements among competing firms and the related problem of oligopoly pricing, which appear to be the principal nongovernmental sources of monopolistic pricing. After a brief overview of the antitrust laws in chapter

3, designed to orient the general reader to the remaining chapters, I argue in chapter 4 that the basic reform necessary to the control of price fixing and oligopoly is to redirect the enforcement of section 1 of the Sherman Act from its present obsession with proving the fact of a conspiracy or attempt to fix prices, in the criminal-law sense of these terms, to a search for evidence, economic in character, of collusive price behavior in the market. Whether there is a lurid conspiracy in the conventional sense of secret hotel meetings, elaborate bid-rotation schemes, and such should be less important than whether the actual price behavior of the market indicates collusion, which may be undetectable by the traditional and very crude tests derived from experience with ordinary criminal conspiracies. I indicate the kinds of economic evidence that might be used both to identify markets prone to collusion and to demonstrate the actual existence of collusion in those markets.

Chapters 5 and 6 discuss two methods of dealing with price fixing, and especially oligopoly pricing, that appeal to people who —unlike myself—despair of dealing directly with the problem of collusive pricing. The first is the dismemberment of the leading firms in oligopolistic industries. Chapter 5 argues that, even if there were no other way of dealing with the problems of collusion and oligopoly, dismemberment would be a bad solution; experience suggests that it would be futile and, if not futile, prohibitively costly both directly and in the perverse incentives that it would create. Chapter 6 examines the major Supreme Court cases that have attempted to prevent the emergence of conditions that favor collusion or oligopoly pricing by forbidding mergers between competing or potentially competing firms, and argues that the luxuriant prohibitions that these decisions have created need to be pruned. In particular, I propose that the judicially created doctrine of "potential competition" be discarded as wholly unworkable. Because market shares are often so decisive a factor in deciding the outcome of a merger case (and of many other types of antitrust case as well), this chapter also examines the crucial step in the litigation of determining which sellers shall be included in and which excluded from the market; a number of changes in the existing approach to market definition are suggested. This chapter also introduces an important subsidiary theme of the book—the extraordinary unwillingness or inability of most Supreme Court justices to apply economics or any other body of systematic thinking to antitrust problems.

Chapter 7 examines, with respect to two specific practices—resale price maintenance and the exchange of price information among competing sellers—the problem of locating the boundary between collusive practices that should be forbidden and apparently similar practices that should be permitted, and the Supreme Court's deficient solutions. My conclusion is that resale price maintenance should be considered presumptively lawful rather than per se unlawful and that the exchange of price information among competitors should be permitted unless it is proved that they are expressly or tacitly fixing prices.

The grand theme of chapters 4 through 7 is the high price that society has paid for the failure of the antitrust enforcement system to develop a genuinely economic approach to the problem of collusive pricing. The inability to determine the existence of collusive pricing directly has led to all sorts of indirect approaches, most of them deeply flawed in either conception or execution, such as the criminalization of the price-fixing rule, the deconcentration proposals, the excessively stringent restrictions on mergers between competitors and between potential competitors, and the inept handling of the problems of restricted distribution and of exchanges of information among competitors.

The focus of the book shifts in chapter 8 to "exclusionary practices." There is an important distinction, both in economics and in law, between practices by which competing firms voluntarily agree not to compete with each other and practices by which a firm or group of firms seeks to obtain or maintain a monopoly by coercing, intimidating, destroying, or otherwise excluding competitors or potential competitors from the market. The economic theory of monopoly was developed to explain practices of the first sort and has relatively little to say about practices of the second sort. This has led the economists and lawyers of the "Chicago School" to the view that there is no economic basis for concern with the exclusionary practices—perhaps they do not exist at all, and, if they do, they must be so rare as not to be worth worrying about. In my opinion, although this view contains a great deal of truth it is overstated. There is an economic basis for concern with at least some exclusionary practices, in at least some circumstances; and a few practices that are not exclusionary (though so classified in the law), like persistent price discrimination, may still be undesirable on strictly economic grounds. Chapter 8 attempts to develop a set of practical rules, grounded in economic analysis, for regulating the alleged exclusionary practices. Among its proposals are a new definition of predatory pricing and drastic curtailment of the prohibitions against tie-in agreements, vertical integration, exclusive dealing, and boycotts.

Chapter 9 asks how the antitrust statutes, and the major judicial doctrines based (often loosely) on them, can be tidied up, both to eliminate the inconsistencies and redundancies of existing antitrust doctrine and to conform to the specific proposals advanced in chapter 8 and earlier chapters. I argue that the doctrines of monopolization and of attempts and conspiracies to monopolize have no proper place in a sound system of antitrust policy and, indeed, that every antitrust provision except section 1 of the Sherman Act could be repealed without serious loss. However, although there would be some value in a sweeping statutory revision along the lines suggested in chapter 9, most of the doctrinal reforms suggested elsewhere in the book could be implemented without statutory change. The body of antitrust doctrine is largely the product of judicial interpretation of the vague provisions of the antitrust laws and thus can be changed by the courts within the very broad limits set by the statutory language and what we know of the intent behind it. What is required is judicial recognition that many of the existing judge-made rules of antitrust are inconsistent with the fundamental, and fundamentally economic, objectives of the antitrust laws.

Finally, chapter 10 discusses the administration of the antitrust laws. It advances a number of patently unrealistic and impolitic, but seriously intended, suggestions for administrative reform, including the abolition of prison sentences for antitrust violators, the elimination of treble damages for most antitrust violations, the award of attorneys' fees to winning defendants, and the radical simplification of the antitrust trial.

2   The Costs
of Monopoly

In addition to furnishing a definition of monopoly, economic analysis offers reasons—some firmly rooted in economic theory, some more conjectural—why monopoly reduces economic efficiency in some (not all) circumstances. My first purpose in this chapter is to explain the theory of monopoly in terms that should be comprehensible to readers without previous knowledge of economics yet (I hope) not wholly uninteresting to those possessed of such knowledge, and to develop the relevance of the theory to antitrust policy. My second purpose is to argue that the economic theory of monopoly provides the only suitable basis for antitrust policy and, not incidentally, an appropriate guide in interpreting our actual antitrust laws. The exposition is in places regrettably but unavoidably difficult and I hope the reader will bear with me, as this chapter is the basis for much that follows.

The Economic Theory of Monopoly and the Case for Antitrust

A monopolist is a seller (or group of sellers acting like a single seller) who can change the price at which his product will sell in the market by changing the quantity that he sells. This "power over price," the essence of the economic concept of monopoly, derives from the fact that the price that people are willing to pay for a product tends to rise as the quantity of the product offered for sale falls. Some people will value the product more than other people do and will therefore bid more for it as the quantity available shrinks in order to make sure that they get it. The seller who controls the supply of a product can therefore raise its price by restricting the amount supplied.

The observant reader may be quick to point out that, even in a highly competitive market, with many sellers selling the identical product, each one would have some power over price; for if any seller reduced his output, the entire output of the market would fall and the market price would therefore rise. This point is formally correct, but, where a seller produces only a small fraction of the market's total output, the change in total output brought about by a fractional reduction in *his* output is unlikely to be great enough to affect the market price significantly; his power over price is slight and can be ignored. Moreover, the smaller his output is in relation to that of the remaining sellers in the market, the likelier it is that any cut in his output will be promptly offset by an increase in the output of the other sellers, each of whom would need to increase his output only fractionally in order to restore the market's total output to its level before the first seller's reduction.

The sole seller of a product, a "monopolist," need not worry that if he raises his price other sellers will expand their output of the product and thereby drive the price back down—by definition there are no other sellers of the product. To be sure, the higher price may give firms in other markets an incentive to enter this one; but presumably entry into the market takes time, and, assuming that the formation of the monopoly was not anticipated, the monopolist will enjoy at least a temporary power over price.

It remains to be considered why and how he will exercise that power. We may assume that every firm wants to maximize its profits—the excess of its total revenue over its total cost. Suppose that just before the market became monopolized the market price was equal to the cost of making and selling the product in question ("cost" to the economist includes a reasonable return on equity capital). In this case the market price would be the competitive price. If the monopolist reduces production below the competitive level, the market price will rise. How will his costs and revenues, and hence profits, be affected? His total cost will be lower since he will be producing less. His total revenue, i.e., price times output, will be higher or lower at the new price and output depending on whether the proportional increase in price is greater or less than the proportional reduction in output or the same. Clearly, if the price increase is proportionally greater than the reduction in units sold, the price increase will be profitable to the firm. Its total revenue will be higher, while its total cost will be lower since it will be producing less, and so the difference between its revenue and cost—profit—will be greater than at the competitive price.

Thus, the monopolist will always charge a price higher than the competitive price if demand at the competitive price is *inelastic*, that is, if the proportional reduction in the quantity demanded as a result of the higher price is less than the proportional increase in price.[1] Moreover, he will increase his price *at least* to the point where a further price increase would cause a proportionally larger redurtion in the quantity demanded, for until that point is reached every price increase raises total revenue while reducing total cost. In other words, the monopolist will always operate in the elastic portion of his demand curve. He may raise his price beyond the point where demand turns elastic and his total revenues therefore begin to shrink, for he is interested in maximizing profits, not revenues. He will stop raising his price only at the point where any further increase would reduce total revenues by more than the reduction in total cost resulting from the smaller quantity produced.[2] That is the point at which the monopolist's profits are maximized. The optimum monopoly price may be much higher than the competitive price, depending on the intensity of consumer preference for the monopolized product—how much of it they continue to buy at successively higher prices—in relation to its cost.

We have established that output is smaller under monopoly than under competition but not that the reduction in output imposes a loss on society. After all, the reduction in output in the monopolized market frees up resources that can and will be put to use in other markets. There is a loss in value, however, because the increase in the price of the monopolized product above its cost induces the consumer to substitute products that must cost more to produce (or else the consumer would have substituted them *before* the price increase), although they are now cheaper to him (assuming that they are priced at a competitive level, i.e., at cost). Thus monopoly pricing confronts the consumer with false alternatives: the product that he chooses because it *seems* cheaper actually requires more of society's scarce resources to produce. Under

---

1. For example, suppose that the output of the firm at the competitive price, $5, is 1,000 units, but at $5.05 would be 999 units. Then demand at the competitive price is inelastic, because the proportional increase in price (1 percent) is greater than the proportional decrease in output demanded (.1 of 1 percent) with the result that the higher price yields a larger total revenue—$5,044.95 compared to $5,000.

2. The determination of the optimum monopoly price is discussed at greater length in the Appendix at the end of the book. See also my *Antitrust: Cases, Economic Notes, and Other Materials* 5–14 (1974).

monopoly, consumer demands are satisfied at a higher cost than necessary.

This analysis identifies the cost of monopoly with the output which the monopolist does *not* produce, and which a competitive industry would. We have said nothing about the higher prices paid by those consumers who continue to purchase the product at the monopoly price. Economic analysis used to treat this transfer of wealth from consumer to producer as costless to society as a whole, since the loss to the consumer is exactly offset by the gain to the producer and both are members of society. The only cost of monopoly in that analysis was the loss in value resulting from substitution against the monopolized product, since the loss to the substituting consumers is not recouped by the monopolist (or anyone else)[3] and is thus a net loss, rather than a mere book-keeping entry on the social books. But the traditional analysis was shortsighted. It ignored the fact that an opportunity to obtain a lucrative transfer payment in the form of monopoly profits will attract real resources into efforts by sellers to monopolize, and by consumers to prevent being charged monopoly prices. The costs of the resources so used are costs of monopoly just as much as the costs resulting from the substitution of products that cost society more to produce than the monopolized product.[4]

Suppose, for example, that a cartel fixes prices somewhere above the competitive level (i.e., cost), and the entry of new firms or the expansion of existing firms (whether members or non-members of the cartel) is for some reason impeded. Each member of the cartel will have an incentive, by expending resources on making his output more valuable to consumers than the output of the other members of the cartel, to increase his sales relative to the other cartelists and thereby engross a larger share of the cartel profits. The process of increasing nonprice competition (higher quality, better service, etc.) will continue until, at the margin, the costs of the cartel members have risen to the cartel price level. The higher costs are a cost of monopoly, although there is a partially offsetting benefit since the additional nonprice

3. The sellers of the substitute product are assumed to sell at a competitive price, and thus to enjoy no profits, in the economic sense, from obtaining additional customers. This assumption is examined critically below.

4. The reader should consult my recent article, "The Social Costs of Monopoly and Regulation," 83 *J. Pol. Econ.* 807 (1975), for a fuller development of this line of argument.

competition has some value, though less than its cost, to the consumer.[5] If for some reason nonprice competition were infeasible, and the expected profits of cartelizing therefore very large, the analysis would be altered, but not fundamentally. Firms would expend real resources on forming or gaining admission to cartels in order to share in the expected profits, and this process of competing to become a monopolist would presumably continue until, at the margin, the expected gains of monopoly were just equal to the costs incurred in becoming a monopolist. Of course, one way of sharing in monopoly profits is by entering a market in which a monopoly price is being charged (thereby adding to the output of the market and depressing the market price) or by expanding one's output if one is already in such a market. Unless the outsider has higher costs than the monopolist—an important qualification—these methods of "monopolizing" do not impose costs on society; quite the contrary. But they are properly analyzed as market responses that reduce the expected gains of monopoly by diminishing the monopolist's power over price rather than as market responses that transform expected monopoly gains into costs.

The tendency of monopoly profits to be converted into social costs, until recently a neglected facet of the economic analysis of monopoly, has, as will appear in subsequent chapters, a number of important implications for antitrust policy. For present purposes, the most important point is that it places the economist's hostility to monopoly on somewhat firmer ground than it would occupy if the only costs of monopoly were those that stem from the reduction in output brought about by monopoly. As shown in figure 1, if we assume that problems of cartel organization and the potential competition of new entrants into the cartelized industry constrain the price level in the typical cartelized or monopolized industry to a level only moderately higher than the competitive price level, then the social loss due to the reduction in output at the higher price—D in figure 1—will be quite small in relation to the total revenues of the industry at either the monopoly or competitive price (pq or $p'q'$).[6] The costs of monopoly become

5. If consumers valued the additional services (or whatever) generated by this competition above its cost, presumably the services would have been produced in a price-competitive market as well.

6. See the Appendix for a more elaborate presentation and an explanation of why D is an appropriate measure of the losses to those consumers induced by the monopoly price to substitute other products.

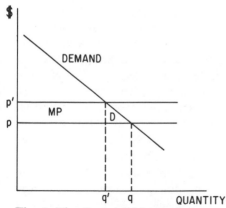

Fig. 1. The Costs of Monopoly

much more imposing if *MP*, the transfer payment from consumers to producers of the monopolized product, is added to *D*. To be sure, *MP* is at best a rough approximation of the actual costs resulting from the competition to become a monopolist—the actual costs could be greater or less[7]—but it is at least a plausible assumption that the total social costs of monopoly will usually exceed *D* by a substantial amount.

Moreover, once *MP* is recognized as being relevant to the costs of monopoly, an objection to the economic analysis of monopoly based on the theory of the "second best" disappears. The objection, in its simplest form, is that if the substitutes for a monopolized product are not being sold at prices equal to their costs, the elimination of the monopoly may encourage rather than discourage inefficient substitutions. To illustrate, suppose that the monopolized product, widgets, is being sold at a price of 10¢, although it costs only 6¢ to produce. A substitute product, gidgets, costs

7. Greater because *MP* ignores expenditures by potential victims of monopoly or by law-enforcement agencies that have the effect of limiting the monopoly price increase and that are properly counted as costs of monopoly; less because expenditures on monopolizing may generate partially offsetting benefits in the form of additional nonprice competition and because some of the "costs" may represent economic rents to the owners of resources specialized to monopolizing rather than social costs.

I am of course speaking here of "bad" monopolies. If the government grants a firm a monopoly precisely in order to evoke greater expenditures by the firm than competition would—this is the economic rationale of the patent laws—the resulting transformation of expected monopoly gains into social costs does not create a net social loss.

only 5¢ to produce but it is also monopolized, and its monopoly price is 8¢. People will tend to buy gidgets, an efficient result since they are cheaper to produce than widgets. Suppose now that the monopoly of widgets is eliminated and the price of widgets therefore falls to the competitive level, 6¢. People will now substitute widgets for gidgets. But this is inefficient, since, although widgets look cheaper to the consumer, they cost society more to produce than gidgets. Nor would the problem that this example illustrates be solved if all monopolies, rather than just some, could be eliminated. Gidgets might be subject to an excise tax that raised their price from 5¢ to 8¢, in which event, just as in the previous illustration, a widget monopoly would encourage efficient substitution.

But in a correct economic analysis of the monopoly problem the possible divergence between the cost and the price of substitute goods is not a decisive objection to taking action against the widget monopoly. The opportunity to obtain a monopoly profit of 4¢ per widget will attract real resources into the activity of becoming a widget monopolist, thereby transforming the 4¢ (or some portion of it) into a social cost that (1) can be eliminated by destroying the monopoly and (2) in all likelihood exceeds the losses (analogous to D) resulting from the fact that widgets are slightly more costly to produce than the substitute product.

The foregoing analysis enables one to conclude, at least tentatively, that the potential social gains from an effective antitrust policy are probably substantial (whether they are greater than the costs of such a policy is a separate question). This point has been obscured in many people's minds by a series of studies that attempt to measure the social cost of monopoly in the American economy and find that it is very slight—perhaps no more than .1 of 1 percent of the Gross National Product.[8] There are several reasons why such studies cannot be used to measure the potential gains from having antitrust laws. The first is that they measure the costs of monopoly *given* the existence of those laws, not the costs of monopoly that could be expected in the absence of such laws. In a sense they measure the degree to which the antitrust laws have failed. The second reason for heavily discounting these

8. See, e.g., Arnold C. Harberger, "Monopoly and Resource Allocation," 44 *Am. Econ. Rev. Papers & Proceedings* 77 (1954).

studies is that their procedure is improper—if the preceding analysis of the costs of monopoly is correct. The estimates of the monopoly price increase are based on the existence of persistently above-average rates of return in some industries, which the authors attribute to monopoly. The difference between those rates and the average rate of return for the industries in the sample is used to estimate the amount of monopoly profits in the revenues of the monopolized industries, and in turn the price increase necessary to produce those profits. This procedure yields an estimate —typically small—of the percentage by which the monopoly price level exceeds the competitive price level. But the estimate is biased downward. It ignores the tendency of competition for a monopoly position to transform expected monopoly profits into costs and thereby push down rates of return in monopolized industries toward the competitive level. A monopolized industry might be charging a price far above the competitive price yet be earning no more than a normal return. Having systematically underestimated the monopoly price increase, the studies compound their error by using the price increase to estimate only the so-called deadweight loss of monopoly (D in figure 1), ignoring the much larger costs (approximated by MP) resulting from the competition to obtain monopoly profits.

Studies such as I have just described have disturbed economists who believed in the antitrust laws; and unaware of the serious deficiencies of the studies, they have cast about for other economic grounds for concern with monopolies. Their search has led them back to the ancient idea that a lack of competition makes a firm less interested and effective in minimizing its costs, whether by careful buying of inputs and supervision of production processes or by inventing new products and processes. A moment's reflection will show that, in some circumstances anyway, the opposite may be true: *competition* may reduce the incentive to minimize cost. The firm that invents a new, cost-reducing process, or a new product, may be unable to recoup its research and development expenses if the process can be promptly copied by a competing firm that has borne no such expenses. The patent laws—laws granting monopolies to inventors—recognize and counteract the tendency of competition to retard innovation; but, since the coverage of these laws is highly incomplete, the process of obtaining and enforcing a patent frequently very costly, and patents limited in scope and duration, the possession of a monopoly not dependent on the patent laws may provide a greater incentive to invent than a patent—let alone competition—does.

Another weakness in the theory that monopoly leads to slack and waste is its inconsistency with the fundamental economic principle that an opportunity forgone is a cost analytically no different from a loss incurred; indeed, forgone opportunity *is* the economic definition of cost. For a monopolist to fail to obtain another $100 in profit by failing to exploit some new process costs him $100, and this is the same amount that is lost by a competitive firm in failing to exploit an opportunity for a $100 cost reduction or product improvement. To be sure, firms and individuals differ in their ability to minimize costs, so that in a market containing a number of firms competition will gradually weed out the less efficient ones and thereby concentrate the assets of the market in the hands of the people who are best at minimizing costs. This process of "natural selection" is attenuated—although not eliminated[9]—in a market that is effectively monopolized in the sense that not only is there only one firm but the entry of new firms is blocked. However, the monopolistic firm has an incentive to *simulate* the competitive struggle for survival in order to minimize its costs and hence maximize its profits, and it can do this readily by establishing competing profit centers within the firm which vie with one another to minimize costs. The wise monopolist eliminates competition only at the level where competition is harmful to the firm—in the pricing of its product. Competition is retained in those areas where it increases profits. The only danger that remains is the lack of a market mechanism other than the takeover bid for displacing unwise or ineffectual management of a monopoly. The empirical significance of this danger is unknown; perhaps the takeover bid is a generally adequate mechanism for this purpose.

The analysis is basically similar if, instead of there being only one firm, the market is effectively cartelized and new entry is blocked. Then each member of the cartel is formally in the same position as the single-firm monopolist in our example, but there are important practical differences. The cartel member has to consider the possibilities (1) that the cartel will break down,

9. A firm that fails to exploit its opportunities is always in danger of being taken over by another firm, which can offer the shareholders a price for their shares in excess of the market price since the assets of the firm will be worth more in the hands of its new management.

throwing him back into the competitive arena where he will be in serious danger if his costs are higher than those of most of the other firms in the market, and (2) that the members of the cartel having the lowest costs will press for a reduction in the cartel price, since the lower a firm's marginal costs, other things being equal, the lower the price that will maximize its profits.[10]

I have thus far assumed that new entry into the monopolist's or cartel's market is blocked. This assumption is in general unrealistic, and where entry is possible the monopolist or the members of the cartel will have a strong incentive to minimize costs in order to avoid being displaced by a more efficient new entrant.

Another important reason for doubting that monopolists are in general less vigorous innovators than competitive firms derives from our earlier analysis of the tendency of expected monopoly profits to be transformed into actual resource costs. (This reason is applicable only where there is more than one seller, and where they are colluding, but that is empirically a much more important type of monopoly than the single-firm monopoly.)[11] Members of a cartel rarely find it practicable to agree not to compete in *every* dimension of possible rivalry. Usually it is just price and other terms of sale that are fixed, and the firms remain free to compete in other respects. As we have seen, the effect of collusive pricing when nonprice competition is not restricted is to channel the profits generated by such pricing into expenditures on nonprice competition, which comprise all sorts of product and service improvements. If anything, therefore, we would expect cartelization to increase the incentive to invent compared to what it would be in a price-competitive market—and even to carry invention beyond the optimal point.

In summary, I do not think that in the present state of our knowledge cartelization or even single-firm monopolization can be condemned on the ground that a lack of price competition retards invention or generates slackness about costs. There is simply no satisfactory theoretical or empirical basis for such concerns. But

10. See Appendix, infra p. 248.
11. This is true even in countries that have no antitrust laws. Presumably diseconomies of large-scale operation make it more economical to have more than one firm in substantial markets, even if some or all monopoly profits are forgone as a result. There will be more than one firm in the market so long as the higher costs that would result from eliminating the last competitor would exceed the resulting loss of monopoly profits.

we need not be troubled by this, since, as we saw earlier, there are other, and powerful, grounds for believing that monopoly, when it is not simply a by-product of superior efficiency, as in the patent example, is a source of substantial social costs.

Sociopolitical Objections to Monopoly

Having considered the economic objections to monopoly, I want to discuss now three broadly political arguments against it. The first is that monopoly transfers wealth from consumers to the stockholders of monopolistic firms, a redistribution that goes from the less to the more wealthy. This appealing argument is undermined by the point made earlier that competition to become a monopolist will tend to transform the expected gains from monopoly into social costs. To the extent that this occurs, consumers' wealth will not be transferred to the shareholders of monopoly firms but will instead be dissipated in the purchase of inputs into the activity of becoming a monopolist.

A second argument is that monopoly, or more broadly any condition (such as concentration) that fosters cooperation among competing firms, will facilitate an industry's manipulation of the political process to obtain protective legislation aimed at increasing the industry's profits. Often such protection takes the form of controls over entry and price competition, coupled with exemption from the antitrust laws, that result in cartelizing the industry much more effectively than could be done by private agreement. This is not the place to pursue the intricacies of the nascent economic analysis of the determinants of political power.[12] It is enough to note that, while concentration may reduce the costs of organizing effectively to manipulate the political process, it may also reduce the demand for public assistance in suppressing competition, since, as we shall see in chapter 4, a concentrated industry, other things being equal, is in a better position to suppress competition through private agreement, express or tacit, than an unconcentrated industry. It is therefore unclear whether on balance concentrated, or monopolistic, industries will obtain greater help from the political process than unconcentrated, or competitive, industries. This theoretical indeterminacy is mirrored in the empirical world, where we observe many unconcentrated industries—agriculture, truck-

---

12. See my article, "Theories of Economic Regulation," 5 *Bell J. Econ. & Management Sci.* 335 (1974), for a summary and critique of this economic analysis.

ing, local broadcasting, banking, medicine, to name a few—enjoying governmental protection against competition.

In any event, however, this political objection to monopoly and concentration is not sharply different from the economic objection. The legislation sought by an industry—a tariff, a tax on a substitute product, control of entry—will usually have economic effects similar or even identical to those of a private cartel agreement. The political argument—which is simply that concentration facilitates monopoly pricing indirectly through the legislative process, as well as directly through cartelization—thus implies no change in the character of an antitrust policy deduced from economic considerations. (This is also true, incidentally, of the wealth-redistribution argument: the implications for public policy are not sharply different whether one objects to monopoly pricing because it wastes resources or because it brings about undesirable changes in the redistribution of wealth.)

The last political argument that I shall discuss has, in contrast, implications for antitrust policy that diverge sharply from those of economic analysis. The popular (or Populist) alternative to an antitrust policy designed to promote economic efficiency by limiting monopoly is a policy of restricting the freedom of action of large business firms in order to promote small business. (It may be possible to conceive of a different alternative to an efficiency-based antitrust policy, but this is the only one suggested with any frequency.) The idea that there is some special virtue in small business compared to large is a persistent one. I am not prepared to argue that it has no merit whatever. I am, however, confident that antitrust enforcement is an inappropriate method of trying to promote the interests of small business as a whole. The best overall antitrust policy from the standpoint of small business is *no* antitrust policy, since monopoly, by driving a wedge between the prices and the costs of the larger firms in the market (it is presumably they who take the lead in forming cartels), enables the smaller firms in the market to survive even if their costs are higher than those of the large firms. The only kind of antitrust policy that would benefit small business would be one whose principal objective was to limit the attempts of large firms to underprice less efficient small firms by sharing their lower costs with consumers in the form of lower prices. Apart from raising in acute form the question of whether it is socially desirable to promote small business at the expense of the consumer, such a policy would be unworkable because it would require comprehensive and continuing supervision of the prices of large firms. There are no effective shortcuts. For example, if mergers between large firms are forbidden because of concern that they will enable the firms to take advantage of economies of scale and thereby underprice smaller firms operating at less efficient scale, one (or more) of the larger firms will simply expand until it has achieved the most efficient scale of operation. If franchise termination is made difficult in order to protect small dealers, the costs of franchising will be higher, and there will be less franchising, which will hurt the very class of small businessmen intended to be benefitted. The tools of antitrust enforcement are poorly designed for effective discrimination in favor of small firms, compared, for example, to the effectiveness of taxing larger firms at higher rates. We shall have frequent occasion in this book to remark how difficult it is to press the antitrust laws into the service of small business. The realistic choice is between shaping antitrust policy in accordance with the economic (and congruent political) objections to monopoly and—if we think that limiting big business and promoting small is more important than efficiency—abandoning it.

This conclusion would have little relevance to judicial interpretation, as distinct from legislative reform, of antitrust if in fact social or political objectives that are inconsistent with the economic approach to monopoly had been embraced by the framers of the antitrust statutes. However, although noneconomic objectives are frequently mentioned in the legislative histories, it seems that the dominant legislative intent has been to promote some approximation to the economist's idea of competition, viewed as a means toward the end of maximizing efficiency.[13] Accordingly, the economic approach outlined in this chapter constitutes a generally reliable guide to the interpretation as well as revision of the antitrust statutes.

This is not to say that there are no statutory pockets of anticompetitive protectionism which the courts are bound to respect until Congress decides to change the law. An example of such a pocket is the failing-company doctrine, an implicit provision of section 7 of the Clayton Act (the antimerger law). The doctrine permits a merger that would otherwise be condemned because of its anticompetitive effects to be spared if it is shown that, but for the acquisition, the acquired firm would have gone bankrupt. If

13. For some evidence on this point see p. 23 and note 1 infra, and pp. 99–100 infra.

the sole concern of the Clayton Act were with competition and efficiency, there would be no need for a failing-company defense as such. To be sure, in some cases the imminent failure of the acquired firm would be relevant in appraising the competitive effect of the acquisition. It might indicate that the acquisition had changed nothing in the market: the competitor eliminated by it was on his way out anyway. But one can imagine cases where competition would be promoted by letting the acquired firm go under. As an extreme but illustrative example, suppose the failing firm is a monopolist. If it is acquired, its monopoly will be preserved. If instead it is forced to declare bankruptcy and to liquidate, its assets and sales may be divided up among a number of firms and competition thereby restored (assuming the market is not a natural monopoly). Yet the legislative history of section 7 makes clear that even a merger which preserved a monopoly would not violate the statute if the alternative to acquisition was bankruptcy, because the intention of Congress was to protect the creditors, employees, and shareholders of failing companies, if necessary at the cost of permitting monopoly pricing.[14] Nor can this result be justified, on economic grounds, by reference to the

14. See, e.g., S. Rep. No. 1775, 81st Cong., 2d Sess. 7 (1950); Derek C. Bok, "Section 7 of the Clayton Act and the Merging of Law and Economics," 74 *Harv. L. Rev.* 226, 340 (1962); International Shoe Co. v. FTC, 280 U.S. 291, 302 (1930). One court of appeals has held recently that the failing-company defense requires proof that the acquired firm could not have been successfully reorganized in bankruptcy proceedings. United States Steel Corp. v. FTC, 426 F.2d 592 (6th Cir. 1970). This holding, which is based on a dictum in Citizen Publishing Co. v. United States, 394 U.S. 131, 138 (1969), is wrong. The legislative history of section 7 makes clear beyond possibility of doubt that the purpose of the failing-company defense is precisely to avert bankruptcy because of the losses that a bankruptcy proceeding is likely to impose on creditors and shareholders of the bankrupt. Indeed, the position adopted in the *Steel* decision had been expressly rejected by the Supreme Court in the *International Shoe* decision, supra (compare 280 U.S. at 301–02 with the Federal Trade Commission's brief at 15, 23–24), which the framers of the amended section 7 expressly approved as the authoritative statement of the failing-company defense. The *Citizen* dictum is probably just an example of Justice Douglas's careless opinion writing and has been abandoned in subsequent Supreme Court statements of the failing-company defense. See United States v. Greater Buffalo Press, Inc., 402 U.S. 549, 555 (1971); United States v. General Dynamics Corp., 415 U.S. 486, 507 (1974). These decisions, which postdate *Steel*, greatly undermine the authority cf that decision. See United States v. M.P.M., Inc., 1975 Trade Cases ¶ 60,312 (D. Colo.).

social costs of business failure. Business failures constitute an essential means of imparting incentives for efficient business behavior, by placing the costs of mistakes on the firms that make them. Condoning monopoly in order to avert business failure protects not only monopoly, but, what is worse, inefficient monopoly.

Examples of anticompetitive doctrines that, like the failing-company defense, are part of the statutory fabric itself are rare. As we shall see in subsequent chapters, there are a great many judicially fashioned antitrust doctrines that are perverse from an efficiency standpoint, but what is at once striking and heartening is how few of these doctrines can be justified by reference to a legislative determination to subordinate efficiency to other values. The scope for judicial reform of antitrust doctrine is enormous.

Efficient Monopolies

Assuming that antitrust policy is to be shaped by economic analysis of the monopoly problem, what is the proper treatment of those practices that, while monopolistic, may on balance be efficient? The costs resulting from monopoly pricing will sometimes be lower than the cost savings generated by such pricing. Imagine the creation of a monopoly in a market so small in relation to the efficient scale of production that a single firm will have much lower costs than more than one firm—so much lower, indeed, that the profit-maximizing monopoly price is actually below the competitive price. Plainly, society's economic welfare would be greater if the monopoly were permitted than if it were forbidden, and since, in an economic analysis, we value competition because it promotes efficiency—i.e., as a means rather than as an end—it would seem that whenever monopoly would increase efficiency it should be tolerated, indeed encouraged. The problem, as we shall see, is that it is very difficult to measure the efficiency consequences of a challenged practice; and thus throughout this book we shall be continually endeavoring to find ways of avoiding the prohibition of efficient, albeit anticompetitive, practices without having to compare directly the gains and losses from a challenged practice. Fortunately, since few economists believe that collusive pricing generates significant economic gains, when a practice has been correctly identified as a form of collusion we can generally suppress it without misgivings. As it happens, collusion has been—and will and should remain—the principal focus of antitrust policy, and it is the principal focus of this book as well.

3   An Overview
of the Antitrust Laws

In the previous chapter, I offered my view of the proper objectives of antitrust policy. Subsequent chapters will examine the extent to which these objectives have in fact informed the interpretation and application of the antitrust laws, while the purpose of the present chapter is to orient that discussion by describing very briefly the evolution and principal features of contemporary antitrust policy.

Antitrust Doctrine

The basic federal antitrust law, the Sherman Act, was passed in 1890 against a background of rampant cartelization and monopolization of the American economy. Section 1 of the Act prohibited contracts, combinations, and conspiracies in restraint of trade; section 2, monopolization and conspiracies and attempts to monopolize. Since "monopoly" and "restraint of trade" were terms that had a common-law history in both England and America, it would be natural to view the act as the culmination of a tradition of legal concern with the monopoly problem; but it would be incorrect to do so. The framers of the Sherman Act appear to have been concerned mainly with the price and output consequences of monopolies and cartels,[1] whereas the common law of monopolies and restraints of trade had a miscellany of objectives mostly unrelated and sometimes antipathetic to competition and efficiency: such as to assert the supremacy of Parliament over the Crown, to prevent people from making improvident contracts, to thwart unionization, and to limit competition in the distribution of goods.[2] Sometimes, to be sure, contracts monopolistic in the economic sense were refused enforcement on grounds

1. See Robert H. Bork, "Legislative Intent and the Policy of the Sherman Act," 6 *J. Law & Econ.* 7 (1966).
2. See, e.g., William L. Letwin, "The English Common Law Concerning Monopolies," 21 *U. Chi. L. Rev.* 355 (1954).

of public policy,[3] but no consistent antimonopoly policy is discernible.[4]

The discontinuity between the common law of trade regulation and the Sherman Act is important to remember whenever one sees a lawyer or judge attempting to buttress his antitrust theories by reference to some common-law doctrine that he contends was incorporated into the antitrust laws by the Sherman Act. Such an argument is almost always unhistorical. The Sherman Act did not enact the common law of restraint of trade. A better guide to interpreting the Sherman Act is the economic analysis of monopoly.[5]

As shown in table 1, few cases were brought during the early years of the act.[6] Yet by 1898 the Supreme Court had firmly established the principle, immensely important to the development of a sound antitrust policy, that cartels and other price-fixing agreements were illegal regardless of the "reasonableness" of the price fixed.[7] Consistent with the economic analysis of the monopoly problem, the Court decided that collusive pricing was inefficient and should be forbidden; the reasonable price was the competitive price.

This was a good rule, but in the course of successive statements its original purpose was largely forgotten and it degenerated into a shibboleth. The rule had been designed to preserve competitive pricing. Accordingly, the early formulations stressed the effect of the challenged conduct on the market price.[8] This did not mean that evidence of actual effect on price was required—evidence that would have eluded, and still would often elude, the best

3. See, e.g., Craft v. McConoughy, 79 Ill. 346 (1975).
4. See Mogul v. MacGregor, 23 Q.B.D. 598 (1889), aff'd, [1892] A.C. 25, discussed in Richard A. Epstein, "Intentional Harms," 4 *J. Leg. Studies* 391, 423–41 (1975).
5. See note 1 supra.
6. Table 1 is limited to cases brought by the Department of Justice; however, few private cases were brought during the early years of the act, although reliable statistics are lacking. The Federal Trade Commission, which shares responsibility for federal antitrust enforcement with the Justice Department, was not created until 1915. Serious state antitrust enforcement activity is a quite recent phenomenon.
7. See United States v. Trans-Missouri Freight Ass'n, 166 U.S. 290 (1897); United States v. Joint Traffic Ass'n, 171 U.S. 505 (1898).
8. See especially United States v. Addyston Pipe & Steel Co., 85 Fed. 271 (6th Cir. 1898), modified and aff'd, 175 U.S. 211 (1899).

Table 1   Justice Department Antitrust Cases, 1890–1974

Period in Which Case was Initiated	Number of Cases Civil	Criminal	Total
1890–1899	10	5	15
1900–1909	17	25	42
1910–1919	68	58	126
1920–1929	83	38	121
1930–1939	48	32	80
1940–1949	147	211	358
1950–1959	181	164	345
1960–1969	276	126	402
1970–1974	170	64	234
Total	1,000	723	1,723

Source: Commerce Clearing House, Federal Antitrust "Blue-book." The nature of this source and the modifications that I have introduced to obtain a meaningful count are described in my article, "A Statistical Study of Antitrust Enforcement," 13 *J. Law & Econ.* 365–67 (1970). In preparing this table, I recomputed and updated the statistics appearing in that article.

efforts of economic science. It meant only that the circumstances in which the behavior complained of occurred, and in particular the degree to which the colluding sellers controlled the market in question, had to support an inference that the defendants were likely to succeed in raising the market price above the competitive level. Yet by 1940, when the Supreme Court uttered its definitive statement of the rule against price fixing in the *Madison Oil* case,[9] the requirement of demonstrating a probable impact on the market price had disappeared. The offense was no longer the charging of a monopoly price—it was the *attempt* to charge a monopoly price; and no evidence that the defendants were likely to succeed in their attempt was required. The rule against price fixing had become a part of the law of conspiracy instead of a part of the law of monopoly.

This transformation of the rule had two effects, which are discussed in detail in the next chapter. It made it possible for the government to try a price-fixing case on the basis solely of the kind of evidence (secret hotel meetings and the like) that it uses in ordinary conspiracy cases, and thus to ignore the economics of price fixing; and because the government soon became accus-

9. United States v. Socony-Vacuum Oil Co., 310 U.S. 150, 224–26, n. 59 (1940).

tomed to place its entire reliance in enforcing the rule against price fixing on this kind of evidence, it obscured the problem of forms of collusive pricing that do not generate such evidence.

An intelligently designed antitrust policy cannot stop with collusive pricing among independent firms and ignore monopoly pricing by a single firm. Such an approach—which would provide competing firms with a strong incentive to merge into a single firm so as to be able to practice monopoly pricing without inviting punishment—was accordingly rejected by the Supreme Court, in 1904, in the *Northern Securities* decision.[10] The Court in that case held that placing the stock of two competing railroads in the hands of a holding company was a combination in restraint of trade. The case was correctly decided on its facts, but in the course of its decision the Court committed an analytical error of major proportions. It reasoned that the union of control over the railroads achieved through the holding-company device was illegal because it had the same effect as a cartel agreement between the railroads—the elimination of competition between them. The idea that transactions which have the same effect on competition *between* the parties to them should therefore be treated by the law in the same way is a recurrent one in antitrust analysis, but is thoroughly unsound. It ignores the possibility that, while the two transactions have the same effect on competition between the parties, they differ in other respects that are crucial in an evaluation of their total economic effect. Suppose that two competing firms, each very small relative to the other firms with which they compete, merge in order to take advantage of economies of large-scale production or to increase the efficiency with which the assets of one of the firms is managed. The merger would eliminate competition between the firms even more effectively than a price-fixing agreement between them, yet it would be absurd to treat the merger as if it were a cartel—the approach suggested by the Court in *Northern Securities*.[11] The merger would not confer on the

10. Northern Securities Co. v. United States, 193 U.S. 197 (1904). Justice Holmes in dissent urged vigorously that the Sherman Act permitted any merger or other form of corporate amalgamation to which the only objection was the elimination of competition among the parties to the transaction.

11. In fairness to the Court, it should be pointed out that the parties were relatively very large firms (two of the four major transcontinental railroads) and the form of the transaction—control of the firms by means

parties any power to increase price and might actually lead to a reduction in the market price, due to the cost reductions it made possible. This is very different from the effect of a cartel.

It was accordingly a relief when, in 1911, in deciding the government's suit against John D. Rockefeller's Standard Oil Trust, the Supreme Court held that the legality of eliminating competition by fusion as distinct from contract between competing firms was to be determined by applying a "Rule of Reason," which would allow a fuller and more flexible inquiry into the economic consequences of a challenged agreement than was permitted or would have been appropriate in a cartel case.[12] Unfortunately, the Court's opinion was murky. In particular it left unclear the extent to which the illegality of the Oil Trust under the Sherman Act depended on various improper practices—such as exacting secret rebates from railroads, selling below cost to destroy or intimidate local competitors, and evading state regulatory authority—that the trust had been found to have engaged in but that might not have been essential to its achieving and exercising power over price. This ambiguity has never been explicitly resolved. The great merger movement that produced the Oil Trust, the Powder Trust, the Tobacco Trust, the Steel Trust, and a number of other single-firm monopolies ended in about 1905, and by 1911 most of the antitrust cases attacking the classic trusts had run their course.[13] Moreover, only one of these trusts, the Steel Trust (created by the formation of the United States Steel Corporation in 1901), had a record clear of improper practices other than the initial consolidation that gave the trust a commanding market share. And in 1920 the Supreme Court held that U.S. Steel had *not* violated the Sherman Act,[14] although there was some language in the Court's opinion which suggested that the case might have been decided differently had the government brought suit promptly after the formation of U.S. Steel, rather than waiting ten years. Since there has never been a recurrence of the merger-to-monopoly movement that swept the country in the period preceding 1905,

of a holding company—did not involve an actual consolidation of the firm's operations that might have created substantial opportunities for efficiency gains.

   12. Standard Oil Co. of New Jersey v. United States, 221 U.S. 1 (1911).

   13. The disappointing results of this legal campaign are discussed in chapter 5 infra.

   14. United States v. U.S. Steel Corp., 251 U.S. 417 (1920).

the precise legal standard governing such mergers is a somewhat academic question. It has been doubly academic since 1950, when Congress passed a stringent antimerger law that clearly forbade monopolistic mergers—and much else besides.[15]

The reference in the *Standard Oil* opinion to the bad practices of the Rockefeller trust, such as predatory price cutting, proved to be exceedingly important for the subsequent development of antitrust law. Price fixing and mergers to monopoly are methods by which cooperating sellers voluntarily eliminate competition among themselves. They are not forms of aggression against non-cooperating competitors. On the contrary, the formation of a cartel, or the merger of competing firms to create a single-firm monopoly, increases the profit-making opportunities both of other sellers in the market and of potential new entrants by raising the market price above the competitive level. Collusion would be more profitable if entry or expansion by nonparticipants in the cartel or monopoly could somehow be discouraged. Predatory price cutting is one of a number of practices by which a seller or group of sellers might be able—or might be thought able—to obtain or maintain monopoly power by eliminating or intimidating competing sellers or potential competitors.

The difference between "collusive practices," the general term that I shall use to denote cooperative anticompetitive arrangements, and "exclusionary practices," the coercion of sellers outside of the collusive group, is fundamental to an understanding of the antitrust laws. The pure collusive practice involves cooperation between competing sellers (in the form of an agreement, express or tacit, limiting competition, or a merger or other method of fusion) to raise the market price above the competitive level. The agreement generates monopoly profits, but it also induces other firms to expand their output of the product sold by the colluding sellers (or to begin making the product if they have not done so previously) in order to capture a share of the monopoly profits. The pure collusive practice thus carries the seeds of its own destruction. An exclusionary practice is generally a method by which a firm (or firms) having or wanting a monopoly position trades a part of its monopoly profits, at least temporarily, for a larger market share, by making it unprofitable for other sellers to compete with it.

15. The Celler-Kefauver Antimerger Act, amending section 7 of the Clayton Act; see chapter 5 infra.

The difference is nicely illustrated by the formation and subsequent experience of the United States Steel Corporation, to which reference has already been made. U.S. Steel apparently had such a large fraction of the productive capacity of the steel industry that it could obtain monopoly profits by limiting its output. Had the remaining firms in the industry been able to expand their output rapidly without incurring higher production costs, or had new firms been able to enter the industry rapidly and operate at a cost level no higher than that of the existing firms, U.S. Steel's limitation of output would not have resulted in any significant reduction in the over-all output of the steel industry, and the market price would therefore have remained at the competitive level. Even if these conditions were not fulfilled, so long as U.S. Steel took no steps to prevent its competitors from gradually increasing their output or new firms from gradually entering the industry, its monopoly position would inevitably diminish over time. The company did make some efforts to collude with competitors, but it made no attempt to exclude them and as a result its market share declined steadily (from about 60 percent when the company was formed in 1901 to about 20 percent today). The history of U.S. Steel illustrates the policy and the eventual position of a monopolistic firm that does not engage in exclusionary practices.[16]

Many practices besides predatory price cutting have at one time or another been thought to belong in the exclusionary-practices category, such as tie-in agreements, vertical integration, reciprocal buying, exclusive dealing, price discrimination, and group boycotts. Of course, the most effective method of excluding a competitor is to have lower costs that make it possible to underprice him without selling at a loss; happily, this method of exclusion has only occasionally been considered actionable under the antitrust laws. As we shall see, some of the practices deemed exclusionary, mainly price discrimination in its various guises (including tie-in agreements), are monopolistic but not exclusionary—and not collusive either. These are the practices that, for want of a better term, I shall call "unilateral noncoercive monopolization," and they will be discussed in chapter 8.

16. See George J. Stigler, "The Dominant Firm and the Inverted Umbrella," in his book *The Organization of Industry* 108 (1968); but see Donald O. Parsons & Edward John Ray, "The United States Steel Consolidation: The Creation of Market Control," 18 *J. Law & Econ.* 181 (1975), which casts some doubt on the dominant-firm hypothesis of U.S. Steel's behavior.

Exclusionary practices, perhaps because they inflict concentrated losses on business competitors rather than diffuse losses on consumers and suppliers,[17] have been magnified into a much greater social problem than the available evidence indicates them to be. For reasons that will become clear when we discuss those practices in detail, it seems unlikely that they have ever played a major role in the growth or persistence of monopoly conditions. Yet they have been the cutting edge of antitrust doctrine since the *Standard Oil* decision in 1911. Three years later Congress enacted the Clayton and Federal Trade Commission Acts. Section 5 of the Federal Trade Commission Act, the principal substantive provision of that act, forbade "unfair methods of competition," and it seems that this prohibition was directed primarily against exclusionary practices,[18] although it was later held to forbid virtually anything forbidden by any other antitrust provision, and then some.[19] Section 2 of the Clayton Act forbade price discrimination, and section 3 tying and exclusive dealing, in circumstances where the effect might be substantially to lessen competition or tend to create a monopoly. Sections 7 and 8 of the Clayton Act limited stock acquisitions and interlocking directorates, which are not readily conceived of as exclusionary practices (although the framers of the Clayton Act may have thought of them in those terms), but neither provision turned out to have any practical importance. Section 7 was easily avoided by substituting a merger or consolidation (that is, an asset acquisition) for the stock acquisition forbidden by the statute,[20] and interlocking directorates never have been an effective method of collusion or monopolization.[21] Moreover, when section 7 was amended many years later to bring mergers and other asset acquisitions within its scope,[22] it provided a legal basis, as we shall see in chapter 6, for condemning a large number of mergers—includ-

17. Collusive practices do not injure consumers alone; the monopolist's reduced output results in a reduction in his demand for inputs, and the suppliers of those inputs will be hurt to the extent that they do not have equally good opportunities to sell their products in other markets.

18. On the background of the FTC Act, see Gerard Henderson, *The Federal Trade Commission* ch. 1 (1924).

19. See, e.g., FTC v. Brown Shoe Co., 384 U.S. 316 (1966).

20. The history of the avoidance of the original section 7 is told in United States v. Philadelphia National Bank, 374 U.S. 321, 337–40 (1963).

21. See George J. Stigler, "The Effect of the Antitrust Laws," in *The Organization of Industry* 259, 260–61 (1968).

22. See note 15 supra; chapter 6 infra.

ing mergers between competing firms—as exclusionary practices.

The Sherman Act has been on the statute books (at this writing) for eighty-five years, and even the most recent substantive amendment of the antitrust laws, the Celler-Kefauver Antimerger Act, has been operative for twenty-five years—time enough, one would have thought, for the major substantive issues of antitrust policy to be resolved in a reasonably satisfactory manner. Yet the body of substantive antitrust doctrine is today in a profoundly unsatisfactory state. The major problem areas—and the central topics of chapters 4–9—are the following:

1. The Sherman Act has proved to be ineffectual in dealing with forms of collusive pricing that do not generate detectable acts of agreement or communication among the colluding sellers.

2. The courts have swept within the rule forbidding price fixing many practices, such as the exchange of price information among competitors and the fixing of maximum or minimum resale prices by a seller, which are often procompetitive rather than anticompetitive.

3. The courts have been unable to formulate consistent, sensible, and workable standards of illegality for mergers either between competitors or between potential competitors.

4. The category of exclusionary practices has been permitted uncritically to expand, embracing many practices that actually reduce the social costs of monopoly.

The errors of legal policy have been errors of both commission and omission. Practices are forbidden that should not be, and other practices that in fact contravene the policy of the antitrust laws are left alone.

Antitrust Enforcement

Besides the confusion of substantive doctrine, the antitrust area has been plagued by problems of remedy and enforcement. The Sherman Act as originally enacted provided that violations of the act were misdemeanors punishable by a maximum fine of $5,000 and/or imprisonment for up to one year. In addition, either the Department of Justice or a private individual or firm injured by a violation of the act could seek injunctive relief. The private plaintiff could also bring a damage suit, and if he won the court would award him an amount triple his actual damages plus a reasonable attorney's fee. The pattern of remedies set in the original act has survived essentially intact to this day. The maximum fine was raised in 1955 to $50,000 and in 1974 to $100,000 for an individual defendant and $1 million for a corporate defendant. The 1974 amendments also increased the maximum prison sentence to three years. The Clayton Act carries no criminal penalties; otherwise it is enforced just like the 'Sherman Act. The Federal Trade Commission Act is enforced exclusively by the Federal Trade Commission, whose only remedy is a type of injunction called a "cease-and-desist order."

The criminal penalties actually meted out under the Sherman Act have been exceedingly mild. Table 2 shows the average fine per case imposed under the Sherman Act, both in dollars and as a percentage of the estimated sales involved in the illegal activity in the average case.[23] Table 3 indicates the infrequency with which imprisonment has been used as a sanction, though some increase in frequency is evident in the most recent period. The 1974 amendments may of course bring about a quantum jump in the severity of the sanctions meted out to convicted Sherman Act violators, though one doubts it.[24] My own opinion, which is developed in

Table 2   Fines in Price-fixing Cases, 1890–1969

Period in Which Case Was Instituted	Average Fine Per Case[a]	Average Fine as Percentage of Sales Involved on Conspiracy
1890–1899	$ 0 (0)[b]	......
1900–1909	20,000 (11)	......
1910–1919	20,000 (24)	......
1920–1929	98,000 (15)	......
1930–1939	61,000 (18)	......
1940–1949	52,000 (149)	......
1950–1959	40,000 (121)	0.08%
1960–1969	131,000 (103)	0.21%

Source: Commerce Clearing House, Federal Antitrust "Bluebook." See table 1.
[a]Rounded to nearest thousand.
[b]Number in parenthesis is number of convictions during the period.

23. For the sake of comparability, the figures in table 2 are limited to price-fixing cases; however, these constitute 70 percent of all criminal proceedings under the Sherman Act.
24. A glance at table 2 will show that the average fine in 1960–69, when the maximum fine was $50,000, was a good deal less than ten times the average fine in 1940–49, when the maximum fine was only $5,000.

Table 3   Prison Sentences in Federal Antitrust Cases

Period in Which Case Was Instituted	Number of Cases in Which Prison Sentence Was Imposed[a]	Length of Sentence	Characteristics of Case
1890–1894	0		
1895–1899	0		
1900–1904	0		
1905–1909	0		
1910–1914	1	4 hours	labor
1915–1919	3	4 hours	labor
		1 year	labor-sabotage
		1 year	labor
1920–1924	5	....	price fixing-labor
		10 days	labor
		10 months	labor
		8 months	
		1 year	labor
1925–1929	3	6 months	labor
		....	price fixing-labor
		10 days	price fixing-violence
1930–1934	6	3 months	monopolization-violence
		6 months	monopolization-violence
		6 mos.-2 yrs.	price fixing-violence
		2 years	price fixing-violence
		2-5 months	price fixing-labor-violence
		3-6 months	labor-violence
1935–1939	1	1 year	labor-violence
1940–1944	0		
1945–1949	0		
1950–1954	2	6 months	price fixing-labor
		9 months	price fixing-labor
1955–1959	2	90 days	price fixing-labor
		1 year	
1960–1964	2	30 days	price fixing
		....	price fixing
1965–1969	2	24 hrs.-60 days	price fixing
		6 months	price fixing-labor-violence
1970–1974	6	3 months	price fixing-threats
		1 month	price fixing
		9 months	price fixing
		70 days	price fixing
		90 days	price fixing
		1 month	price fixing

Source: Commerce Clearing House, Federal Antitrust "Blue-book." See table 1.
[a]Suspended sentences and probation omitted.

Table 4   Private Antitrust Suits, 1937–1974

Period (Fiscal Year)	Number of Cases Filed[a] (Other Than Electrical Equipment)	Average per Year During Period	Number of Electrical-Equipment Cases Filed[a]	Total	Average per Year During Period
1937–1954	1,874	104	0	1,874	104
1955–1959	1,144	229	0	1,144	229
1960–1964	1,435	287	1,919	3,354	671
1965	443	443	3	446	446
1966	444	444	0	444	444
1967	536	536	0	536	536
1968	659	659	0	659	659
1969	740	740	0	740	740
1970	877	877	0	877	877
1971	1,003	1,003	0	1,003	1,003
1972	1,203	1,203	0	1,203	1,203
1973	1,089	1,089	0	1,089	1,089
1974	1,162	1,162	0	1,162	1,162

Source: U.S. Admin. Office of the U.S. Courts, Ann. Reps. 1940–1974.
[a]Excluding transferred cases.

chapter 10, is that the use of the criminal laws to punish antitrust violations is fundamentally misconceived.

Although data on private actions to enforce the antitrust laws are unavailable for years prior to 1937, such actions were apparently rare during that period. Since then, they have grown explosively, as shown in table 4. Private actions for *price fixing* were probably rare until the private damage suits arising out of the great electrical conspiracy of the early 1960s demonstrated the opportunities for large awards in such cases (some $400 million was awarded in the electrical cases). In recent years the opportunities for substantial damages in price-fixing cases have become even greater as a result of the development of the consumer class action.

The burgeoning of the private antitrust action has induced enormous, and I think justified, concern about the overexpansion of the antitrust laws and their increasing use to retard rather than promote competition. If there were less substantive confusion in antitrust policy, the creation of effective remedies would not be a source of concern—quite the contrary. But to the extent that such confusion seems likely to remain a permanent feature of antitrust policy, we may be forced to the unappetizing choice between failing to provide effective remedies for those violations of the antitrust laws that really harm competition and efficiency, and providing remedies that can be used by private plaintiffs to block takeover attempts by more efficient firms, to harass competitors that have lower costs, and otherwise to frustrate the fundamental goals of antitrust policy. Chapter 10 attempts to resolve this dilemma.

II The Problem of Collusion

4 Price Fixing and the Oligopoly Problem

At the time that the Sherman Act was enacted, cartels were a common phenomenon of American industry. Although sometimes the term "cartel" is used to refer to any collusive arrangement, it is more often limited to the kind of formal, aboveboard agreement among firms to limit their competition that one finds in markets, here and abroad, not subject to the Sherman Act. Because of the temptations to "cheat" (about which more shortly) that collusive agreements create, colluders who don't have to worry about legal harassment will often establish an elaborate machinery for effectuating noncompetitive pricing. The machinery of cartelization includes sales quotas, exclusive sales agencies, price-fixing committees, the levying of penalties for infractions, provisions for arbitration of disputes, investigative apparatus, customer allocation, geographical-market division, and the like. As noted in the last chapter, the illegality of cartels under the Sherman Act was established in the early years of the act; and, since cartels are difficult to conceal, the act, despite its rather feeble sanctions and lackluster enforcement, apparently succeeded in virtually eliminating them from the industries subject to it. The elimination of the formal cartel from those industries is an impressive, and remains the major, achievement of American antitrust law.[1] But the disappearance of the formal cartel did not solve the problem of monopoly pricing. Apart from the fact that some cartels were able to convert into single-firm monopolies without being molested by the antitrust enforcement agencies,[2] and others were able to obtain immunity from the antitrust laws, two major opportunities for monopoly pricing remained. First, a cartel might simply be driven underground by the antitrust laws, thus becoming a secret price-

1. See the Appendix at the end of the book for a stab at estimating the social-cost savings from eliminating the formal cartel.
2. For a striking example of this, see 2 Simon N. Whitney, *Antitrust Policies: American Experience in Twenty Industries* 7 (1958).

fixing conspiracy. Such a conspiracy would be less effective than an overt cartel. The exigencies of concealment would compel abandonment of much of the elaborate machinery that enables a full-fledged cartel to overcome the potentially serious problems of arriving at the optimum cartel price and of preventing the chiseling of that price by cartel members. Yet in the aggregate even these underground conspiracies might pose a substantial social problem. Second, in some circumstances competing sellers might be able to coordinate their pricing without conspiring in the usual sense of the term—that is, without any overt or detectable acts of communication. This is the phenomenon that lawyers call "conscious parallelism" and some economists term "oligopolistic interdependence," but which I prefer to call "tacit collusion" in contrast to the explicit collusion of the formal cartel or its underground counterpart.

The Criminalization of the Price-Fixing Rule

The law responded to these two problems in quite different ways. The response to explicit (albeit covert) collusion took the form of what I have already described in the last chapter as the criminalization of the price-fixing rule. The weapons that the criminal law had developed to deal with conspiracies in other areas were simply trained on price fixing, with the result that the inquiry in a price-fixing case became focused on the question whether the defendants had met or communicated with one another for the purpose of limiting competition. Once the conspiracy approach to explicit collusion became firmly ensconced in the minds of bench and bar, it was perhaps inevitable that tacit collusion would be considered beyond the reach of the antitrust laws because, by definition, it did not involve explicit, detectable acts of agreement or communication. This tendency in legal thinking was reinforced by an economic approach that treated tacit collusion as fundamentally different from the price-fixing conspiracy—as being, in fact, a form of noncollusive, albeit "interdependent," behavior dictated by the concentrated, or "oligopolistic," structure of the market rather than by actual agreement among the sellers.

As a consequence of these developments in legal policy and economic thought, the law relating to collusive pricing became emptied of economic content. Although the purpose of the rule was to prevent monopoly pricing, the only proof of price fixing required or ordinarily offered was proof that the defendants conspired. Whether the conspiracy actually resulted in a substantial increase in price or reduction in output was immaterial. In short, the law punished the *attempt* to fix prices; the completed act—an actual restriction of output—was incidental. And substantial output restrictions not accomplished by methods yielding evidence of a conspiracy were simply beyond the reach of the law.

Partly as a result of the ingenuity of the lawyers for plaintiffs in private antitrust cases, the gulf between economics and price fixing is gradually narrowing. I shall have more to say about this development shortly. It remains generally true, however, that the law of price fixing punishes the attempt to fix prices regardless of its consequences and ignores supracompetitive pricing, however serious, that does not generate the kind of evidence which can be used to establish a traditional criminal conspiracy.

Since lawyers and judges are more comfortable with conspiracy doctrine than price theory, the displacement of emphasis from the economic consequences to the fact of conspiring is natural. But it is inconsistent with an effective antitrust policy. Many attempts to fix price may have negligible consequences, while much serious price fixing may escape detection altogether because overt communication is required to establish an attempt but may not always be necessary to effectuate price fixing.

Several reasons have been suggested for emphasizing the attempt to fix prices rather than the completed act. One is that businessmen would not attempt to fix prices in situations where they were unlikely to succeed; therefore by forbidding the attempt we prevent actual price fixing, and since price fixing is devoid of social utility, no harm is done if attempts that would not have succeeded are also sometimes punished. However, while obviously firms would not participate in price-fixing conspiracies if they were sure they would not succeed, they may sometimes be mistaken, and such mistakes, even if rare, could account for a large proportion of the small number of price-fixing cases that the public enforcement agencies bring. Moreover, if the costs of price fixing (including punishment costs, discounted by the small probability that the conspirators will actually be apprehended) are low, conspiracy may be a perfectly rational business strategy even if most attempts fail. And it is incorrect that no harm is done by pursuing attempts to fix prices that would not succeed: enforcement resources consumed in marginal cases are unavailable for more important ones.

Another reason that has been suggested for the emphasis of the law on the attempt to fix prices rather than on economic effects is that the methods of litigation are ill suited to the resolution of the complex economic questions that an "effects" case would frequently involve. This argument depends on just how complex such a case must be and in any event it could at most justify the refusal of the courts to apply economic criteria—not the refusal of the public enforcement agencies to use such criteria informally in deciding where to concentrate their resources.

A related, and by far the weightiest, reason offered for the emphasis on attempts is that we do not know enough about cartelization to use any other approach. I believe that this attitude is too pessimistic. As we shall see, economic data could be used to identify serious limitations of output due to either explicit or tacit collusion, both by identifying those markets whose characteristics predispose them toward price fixing—markets, in other words, where a search for evidence of actual price fixing is most likely to be rewarded—and by applying certain tests in the suspect markets to determine whether the market price is in fact substantially above the competitive level.

The Interdependence Theory of Oligopoly Pricing

I am also critical of the other branch of the conventional analysis of collusive pricing, the branch that asserts that what I have termed "tacit collusion" is fundamentally different from explicit collusion and cannot be punished as a form of price fixing. This point of view was given its authoritative expression in an article by Donald Turner, published in 1962,[3] which argues strongly that oligopoly pricing (tacit collusion in my terminology) is beyond the reach of section 1 of the Sherman Act. The argument is based on the "interdependence" theory of pricing under oligopoly. That theory can be briefly summarized as follows. In a market of many sellers, the individual seller is too small for his decisions on pricing and output to affect the market price. He can sell all that he can produce at that price and nothing at a higher price. He can shade price without fear of retaliation because the expansion of his output resulting from a price reduction will divert only an imperceptible amount of business from each of his competitors. (For example, in a market of 100 sellers of equal size, an expansion in output of 20 percent by one of them will result in an average fall

3. Donald F. Turner, "The Definition of Agreement Under the Sherman Act: Conscious Parallelism and Refusals to Deal," 75 *Harv. L. Rev.* 655 (1962).

in output of only about .2 of 1 percent for each of the others, so a seller need not worry in making his pricing decisions about the reactions of his rivals.) In contrast, in a market where there are few sellers (an "oligopoly"), a price cut that produces a substantial expansion in the sales of one seller will result in so substantial a contraction in the sales of the others that they will promptly match the cut. If, for example, there are three sellers of equal size, a 20-percent expansion in the sales of one will cause the sales of each of the others to fall by an average of 10 percent—a sales loss the victims can hardly overlook. Anticipating a prompt reaction by his rivals that will quickly nullify his gains from price cutting, the seller in a highly concentrated market will be less likely to initiate a price cut than his counterpart in the atomized market. Oligopolists are "interdependent" in their pricing: they base their pricing decisions in part on anticipated reactions to them. The result is a tendency to avoid vigorous price competition.

Turner asks whether oligopolistic interdependence should be viewed as a form of agreement to fix prices that violates section 1 of the Sherman Act. Turner is prepared to allow that, "considered purely as a problem in linguistic definition,"[4] interdependent pricing could be deemed a type of collusion. But to him a more important consideration is that "the rational oligopolist is behaving in exactly the same way as is the rational seller in a competitively structured industry; he is simply taking another factor into account [the reactions of his rivals to any price cut] . . . which he has to take into account because the situation in which he finds himself puts it there."[5] Since the oligopolist is behaving just like the seller in an atomized market, oligopoly pricing can be described as "rational individual decision in the light of relevant economic facts" as well as it can be described as collusion.[6]

Turner's decisive argument, however, is that no effective remedy against oligopolistic interdependence can be fairly implied from section 1. An injunction that merely "prohibited each defendant from taking into account the probable price decisions of his competitors in determining his own price or output" would "demand such irrational behavior that full compliance would be virtually impossible."[7] To be effective, the injunction would have to require

4. Id. at 665.
5. Id. at 665–66.
6. Ibid.
7. Id. at 669.

the defendants to reduce their prices to their costs, and the enforcement of such a decree would involve the courts in a public-utility type of rate regulation for which they are ill equipped. Dissolution of the guilty firms would also be inappropriate in a section 1 setting: "If effective and workable relief requires a radical structural reformation of the industry, this indicates that it was the structural situation, not the behavior of the industry members, which was fundamentally responsible for the unsatisfactory results."[8]

Oligopolistic interdependence, in short, is inherent in the structure of certain markets. Only semantically can it be equated with collusive price fixing, for it is unresponsive to the remedies appropriate in price-fixing cases. How, then, to deal with the phenomenon? Turner's answer is to break up oligopolistic firms into small units, either through special legislation or in proceedings under section 2 of the Sherman Act charging oligopolists with jointly monopolizing their market. We shall examine the problems of implementing a "deconcentration" approach to oligopoly in the next chapter. For now, we are concerned only with Turner's analysis of the unsuitability of section 1, and of section 1-type remedies (injunctions, treble damages, criminal sanctions), for dealing with oligopoly pricing.

Turner's analysis is a logical application of the interdependence theory of oligopolistic pricing. But the theory is inadequate. The idea that a seller in a concentrated market will be reluctant to initiate price reductions—simply because he knows that, unlike the situation in an unconcentrated market, a price cut will have so large an impact on the sales of his competitors as to force them promptly to match the cut, thereby wiping out the price cutter's gains and leaving everyone worse off than before—depends on a number of critical, but unexamined, factual assumptions. One is that there will be no appreciable time lag between the initial price cut and the response; if there is, the price cutter may obtain substantial interim profits from his lower price. Yet there may well be such a lag, if the price cut can be concealed or, in cases where concealment is impossible, if the other sellers cannot expand their output as rapidly as the first to meet the greater demand at the lower price.

The interdependence theory also overstates the impact of one oligopolist's price reduction on the sales of the others, and hence

8. Id. at 671.

the incentive to react immediately to such a reduction. When a seller increases his output by lowering his price, only part of the additional output consists of sales diverted from his rivals. The rest consists of sales to new buyers who bought less or none of the product at the higher price. Depending on the elasticity of demand, much of the price cutter's new business may come from outside the market rather than from the former customers of his rivals. This effect will diminish the impact of the price cut on them, thus reducing the likelihood of their responding immediately. The impact will also be diminished if the price cutter initially reduces price on only a portion of his output, or if his output is not perfectly substitutable for the output of the other sellers in the market.

Moreover, the basic distinction claimed between concentrated and unconcentrated markets with respect to price competition depends on an artificial convention. The different changes in output that are compared are related only in that each represents the same percentage of each seller's previous output. It is true that if there are 100 sellers of equal size in a market having a total output of 1,000 units and one increases his output by 2 units—20 percent —the effect on the sales of the other firms will be slight. But if there were only 3 sellers in the market (each the same size) and one increased output by 2 units, the effect on his rivals would be negligible too. To produce dramatic effects under oligopoly, a much larger expansion of output by the price cutter must be assumed. Let the oligopolist in our example expand output by 20 percent of his previous output (67 units) and, true enough, his rivals will lose such a large fraction of their sales as to make them want to match the lower price. But if the same market were unconcentrated and a seller (or several sellers) increased output by 67 units, the remaining sellers would respond too. The interdependence theory assumes both that an individual seller can expand output by only a fraction of his previous output and that individual sellers in an unconcentrated market, unlike their counterparts in concentrated markets, will lack the foresight to realize that a price cut by several of them may have an aggregate impact on the remaining sellers so large as to provoke a prompt matching response by those sellers. These assumptions may be generally valid, but more than assertion is required to make them so.

A further difficulty arises from the emphasis that the interdependence theory places on price *reductions*. The supposed reluctance of oligopolists to reduce prices is cause for concern only if there is reason to believe that their prices are above the competitive level. The interdependence theory does not explain, however, how oligopolistic sellers ever establish such a price in the first place. To be sure, if costs or demand in a market decline, a failure to reduce price may have the effect of transforming a previously competitive price into a monopolistic one. But, given our seemingly chronic inflation, a higher than competitive price normally could not be maintained without occasional market-wide price increases. How are these effected? The unsatisfactory answer given by interdependence theorists is "price leadership."

Consider an unconcentrated market in which price is equal to cost (including in cost an allowance for a fair return to the investors). As the result of a series of mergers, the market becomes oligopolistic. One of the leading firms then raises its price to the monopoly level. It knows that it will be unable to maintain a supracompetitive price if its rivals do not match the increase, but it relies (so the argument goes) on their having the good sense to realize that all would be better off at the higher price. However, to the extent that this reasoning is plausible it undermines the proposition that oligopolists are reluctant to *reduce* prices. That proposition depends on each oligopolist's reasoning that, if his rivals match his price reduction, everyone, himself included, will end up worse off than before, because they will be at a lower price level. But why will that unhappy result not be prevented on the way down by an appropriate exercise of price leadership? Anticipating that it will, an oligopolist should be unafraid to shade price, reasoning that if his rivals do not match his lower price his profits will increase, while if they do match it he can promptly restore his price to the original level, since his rivals are sure to follow his leadership. There is, of course, the danger that one of the other firms, reasoning similarly, will *not* follow him back up but will instead reason as follows: "If I raise my price more slowly than the others, I can increase my profits at their expense; should they come back down to my price, it will be time enough to raise my price then, and they will follow." If oligopolistic sellers reason this way, they may indeed regard price reductions as a dangerous tactic. But if such reasoning is common it will be difficult for oligopolists to reach noncompetitive price levels in the first place. Each will be reluctant to exercise price leadership knowing that the others will be tempted by the prospect of short-term gains at his expense to lag in matching his higher price.

A Unified Theory of Collusive Pricing

The internal difficulties of the interdependence theory argue for an alternative approach to the question of collusive pricing in the absence of provable conspiracy. George Stigler has developed an alternative approach that is at once subtle and simple: to treat oligopoly pricing as a special case in the general economic theory of collusive pricing.[9] In this analysis, which has been surprisingly neglected by antitrust lawyers and economists, cartels (here broadly defined to include any method of collusive pricing) are assumed to vary in formality from the full-blown cartel that the Sherman Act has substantially eliminated in the industries subject to it to the "cartel" that requires no detectable machinery of collusion—the "cartel" in which collusion is effectuated by a purely tacit meeting of the minds, a mutual forbearance to carry production to the point where price equals marginal cost. This approach opens up the possibility that the same basic legal doctrines and remedies might be employed effectively across the entire range of cartel formality.

A firm's decision to collude, whether expressly or tacitly, is presumably made by balancing the potential gains of collusion to the firm against the costs of collusion to it, including any expected punishment costs. By examining the factors that bear on the private benefits and costs of colluding, we can identify the kinds of market settings in which collusion is likely to be attempted and the amount of communication, formality, etc., that would be required to enable the attempt to succeed. We may even be able to identify the specific economic symptoms of effective collusion. In short, we may be able to go beyond the "cops-and-robbers" approach to price fixing that has heretofore dominated the law, and in so doing incidentally solve the problem of how to prevent tacit collusion.[10]

9. George J. Stigler, "A Theory of Oligopoly," in his book *The Organization of Industry* 39 (1968).

10. See Richard A. Posner, "Oligopoly and the Antitrust Laws; A Suggested Approach," 21 *Stan. L. Rev.* 1562 (1969); cf. John M. Kuhlman, "Nature and Significance of Price Fixing Rings," 2 *Antitrust Law & Econ. Rev.* 69 (1969). For background on the economics of cartelization see

The potential gains from collusion[11] are determined by the (price) elasticity of demand facing the colluding sellers. For our purposes, the elasticity of demand may be defined as the percentage change in quantity demanded as a result of a 1-percent change in price; it is always negative since a price increase results in a reduction in quantity demanded and a price reduction in an increase in the quantity demanded. The less elastic the demand for a product at the competitive price, the greater are the potential gains from collusion. Suppose, for example, that a 1-percent increase in price will result in only a .5 of 1-percent decline in quantity demanded; since total revenue is simply the product of price charged and quantity sold, the higher price will yield a larger total revenue to the sellers of the product,[12] while their total costs will be lower since fewer units will be produced. The higher price is clearly more profitable. If demand were instead highly elastic at the competitive price, the quantity effect of a price increase might be so drastic as to reduce both the total sales of the sellers and their net revenues.

Unfortunately, elasticities of demand are difficult both to measure and to interpret. A high measured elasticity might indicate that collusion was unattractive to the sellers in the market because a price increase would result in a sharp contraction in total revenues; or it might indicate that the sellers were successfully colluding and had forced the market price into the region of the demand curve where a *further* increase in price would be unprofitable, which as we saw in chapter 2 is precisely the region in which the successful monopolist or cartel will sell. Thus it may be difficult to tell in specific cases whether a group of sellers is in fact likely to consider collusion a potentially profitable strategy. But sometimes there is persuasive indirect evidence. As explained more fully in chapter 6, if other sellers make a product identical to that of the potential colluders, it may be possible to infer that the demand

Donald Dewey, *Monopoly in Economics and Law* 7–24 (1959); John S. McGee, "Ocean Freight Rate Conferences and the American Merchant Marine," 27 *U. Chi. L. Rev.* 191 (1960); George A. Hay & Daniel Kelley, "An Empirical Survey of Price-Fixing Conspiracies," 17 *J. Law & Econ.* 13 (1974); Richard A. Posner, "A Statistical Study of Antitrust Enforcement," 13 *J. Law & Econ.* 365 (1970).

11. I am speaking here of the *gross* benefits to the colluding sellers; the costs of collusion are discussed separately below.

12. For an example of this effect see supra note 1 at p. 10.

facing the latter at the competitive price must be highly elastic, since presumably a slight increase above that price would induce consumers to switch promptly to the other sellers of the product. But this presumption is not absolute. The other sellers may have higher marketing costs—perhaps higher transportation costs—because of their greater distance from the buyers, or higher production costs because of lack of access to patented production processes used by the putative colluders.[13] Thus, it is necessary in some cases to recognize the existence of geographical submarkets within which the competition of distant sellers of the same product will be ineffective in compressing price to cost, or distinct product submarkets such as for "cracked" and "straight" gasoline.[14] And even if other sellers have the same costs in general as the members of the cartel, they may not be able to expand output rapidly enough to offset an output restriction without incurring sharply higher costs than the cartel. It is in this connection that the combined market share of the colluding sellers—a factor quite properly stressed in the early cartel cases,[15] though later forgotten—becomes relevant. The larger that share, the less likely it is that the remaining sellers will quickly nullify the effect of the cartel on the market price by expanding their output, since each would have to make a proportionately very large increase in his output and this is usually difficult to do in a short time. Hence the cartel will be able to enjoy monopoly profits for some period.

Existing sellers are not the only source of additional output in a market. Sellers of other products (or of the same product in a different region) will have an incentive to enter a market in which the sellers are earning monopoly profits. Again, the speed with which new entry can be expected to bring about a substantial expansion in the output of the market is crucial in evaluating how the possibility of new entry affects the expected gains from collusion. A further complication is that even if there are no other sellers of the product in question, and new entry into the market is for some reason completely blocked, the elasticity of demand at

13. See, e.g., Standard Oil Co. (Indiana) v. United States, 283 U.S. 163 (1931), discussed in John S. McGee, "Patent Exploitation: Some Economic and Legal Problems," 9 *J. Law & Econ.* 135, 150–60 (1966).

14. See supra note 13.

15. The most sophisticated discussion is in United States v. Addyston Pipe & Steel Co., 85 Fed. 271 (6th Cir. 1898), modified and aff'd, 175 U.S. 211 (1899).

the competitive price may be so high as to make collusion an unprofitable strategy. The consumer may have plenty of good substitutes for the various end uses to which the product in question is put, albeit none of these substitutes is identical, or even very similar, to the product.[16]

The sorts of evidence that might be used to estimate the elasticity of demand facing a group of sellers at the competitive price will rarely yield unambiguous inferences. For example, the fact that there may have been a number of new entrants into a market in the recent past may indicate only that the sellers in that market were charging such a high price that they attracted firms which would not have entered the market at the competitive price. Yet there are easy cases as well as hard, and whatever the ultimate decision on how much evidence should be admitted in a judicial proceeding given the cumbersome evidentiary processes of litigation, it is inexcusable that the enforcement agencies should fail to consider such evidence in deciding how to allocate their limited resources. The small market share of the mattress manufacturers accused of price fixing in the *Sealy* case should have alerted the Justice Department to the fact that the purpose and effect of the challenged arrangement could not have been price fixing, however much it resembled it.[17] The manifest ease and rapidity of entry into the retail grocery business at competitive price levels should have deterred the Justice Department from bringing suit to challenge a merger of competing supermarket chains on the ground that the merger might create a market structure conducive to collusion.[18] In many cases of alleged or suspected collusion it will be possible to make a threshold judgment as to whether the conditions in the market indicate that the elasticity of demand at the competitive price is probably so high that collusive pricing would be an unprofitable strategy to follow even if it were costless to collude. Such a judgment will help the enforcement agencies to

16. It is necessary to distinguish between the ultimate satisfactions that a product yields—nutrition, comfort, prestige, or whatever—and the product itself. Although two products may not be substitutable for all the satisfactions that they yield, they may be perfect substitutes for one, say prestige (a Rolls-Royce versus a yacht). Conceivably, there might be perfect substitutes in each of the ultimate dimensions of satisfaction in which a given product competed with other products. But see pp. 149–50 infra.

17. United States v. Sealy, Inc., 388 U.S. 350 (1967); see pp. 165–66 infra.

18. See pp. 105–9 infra.

allocate their resources intelligently and avoid the pursuit of shadows and chimeras—which unfortunately is a very large part of the antitrust enforcement process today.

Even if the potential gains from collusion are substantial because demand is relatively inelastic at the competitive price, collusion will not be attempted if those gains are outweighed by the costs of collusion. The costs are of two types,[19] costs of arriving at a common price above the competitive price level and costs of preventing chiseling of the agreed-upon price by members of the group. Among the problems of fixing a mutually satisfactory price are the conflicting interests of sellers having different costs; the optimum cartel price will be lower for a seller with lower costs.[20] A similar conflict will arise if the output of one or more sellers in the group is not perfectly substitutable for the output of the others (a likely circumstance since sellers will differ in their reputation for reliability, in quality control, in detailed product specifications, and in other respects relevant to consumer choice). The sellers whose output is more highly valued by the consumer will want a higher market price than the others.[21] Still another problem in arriving at the initial price-fixing agreement is that the industry may not, and indeed is quite unlikely to, produce a single item. The steel industry does not sell "steel"; it sells sheets, bars, and other shapes, of varying thickness, strength, ductility, etc.—in short a large variety of product types—and a separate collusive price would have to be set for each one because of the ease of substituting one for another. Moreover, once the price schedule is fixed there must be a mechanism for renegotiating it from time to time as changes in the conditions of cost or demand alter the optimum price. Finally, agreeing on price alone may not be enough to get the cartel going. The transition from a competitive to a monopolistic market entails a reduction in the output of the market, and a decision must be made as to how this reduction is to be shared among the members of the cartel. It will not do for each member to continue producing at his old level of output—goods that cannot be sold at the monopoly price will pile up and eventually exert irresistible pressure to reduce price. Yet each seller will be reluctant to curtail *his* production, since the more he can

---

19. I put to one side punishment costs, since we are trying to figure out when punishment is necessary to deter collusion.

20. See Appendix, infra p. 248.

21. Cf. id. at 249.

sell at the monopoly price the greater will be his profits. He would prefer the other sellers to curtail their production. It may therefore be necessary for the cartel to assign sales, and even production, quotas.

Another reason why just agreeing on a price may not be enough to make collusion effective was suggested in chapter 2. Setting the price above a seller's costs will induce him to expend resources on upgrading his output in the consumer's eyes so as to take sales away from his competitors and thereby engross a larger share of the profits generated by the higher than competitive price. If all the sellers do this, they will compete away all of the monopoly profits and end up earning a competitive return at the monopoly price. Thus it may be necessary to agree to limit not only price competition but the important forms of nonprice competition as well, a difficult thing to do since there are so many ways in which sellers can vie for the buyer's patronage.

In short, launching a cartel may require quite elaborate negotiations among the parties, which must of course be carried on in a clandestine manner to avoid immediate detection by the antitrust enforcers. The requirement of concealment would appear greatly to diminish the possibility of effective collusion in industries subject to the Sherman Act that are not highly concentrated or oligopolistic. In such industries a few sellers account for a sufficiently large share of the market to be able to maintain a supracompetitive price without immediately losing most of their business to their competitors. The costs of negotiation rise, probably quite rapidly,[22] with the number of parties to the negotiation; so, of course, does the likelihood of detection. It seems unlikely that a large number of firms could accomplish the complex and delicate task of effectively coordinating their pricing without generating abundant evidence of conspiracy. Some degree of concentration thus appears to be a necessary condition of successful collusion in markets governed by the Sherman Act.

This conclusion is reinforced by a consideration of the costs incurred in maintaining a collusive pricing scheme once it has been created. A collusive price cannot be expected to persist through

22. A two-party negotiation requires establishing one communication path; a three-party, three; a four-party, six; and a five-party, ten. The general formula for the number of two-way communications necessary to link up all the members of a group is $N(N\text{-}1)/2$, where N is the number of members of the group.

sheer inertia, since each member of the colluding circle has an incentive to shade the price and thereby increase his profits.[23] It might seem that no member of the cartel would be so shortsighted as to cheat in this way, since he must know that cheating is self-defeating in the long run. Even so, the cartel price might be under-cut inadvertently, because of a computational mistake or a failure of communication either of the agreed price or of a change in it. Mistakes of this sort must be common when coordination is effected, as it must be in industries subject to the Sherman Act, by clan-destine means. Yet competing sellers will not know that the "cheat-ing" was inadvertent, and may retaliate; in this way a mistake can easily trigger a general round of price cutting. Moreover, one mem-ber of a cartel may cheat because he suspects that others are cheating and therefore wants to teach them a lesson, or because he lacks confidence that the cartel will endure and sees no reason why he should forgo the short-run advantages of a lower price in exchange for long-run advantages unlikely in fact to accrue to him. A clandestine cartel is rife with inducements and temptations to cheating, as is confirmed by the history of actual cartels, which are usually quite unstable even when not forced underground by antitrust enforcement.[24]

Cheating is presumably least likely when detection is prompt and certain, for in that case the cheater gains no advantage from his lower price—it is promptly matched. As Stigler has shown, ease of detection is directly related to the concentration of the selling side of the market and inversely related to the concentra-tion of the buying side.[25] The fewer the sellers in the colluding group, the easier it will be to tell whether a loss in sales is the

23. Suppose, for example, that the agreed-upon price is $5 per unit, but unit cost is only $3 (and does not, I shall assume for purposes of this example, vary with the number of units produced). The implicit sales quota of each member of the cartel is, let us assume, 100 units. Each member's expected profits are therefore $200. Suppose, however, that by granting secret discounts that would reduce his average revenue from $5 to $4.80 per unit a seller could increase his output—mainly of course at the expense of the other members of the cartel—to 125 units. His total profits would rise to $225. He would be making less profit on each unit sold but the proportional increase in the number of units sold would be greater than the price decrease.

24. See, for example, the case studies presented in George W. Stocking & Myron W. Watkins, *Cartels in Action* (1946).

25. See note 9 supra.

result of price cutting by another member of the group. Conversely, the fewer the number of major buyers, the more difficult it will be to attribute even a substantial loss in sales to cheating by another seller, since the loss may have resulted from the defection of a single buyer, conceivably a random event. In addition, cheating is more attractive when it takes the form of granting a lower price to a single large buyer rather than to many small ones, since the likelihood of detection presumably increases with the number of customers who are favored. In principle, a cartel could establish an investigative apparatus for detecting cheating, but this would greatly increase the probability that the cartel itself would be detected.

Oligopoly or seller concentration thus has a double significance in the analysis of the clandestine cartel. It facilitates the initial formation of the cartel by reducing the immense practical difficulties of conducting elaborate negotiations clandestinely, and it facilitates the maintenance of the cartel in the face of the inevitable self-destructive tendencies by making it possible to detect cheating without elaborate policing efforts that would inevitably be discovered by the authorities. The impermissible analytical leap (which proponents of the "interdependence" theory of oligopoly often make) is from the proposition that concentration is probably a necessary condition of clandestine collusion to the proposition that it is a sufficient condition. There is nothing in the theory of cartels to suggest that if there are just a few major sellers in a market competition will automatically disappear. Each seller must still decide whether to limit output, and this implies at least tacit agreement with his major competitors. The problems of arriving at a mutually agreeable price and then maintaining it in the face of temptations to cheat exist whether few or many sellers are trying to collude. The only difference is that these problems are more easily overcome, without the need to create the kind of elaborate apparatus of communication and enforcement that is bound to be detected eventually, in a market where effective collusion requires the cooperation of only a few sellers than in an otherwise identical but less concentrated market. And even this difference is important only in a system where antitrust liability hinges on proof of overt communication. It would disappear in a system that punished effective collusion, however administered, rather than just a particular method of colluding. In terms of the substantive economic objectives of antitrust policy, it is a detail whether a cartel is buttressed by all or any of the facilitating devices that cartels in markets not governed by the Sherman Act employ, or whether it achieves its end by purely tacit collusion; in either case the objection is to the cartel price rather than to the means by which that price is set initially and then maintained.

Implementing an Economic Approach to Detection and Proof of Collusion, Explicit or Tacit

The foregoing discussion lays the basis for what I shall call the economic approach to punishing collusion—explicit and tacit—to distinguish it from the traditional legal approach based on proof of a conspiracy. The economic approach as I envisage it would proceed in two stages. The first would involve identifying those markets in which conditions are propitious for the emergence of collusion; the second, determining whether collusive pricing in fact exists in such a market. The reader may wonder whether the first stage is either necessary or appropriate: one could hardly punish firms simply for finding themselves in a situation where collusion would appear to be an advantageous strategy; and if they *are* in fact colluding why worry whether the circumstances in the market are favorable to collusion? The reasons for the first stage of the inquiry are twofold: first, to enable enforcers to concentrate their resources in markets where the resources are likely to be employed most productively; second, to permit ambiguous conduct to be evaluated. For example, as we shall see in chapter 7, in a market where conditions are favorable to collusion an exchange of price information may be persuasive evidence of collusive pricing, whereas in a market in which conditions are unfavorable to collusion the same such exchange may be no evidence of collusive behavior at all—may be, in fact, a procompetitive element of the market.

Let us now examine the conditions favorable to collusion in more detail:

(1) *Market concentrated on the selling side.* There are various indexes of seller concentration, of which the most common (but not the best) is the aggregate market share of the 4 or 8 largest firms.[26] Unfortunately, there is no consensus among economists

---

26. A better index is the Herfindahl, which automatically incorporates the effect on the likelihood of collusion of the presence of a fringe of small firms in the market—a factor that I discuss separately as item (2) below.

with respect to the threshold above which collusion becomes an attractive proposition. Indeed, it is unclear that there can be "a" threshold. Concentration interacts with the other predisposing characteristics; a level of concentration that might be insignificant in an industry selling a customized product to a concentrated market and facing a substantial probability of new entry should prices rise above the competitive level might become the decisive factor inducing collusion in an industry where the other conditions were propitious. About the most that can be said on the question is that different levels of concentration create a presumptive danger of collusive pricing in the minds of different economists. Some would not begin to worry until the 4 largest sellers in the market had a combined market share of 70–80 percent,[27] and others would begin to worry when the share of the 4 largest sellers reached 40 percent.[28] But no responsible economist would claim today that concentration was the *only* factor predisposing a market to collusion.

(2) *No fringe of small sellers.* A disadvantage of expressing concentration in terms of the combined market share of the largest sellers is that it does not tell us very much about the remaining sellers. Yet it surely makes a difference in a market where the 4 largest firms have 80 percent of the market whether there is 1 other firm or 100. The coordination of the pricing of 5 firms is obviously much easier than that of 104 firms, and while it may of course be unnecessary to obtain the agreement of the little firms in order to collude effectively—they may not be able to expand their output rapidly enough to offset the output restriction of the colluding sellers and may in any event have higher costs than the colluders—still, any part of the market that is outside of the colluding circle constitutes a limitation on the power of the colluding sellers over the market price.

(3) *Inelastic demand at competitive price.* The relationship between the elasticity of demand facing a group of sellers at the competitive price and the potential gains to them from collusion has already been discussed, and I have acknowledged that elastici-

See Richard A. Posner, supra note 10, at 1602–03, for a discussion of how the Herfindahl index might be used in formulating antitrust guidelines in the merger area.

27. See, e.g., George J. Stigler, supra note 9; Oliver E. Williamson, Book Review, 83 *Yale L. J.* 647, 658 (1974).

28. See, e.g., Frederick M. Scherer, *Industrial Market Structure and Economic Performance* 185 (1970).

ties are difficult to measure, especially where the point on the demand curve at which the elasticity of demand is to be measured (the competitive price) may be different from the point at which the industry is actually selling. Yet economists spend a good deal of time trying to estimate demand elasticities,[29] with at least partial success, and they would spend a great deal more time at it were there a greater demand for such work, and in the process they would improve their techniques. Moreover, while a finding that demand is highly elastic is bound to be of ambiguous import, since one can never be sure that it is not the result of the sellers' having jacked the price up into the elastic region of the demand curve in order to maximize monopoly profits, a finding that demand is *in*elastic at the current market price is rather good evidence that the sellers are not colluding—at least, not effectively. Further, even if direct measurements of the elasticity of demand are deemed hopelessly unreliable, it is often possible to estimate the elasticity indirectly—as antitrust lawyers, judges, and economists do all the time, often poorly to be sure, in determining the existence of a "relevant market" in which to appraise the effects of a challenged practice. If, for example, a product has no good substitutes at the current price, that is at least some evidence, albeit not conclusive, that the demand for the product is inelastic at that price. If, on the other hand, the product has good substitutes at the current price but these substitutes cost a good deal more to produce, that is some evidence that the product is in fact being sold at a monopoly price; at the competitive price, which would equal cost, the higher-cost substitutes would disappear from the market. We return to this point in chapter 6.

(4) *Entry takes a long time.* Strictly speaking, this factor is part of the last one since the effect of a price increase in inducing the prompt entry of new firms and a consequent shift of business away from the firms in the market will affect the elasticity of demand other than in the very short run.[30] But to the extent that the

---

29. See, e.g., H. S. Houthakker & Lester D. Taylor, *Consumer Demand in the United States, 1929–1970* (1966).

30. The elasticity of demand varies with the time period under consideration. In the very short run, demand is likely to be quite inelastic because it is difficult for either sellers or buyers to adjust immediately to a change in relative prices. But, if demand is inelastic only in the very short run, collusion will not be attractive to the sellers in the market because the total profits that it would yield would be very small.

elasticity of demand cannot be measured directly and must instead be inferred from qualitative evidence, the rapidity of entry is an important piece of evidence. To be sure, it is, as noted earlier, a somewhat ambiguous one since the very fact that the market price is above the costs of production will provide an incentive for prospective entrants to accelerate their entry, even if they must incur higher costs because of their haste and, as a consequence of the higher costs, will not be able to sell at the (old) competitive price level. In short, the fact that new entry is frequent and rapid may be a symptom of collusive pricing rather than a deterrent to it.

But we are not condemned to complete agnosticism. A rough estimate of the likely rapidity of new entry at competitive price levels can often be made on the basis of the production characteristics of the industry in question. A firm's cost of production is inversely related to the time interval between the decision to produce and the delivery of the output to the purchaser.[31] Since increases in the interval reduce the present value of the firm's output as well as its costs, the firm will not delay production and delivery indefinitely. The optimum delay will depend in part on the rate at which cost falls with delay, and one imagines that the rate will be higher for more complicated production processes. That is presumably why U.S. Steel's monopoly position was not instantaneously eliminated by the entry of new firms or the expansion of existing ones: the cost of quickly creating, or rapidly expanding, a complex enterprise such as steel production is prohibitively high.[32] Consider by way of contrast an attempt to fix a monopoly price in the retail grocery business. Even if the monopoly price were completely unanticipated, and faithfully honored by the firms already in the market, it would persist for only a short time because the activities that must be coordinated in order to start a new supermarket—finding suitable premises, hiring the necessary personnel, financing, making arrangements with suppliers and customers—are

31. See Armen A. Alchian, "Costs and Outputs," in *Readings in Microeconomics* 159, 165 (William Breit & Harold M. Hochman eds., 2d ed. 1971).

32. This does not explain why the formation of U.S. Steel was not anticipated far enough in advance to enable competing firms or new entrants to complete their preparations for expansion by the time U.S. Steel was formed. Perhaps, however, its formation was too uncertain to justify the kind of investment that would have been necessary for the firms not included in the merger to expand their productive capacity sufficiently to offset U.S. Steel's output restriction.

few and simple, and the optimum delay between the decision to enter and actual entry is therefore short. This example suggests, incidentally, that a national (or international) monopoly is apt to be a good deal more durable than a local or regional one; entry is likely to occur much more rapidly when it can be accomplished by the expansion of an existing enterprise into a new geographical area (e.g., Safeway opening its first supermarket in Fairbanks, Alaska), rather than by the creation of a brand-new firm.

In discussing the relevance of new entry to the propensity to collude I have carefully avoided using that confusing term "barrier to entry." A barrier to entry is commonly used in a quite literal sense to mean anything which a new entrant must overcome in order to gain a foothold in the market, such as the capital costs of entering the market on an efficient scale. This is a meaningless usage, since it is obvious that a new entrant must incur costs to enter the market, just as his predecessors, the firms now occupying the market, did previously. A more precise definition has been offered by Stigler: a barrier to entry is a condition that imposes higher long-run costs of production on a new entrant than are borne by the firms already in the market.[33] A barrier to entry in Stigler's sense has important policy implications: it implies the existence of a range within which the firms in the market can increase the market price above the competitive level without having to worry at all about losing sales to a new entrant. But, as we shall see in the next chapter, barriers to entry in this sense appear to be rare. Of greater practical importance are factors that do not create a barrier to entry but increase the length of time required for new entry to take place, by making the production process a complex one which requires substantial time to organize efficiently. Such factors include vertical integration and economies of scale, which increase the optimum size of the new entrant.

(5) *Many customers.* There is no need to repeat the earlier discussion of the relevance of concentration on the buying side of the market to the propensity to collude.

(6) *Standard product.* The less standardized (more customized) a product is, in the sense that the specifications of the product differ in important respects from order to order rather than being uniform across orders, the more difficult it will be for the sellers of the product to collude effectively. The heterogeneity of the

33. George J. Stigler, "Barriers to Entry, Economies of Scale, and Firm Size," in *The Organization of Industry* 67 (1968).

orders will make it impossible to agree upon a single price that would be appropriate for all orders. The sellers will instead have to agree on a complex schedule of prices for different grades and qualities and this may be impossible to do without overt negotiations of the sort likely to be detected by the antitrust enforcers. Moreover, the detection of cheating by members of the cartel will be complicated by the difficulty of knowing whether a competitor's price is below the agreed level or is simply a lower price for a lower grade or quality of the product.

Although there is, unfortunately, no quantitative index of standardization, there are qualitative indications that may be decisive in particular cases. If an industry does not inventory any stock items, this is a good indication that the industry is producing a custom product; presumably, each order is so unique that it would be pointless to maintain an inventory in the hope that a customer would find what he wanted among the items on hand. The absence of second-hand and spot markets, and of price lists or pricing manuals, is also, and for a similar reason, evidence that the industry is producing a custom product in the sense relevant to the feasibility of collusion.

(7) *The principal firms sell at the same level in the chain of distribution.* The enforcement of a cartel is complicated, and the feasibility of collusion therefore reduced, when some members sell at lower levels in the chain of distribution than others. Suppose that although the cartel price to the retail dealer is 10 cents, a vertically integrated member of the cartel, who sells only to the ultimate consumer, charges 13 cents. In order to determine whether or not this seller is cheating, the cartel members must determine the reasonable spread between wholesale and retail price; if the cost of retail distribution is more than 3 cents, the seller is cheating.

(8) *Price competition more important than other forms of competition.* Where the product is a fungible commodity, cutting prices may be the only way of getting business away from a competitor; if so, eliminating price competition is sure to yield higher profits. But if other forms of competition—inventory, product quality, service, or whatever—are very important, the only effect of eliminating price competition may be to channel competitive energies into other, and costly, forms of competition. Indeed, as we have already discussed, firms may increase their expenditures on the other forms of competition until they have competed away all of the higher profits that they hoped to obtain by increasing prices above the competitive level.

(9) *High ratio of fixed to variable costs.* In a market where fixed costs are a high proportion of total costs, competition may be relatively unstable and may lead to frequent bankruptcies among the competing firms.[34] If bankruptcy is more costly to the owners and managers of a firm than a simple failure to obtain the difference between a competitive and monopolistic rate of return would be, then firms will rate the benefits from monopoly pricing higher than they would in an industry where competitive pricing might lead them into bankruptcy. (Of course other factors besides a high ratio of fixed to variable costs might place the firms in an industry in danger of going bankrupt.)

(10) *Demand static or declining over time.* Collusion is more difficult to police in a market where demand is growing over time than in one where demand is static or declining. If demand is growing, a firm that is the victim of cheating by other members of the cartel may be hurt not by losing customers but by failing to obtain its fair share of new customers; and failure to grow as rapidly as competitors are growing will be less convincing evidence of cheating than loss of existing customers.

(11) *Sealed bidding.* In markets where business is awarded on the basis of sealed bids, it is easier for colluding sellers to detect cheating. If a seller other than the one whom the cartel has designated to submit the low bid wins the contract, it can only be because he submitted a lower bid than agreed upon—there can be no alternative explanation for the diversion of business from the seller who was supposed to obtain the contract. Thus the use of sealed bidding by buyers facilitates collusion.

(12) *The industry's antitrust "record."* In a market where collusion is attractive, there is likely to be a history of attempts at express collusion, some of which may have been detected by the antitrust enforcers. Accordingly, a "record" of price fixing or related antitrust violations is some evidence that the structure of the market is favorable to collusion. However, the absence of a record of antitrust violations is of course not decisive, since such absence is consistent with an inference that the market is so propitious to collusion that the firms have been able to collude without ever being detected.

34. Fixed costs are those that do not vary with the level of output. Since they cannot be reduced to adjust to a fall in demand, a firm that has heavy fixed costs is peculiarly vulnerable to an economic downturn or other unexpected development that forces it to curtail its output or to reduce its price.

The foregoing criteria could help the enforcement agencies to identify those markets in which collusion was likely and therefore in which the agencies should concentrate their search for evidence of price fixing. If the search yields proof of an actual conspiracy, well and good; a conspiracy in a market where collusion is likely to be effective is a serious matter and should be punished. In some cases, however, it may be possible to demonstrate the existence of collusive pricing even though no overt acts of collusion are detected. The sorts of evidence—evidence of collusive behavior—relevant to such a demonstration are the following:

(1) *Fixed relative market shares.* If the major firms in a market have maintained identical or nearly identical market shares relative to each other for a substantial period of time, there is good reason to believe that they have divided the market (whether by fixing geographical zones or sales quotas or by an assignment of customers), and thereby eliminated competition, among themselves. Under competition, market shares will fluctuate as now one firm, now another, pulls ahead of its rivals in the struggle for customers and sales. Divisions of markets have figured in many Sherman Act cases; but it has not always been recognized that proof that market shares have been abnormally stable can in itself constitute evidence that the market has been divided.

(2) *Price discrimination.* Price discrimination is a term that economists use to describe the practice of selling the same product to different customers at different prices even though the cost of sale is the same to each of them.[35] A glance at figure 1[36] will show that the monopolist who is able to move down the demand curve from its highest point to its intersection with the marginal-cost curve, charging a different price for each sale according to the strength of the consumer's desire for it, will obtain greater profits than the monopolist who charges a single price. Although perfect discrimination (where the schedule of prices charged lies precisely along the demand curve) is never feasible, some degree of dis-

35. More precisely, it is selling at a price or prices such that the ratio of price to marginal cost is different in different sales. Thus, two sales that involve different costs but are made at the same price would be discriminatory. The economic meaning of price discrimination must not be confused with the legal meaning of price discrimination under the Robinson-Patman Act, whose intricate and often perverse requirements will not be discussed in this book.

36. P. 13 supra; see also Appendix, infra pp. 242–43.

crimination often is, and it is commonly found in monopolistic markets. Persistent discrimination is very good evidence of monopoly because it is inconsistent with a competitive market; it implies that some consumers are paying more than the cost of serving them, a situation that would disappear with competition. However, it is very important to distinguish the persistent or systematic discrimination that is a symptom of monopoly from the temporary or sporadic discrimination that commonly accompanies (1) the movement from one equilibrium to another in a competitive market and (2) the disintegration of a cartel due to chiseling, which will often take the form of selective, i.e., discriminatory, discounts from the cartel price.

There are various objections to using discrimination as evidence of unlawful collusion. One is that discrimination may result not from collusion but from the monopoly power of individual firms in the market.[37] For example, the traditional price difference between first-run and subsequent-run motion pictures is discriminatory, but it is probably due to the individual monopoly power of the film producers, stemming from their copyrights, rather than to collusion among the producers. This point illustrates the broader problem of properly characterizing price differences. They may be discriminatory yet not good evidence of collusion, either because they are merely incidental to a shift in the competitive equilibrium or because they result from individual exercises of monopoly power rather than from collusion; they may be incidental to the collapse of a cartel rather than to the cartel's exploitation of its monopoly power; or they may not be discriminatory at all—a price difference may, of course, reflect simply a difference in cost. Where there are joint or common costs, prices to different customers may be proportioned differently to the marginal costs of serving each customer without being discriminatory in any sense relevant to inferring monopoly power. While I concede the acute difficulties of properly interpreting evidence of alleged price discrimination,

37. This point is stressed in Richard S. Markovits, "Oligopolistic Pricing Suits, the Sherman Act, and Economic Welfare, Part I," 26 *Stan. L. Rev.* 493, 512–13 and n. 47 (1974). Other criticisms of my proposal to use economic evidence to establish collusive pricing appear in Part III of this massive article, 27 *Stan. L. Rev.* 307, 319–29 (1975). I have answered Markovits in my "Oligopoly Pricing and the Sherman Act: A Reply to Professor Markovits," forthcoming, *Stan. L. Rev.* (May 1976), to which the interested reader is referred.

it seems to me unduly pessimistic, despite the unhappy experience with the Robinson-Patman Act, to regard these difficulties as in all cases insuperable.

Another objection to the use of evidence of price discrimination in proving collusion is that discrimination should be encouraged rather than discouraged because it results in an expansion of output over the level produced by the single-price monopolist. However, only perfect price discrimination, which is never possible in practice, is certain to result in a larger output than single-price monopoly (in fact, in the competitive output). Whether the much cruder forms of discrimination that one encounters in the real world lead on average to a greater or smaller output than single-price monopoly is an empirical question.[38] Suppose, for example, that a monopolist who formerly sold his entire output at a price of $5 now divides his customers into two classes, and sells to one at $3 and to the other at $7. The lower price will increase demand for the product, but the higher price will reduce it because some consumers who were willing to pay between $5 and $6.99 are bound to be placed in the $7 rather than the $3 class and will therefore switch to other products. Of course, if the monopolist could discriminate perfectly he would never charge a customer willing to pay a price greater than the marginal cost of serving him a price that exceeded his willingness to pay. But all price discrimination in the real world is imperfect, which means that sales will be lost as well as gained when the monopolist substitutes a discriminatory for a uniform price schedule. To be sure, if the monopolist were forbidden to charge a price higher than the single price that he would have charged if he were not allowed to discriminate, price discrimination, even if imperfect, would always result in a larger output; but such a regulation would be impractical.

Even in the purely hypothetical case of perfect price discrimination, it is unclear that the total social costs of monopoly would be lower than under nondiscriminating monopoly. The expected gains of a price-discriminating monopolist are higher, and this will result in a greater investment of resources in obtaining the monopoly. If as in chapter 2 it is assumed as a first approximation that the costs of monopoly are equal to its expected gains, then it

38. See Paul A. Samuelson, *Foundations of Economic Analysis* 42–45 (1947); Joan Robinson, *The Economics of Imperfect Competition* 188–95 (1933).

can be shown that a perfectly price-discriminating monopoly will be more costly to society than a single-price monopoly of the same market, albeit the output of the discriminating monopolist will be larger and indeed equal to the competitive output.[39] A similar conclusion is reached in the case of the imperfectly discriminating monopolist. On average, the output under imperfectly discriminating monopoly is not expected to be either greater or less than under single-price monopoly. The only difference is that the expected gains from imperfectly discriminating monopoly are greater than those from single-price monopoly. This means that the costs of discriminating monopoly will be greater than those of single-price monopoly, with no offsetting social gain from a larger output in the monopolized markets.[40]

The remaining objection to using evidence of price discrimination to prove collusion is that the only consequence will be to deter price fixers from discriminating, thereby eliminating simply a symptom of collusion. But more than symptomatic relief is involved. Since price discrimination increases the gains from monopoly, a policy that discourages discrimination will reduce the incidence, and hence aggregate costs, of monopolization.

I want to emphasize that I am not suggesting that price discrimination be enjoined as part of the remedy in a collusion case based in part on evidence of discrimination. It would be very difficult to draft a decree forbidding systematic price discrimination that did not constrain or inhibit legitimate pricing behavior as well. The appropriate remedy in a collusion case is the same regardless of the nature of the evidence used to support the inference of collusion: an injunction, fine, or damage award which allows the defendants complete competitive flexibility, and forbids only the (explicit or tacit) collusive agreement itself.

(3) *Exchanges of price information.* In a market of many small sellers, the exchange of price information may serve the salutary purpose of reducing price dispersions based on inadequate knowledge and thereby improving competition. Where there are few sellers, however, the problem of inadequate knowledge is probably less serious—it is easier to keep tabs on the pricing of a few rivals—and the inference that complete certainty as to the

39. This is demonstrated in the Appendix, infra pp. 242–43.
40. A further inefficiency created by price discrimination is distortion in the costs of the customers of the discriminating seller. They pay different prices for inputs that cost society the same to produce.

actual transaction prices of competitors is sought primarily to facilitate cartelization is stronger. Systems of price exchange are likely to be good evidence of price fixing in the second case, but not in, the first. Exchanges of price information may take quite subtle forms. Public discussions of the "right" price for an industry to maintain, conducted by the businessmen in the industry, and announcements of price increases far in advance of their actual implementation, may be stages in the formation and implementation of a cartel agreement, and they should be scrutinized carefully. The proper legal treatment of information exchanges is an issue of the first importance which is discussed in some detail in chapter 7.

(4) *Regional price variations.* If a product is sold in separate geographical markets (like cement), and if prices are fixed in some of these markets but not others, one will observe a regional price variation. To be sure, such a variation may stem from factors other than price fixing; costs may be different in the different areas. But, at least in some cases, it should be possible to correct for such differences. The method is of limited utility where the market for a product is nationwide (like locomotives), although comparison with foreign markets may be possible. Most price-fixing cases, however, have involved regional or local rather than national conspiracies.

(5) *Identical bids.* A useful method of proving price fixing is to show that identical sealed bids were submitted for a contract to supply a nonstandard item. The qualification is critically important: the item is standard, or composed of standard items,   bids are consistent with competition because the bidders'   ay be identical. This method of proof is of course limited   ed-bid situations, and moreover to those sealed-bid situations where the conspirators are not clever enough to rotate the   bid in a nonobvious manner.

(6) *Price, output, and capacity changes at the formation of the cartel.* The formation of a successful cartel will be followed (in the usual case) by a rise in price and a reduction in output, unless demand for the product is increasing—an effect that can sometimes be netted out. Simultaneous price increases and output reductions unexplained by any increases in cost may therefore be good evidence of the initiation of a price-fixing scheme,[41] while

41. Cf. Bray v. Safeway Stores, Inc., 392 F. Supp. 851 (N.D. Calif. 1975).

changes in the opposite direction might be used as evidence that a cartel had just collapsed. Notice that it is not necessary to determine what the firms' marginal costs are or what the competitive price and output would be. One simply observes price and output changes and asks whether changes in costs or in demand explain them, or whether it is necessary to posit cartelization.

Another clue to the initiation of a price-fixing scheme is the unexplained creation of substantial excess capacity. When firms contract output pursuant to a price-fixing scheme, their previous capacity, geared to the larger competitive output, becomes in part excess. The history of cartels contains some dramatic examples of this phenomenon.[42] Excess capacity that arises suddenly and cannot be explained by changes in demand or mistakes in planning is evidence of price fixing.

If the cartel is reasonably stable, capacity will gradually be reduced to a level appropriate to the reduced scale of output. If the cartel is unstable and the participants suspect it may soon break down, they may decide to maintain extra capacity in reserve; or they may do so in order to enhance their bargaining power within the cartel. In either event one would observe persistent excess capacity, which would be additional evidence of price fixing. Particularly suggestive would be a combination of persistent excess capacity with frequent new entry, a combination difficult to explain without positing cartel pricing. Unfortunately, determining when capacity is excess is normally very hard to do, due to the difficulty of distinguishing excess capacity from peak-load or standby capacity.

(7) *Industry-wide resale price maintenance.* Where the resale price is fixed, it is more difficult for a member of the cartel to cheat. He will gain no additional sales by granting a secret discount to a dealer; the discount will be a pure windfall to the dealer. But the fact that competing sellers engage in resale price maintenance is an ambiguous sign of cartelization; it may mean only that each of the sellers in the industry has decided that his own ends would be furthered by controlling the resale price of the product. Normally (as we shall see in our detailed analysis of resale price maintenance in chapter 7), this will happen only when the product is sold in conjunction with expensive services performed by the dealer, such as elaborate display. A dealer

42. See, e.g., United States v. American Tobacco Co., 221 U.S. 106, 157, 159, 163, 174–75 (1911).

might be tempted to dispense with the services and cut his prices, thereby attracting sales away from dealers who continued to provide them. Inevitably, the amount of services provided would diminish. Resale price maintenance is a way of preventing such "freeloading" and the consequent erosion of service. Where a product is normally not sold together with services, this explanation fails and we can assume that the purpose of industry-wide resale price maintenance is to facilitate price fixing among the sellers.

The same test might enable an enforcement agency to distinguish between resale-price-maintenance schemes imposed by a single seller for his own ends and those nominally imposed by a single seller but actually imposed by his dealers to eliminate competition among themselves. If the product is not one sold with services, the latter inference can be drawn. Unfortunately, the use of this test encounters a difficulty here that should come as no surprise to the reader of this book: the "customary" provision of services in conjunction with a product may be nothing more than a symptom of a dealer's cartel that has led each member to increase nonprice (i.e., service) competition in an effort to engross the largest possible share of the cartel profits.

(8) *Declining market shares of leaders.* The establishment of a monopoly price will attract new competitors to a market, who will perceive opportunities for unusual profits. The existing firms could seek to repel entry by reducing their price to the competitive level, but this would defeat the purpose of the cartel; they will normally do better by maintaining a supracompetitive price and allowing their market share to decline gradually, the strategy of U.S. Steel discussed in chapter 3. A long-term decline in the market shares of the leading firms in a market, accordingly, is a symptom of price fixing, though an ambiguous one since it may be attributable to other factors. In some cases it may be possible to rule out the other factors.

(9) *Amplitude and fluctuation of price changes.* There is some basis in economic theory for believing both that a monopolist (or cartel) will react to cost or demand changes by smaller percentage changes in price than the sellers in a competitive but otherwise identical market,[43] and that a cartel will change price less frequently than competitive firms would, because of the difficulty

43. See Appendix, infra pp. 248–49.

and legal risk in renegotiating the cartel price. The Supreme Court has on one occasion attached great weight to such evidence—but with intellectually disastrous results![44]

(10) *Demand elasticity at market price.* As we have seen, a monopolist will never sell at a price where demand is inelastic, for he could increase his total revenues and profits by reducing his output. Therefore, if demand is inelastic at the current market price that price is not the monopoly price, though it might be higher than the competitive price as a result of efforts, not wholly successful, at cartelization. An inference of monopolization could be drawn if demand was elastic at the current price but the product did not have good substitutes as measured by relative cost (not price).

(11) *Level and pattern of profits.* In a few cases it may be possible to infer collusion from the presence or pattern of abnormally high rates of return. To be sure, the measurement problem is acute; unusually high rates may be due to superior efficiency rather than to collusion; and the absence of abnormally high profits need not imply the absence of collusion since the members of the cartel may have competed away their monopoly profits in various forms of nonprice competition. But profit data, where obtainable in reasonably reliable form, may sometimes have evidentiary value. For example, the theory of collusion suggests that, at the initial formation of a cartel, the profits of the smaller firms in the market will increase by a greater proportion than the profits of the larger firms. The reason is that the smaller firms are likely to remain outside of the cartel (it doesn't pay to get them to join) and hence to produce the same output as, or a higher output than, they were producing previously, while the larger firms are reducing their output in order to increase the market price. Over time, however, the profits of small firms as a group in the market should decline as the monopoly price attracts into the market new firms (which are presumably small, at least initially) that earn only a normal return. Thus the profitability gap

44. In American Tobacco Co. v. United States, 328 U.S. 781 (1946), the Supreme Court inferred conspiracy in part from the defendants' action in simultaneously raising their prices in the face of allegedly falling demand and costs. However, as demonstrated in the Appendix, infra pp. 248–49, a monopolist would lower, not raise, his price in these circumstances. An alternative explanation for the price increase is suggested in Richard A. Posner, *Antitrust: Cases, Economic Notes, and Other Materials* 109 (1974).

will tend to close. Moreover, the profits of both the small and the large firms in the market should decline over time as the firms devote more and more resources to nonprice competition. In short, while proof that firms in a market are obtaining monopoly profits may be very difficult to obtain, changes in the level of profits of the firms in the market and of particular subsets of those firms may be useful evidence of collusion—and much easier to establish than whether the level of profits in the market at any time is above or below the competitive level.

It should go without saying that I am *not* proposing that tacit colluders be subjected to a public-utility type of control over their prices and profits. Evidence of profitability would be used together with other evidence to support an inference of collusion. Collusion would be punished, with a view to preventing its continuation or recurrence, but the individual firms would be free to charge any price they wished.

(12) *Basing-point pricing.* A basing-point pricing system is a system under which sellers, in quoting a delivered price (that is, a price that includes the transportation of the good to the buyer), compute the transportation component of the price not from the seller's factory but from a standard point that may be far away from it. If, for example, Pittsburgh were the basing point for the steel industry, a steel company located in Gary, in quoting a price to a buyer in New York, would add to the factory price the freight cost from Pittsburgh to New York, rather than the actual freight cost (from Gary to New York) that the seller would incur in making delivery. Where the basing point is nearer the customer than the seller's factory is, the freight cost included in the price is less than the actual freight cost; the result is "freight absorption" by the seller. Where the basing point is farther from the customer than the seller's factory is, the seller's actual freight cost is less than the cost he adds on to the factory price in computing the delivered price; the extra freight cost is referred to as "phantom freight." Basing-point pricing involves both freight absorption and phantom freight.

The purpose of basing-point pricing is to facilitate collusion by simplifying the pricing of the colluding firms.[45] It is plainly inconsistent with competition, which would quickly eliminate any phan-

---

45. Merely absorbing freight in order to compete with a seller located nearer to the customer would not be evidence of collusive pricing.

tom freight charges. With one exception,[46] in all of the cases in which basing-point systems have been challenged as a violation of the Sherman Act, there has been evidence that the sellers had agreed to set up a basing-point system.[47] It should be clear by now that I regard such evidence as unnecessary to establish a violation of the Sherman Act.

The Legality and Practicality of the Suggested Approach

In suggesting the relevance of economic evidence to proof of price fixing, I am not breaking new ground. Such evidence already plays an important role in the trial of price-fixing cases,[48] and would play a much larger role if lawyers and judges had a firmer grasp of the economics of cartelization. But it is widely assumed that the only use of such evidence is to help the trier of fact infer the existence of a price-fixing conspiracy—i.e., an overt agreement—and that such an inference is indispensable to finding that the Sherman Act has been violated. This is where I part company with many other students of antitrust policy. If the economic evidence introduced in a case warrants an inference of collusive pricing, there is neither legal nor practical justification for requiring evidence that will support the further inference that the collusion was explicit rather than tacit. Certainly from an economic standpoint it is a detail whether the collusive pricing scheme was organized and implemented in such a way as to generate evidence of actual communications.

The language of section 1 of the Sherman Act, though confined to restraints of trade imposed by "contract, combination . . . , or conspiracy," is not an obstacle to the suggested approach. There is no distortion of accepted meanings in viewing tacit collusion as a form of concerted rather than unilateral activity. If seller A restricts his output in the expectation that B will do likewise, and B restricts his output in a like expectation, there is a literal meeting of the minds, a mutual understanding, even if there is no overt communication. In forbearing to seek short-term gains at each other's expense in order to reap monopoly benefits that only such

---

46. See Triangle Conduit & Cable Co. v. FTC, 168 F.2d 175 (7th Cir. 1948), aff'd by an equally divided Court sub nom. Clayton Mark & Co. v. FTC, 336 U.S. 956 (1949).

47. See, e.g., FTC v. Cement Institute, 333 U.S. 683 (1948).

48. An excellent example is Wall Products Co. v. National Gypsum Co., 326 F. Supp. 295 (N.D. Calif. 1971). See note 52 infra.

mutual forbearance will allow, A and B are like the parties to a "unilateral contract," which is treated by the law as concerted rather than individual behavior. If someone advertises in a newspaper that he will pay $10 to the person who finds and returns his dog, anyone who meets the condition has an enforceable claim against him to the promised reward. The finder's action in complying with the specified condition is all the indication of assent that the law requires for a binding contract. Tacit collusion is similar: one seller communicates his "offer" by restricting output, and the offer is "accepted" by the actions of his rivals in restricting their outputs as well. I am arguing simply that it may be appropriate in some cases to instruct a jury to find an agreement to fix prices if it is satisfied that there was a tacit meeting of the minds of the defendants on maintaining a noncompetitive pricing policy.

To be sure, there are dangers in pressing the "meeting-of-the-minds" approach too far. Suppose that a group of competing firms simultaneously experience an increase in the cost of some raw material that each one uses. In deciding how to respond to the common cost increase, each firm will consider the probable response of its competitors to the increase, since its ability to pass on the cost increase in whole or in part to its customers by raising price will depend on the pricing decisions of its competitors. The process by which the firms arrive at the new equilibrium at a higher price may thus have elements of "tacit agreement." The process is not an anticompetitive one; yet if the firms explicitly coordinated their pricing in reaction to the cost change, the law would treat their agreement as illegal collusion—and rightly so, since there would be justifiable suspicion that the agreement was both unnecessary to smooth adjustment to the cost increase and motivated, at least in part, by a desire to raise the market price by more than the cost increase actually requires.

This example shows that the law should not always equate tacit and explicit pricing agreements. Some degree of tacit coordination of pricing in reaction to external shocks, such as the increase in raw-material costs examined above, is inevitable and unobjectionable. What is not inevitable, and is objectionable, is a tacit agreement to limit output and charge a higher than competitive price.

The approach that is proposed here is consistent not only with the language of section 1 of the Sherman Act but also with the decisions authoritatively construing the requirement of agreement.

American Tobacco Co. v. *United States* teaches that "a tacit meeting of the minds" satisfies the requirement.[49] And read in context the famous passage in *Theatre Enterprises, Inc.* v. *Paramount Film Distrib. Corp.*[50]—" 'conscious parallelism' has not yet read conspiracy out of the Sherman Act entirely"—is not inconsistent even if one declines to speculate on the possible implications of "entirely." The evidence in *Theatre Enterprises* suggested that the separate actions of the defendant movie distributors in refusing to grant the plaintiff exhibitor first-run status reflected the individual judgment of each of the distributors that the location of plaintiff's theater was unsuitable for a first-run theater. There was even evidence that the distributors doubted the good faith of the plaintiff in applying for first-run status. In these circumstances, the parallel refusals did not connote agreement, tacit or otherwise. There were even fewer elements of agreement than in the example discussed above in which competing sellers raised their prices in response to a cost increase affecting all of them; the evidence in *Theatre Enterprises* indicated that each of the distributors would have refused to grant plaintiff first-run status regardless of what any competing distributor would have done; the parallel action of the distributors was not even conscious.

Recently, a federal district court inferred unlawful collusion from the simultaneous action of competing producers in withdrawing discounts.[51] A careful examination of the circumstances surrounding the withdrawal suggested that its only purpose could have been to implement a scheme of collusive pricing.[52] There

---

49. 328 U.S. 781, 810 (1946). See also Interstate Circuit, Inc. v. United States, 306 U.S. 208 (1939).

50. 346 U.S. 537, 541 (1954).

51. Wall Products Co. v. National Gypsum Co., supra note 48. But see Bogosian v. Gulf Oil Corp., 1975 Trade Cases ¶ 60,283 (E.D. Pa.).

52. The court stressed structural characteristics of the relevant market predisposing it to collusion, such as concentration of sellers, homogeneity of the product, inelasticity of demand (though the court neglected to distinguish between inelasticity of demand at the competitive price and at the market price, which was presumably supracompetitive), unimportance of nonprice competition, and the high ratio of fixed to variable costs in the industry. As evidence of collusive behavior, the court noted that right after the alleged formation of the collusive scheme the market price had risen notwithstanding the fact that demand was falling. The court's opinion also notes the secular decline in the market shares of the leading sellers,

was also evidence that the defendants had actually communicated with one another, but the court did not rely on that evidence, holding that the actual communications had been limited to exchanges of price information necessary to avoid violating the Robinson-Patman Act.

Professor Turner has argued that if section 1 were interpreted to forbid tacit collusion it would be impossible to expect the sellers in oligopolistic markets to comply with the law, because compliance would involve irrational behavior by the sellers.[53] This is tantamount to arguing that oligopoly is a sufficient as well as necessary condition of tacit collusion. Yet surely Turner does not believe that *all* oligopolists charge supracompetitive prices. Even in the absence of legal penalty, an oligopolist might decide not to restrict output, because of inability to predict his rivals' reactions or fear that they would cheat. If tacit collusion were punished, fear of punishment would provide an additional reason to abjure noncompetitive pricing. This would be true even in the example that Turner offers as the clinching argument for his view: where demand is declining and competitive prices would entail losses to the industry.[54] Explicit collusion is sometimes the only expedient that will enable an industry to avoid losses in a period of declining demand, yet one assumes that the prohibition against such collusion retains a deterrent effect even in those circumstances. Firms faced with losses will not collude if they anticipate that the cost of collusion, as a result of punishment, will exceed the benefits in averting business losses. Oligopolists would reason the same way if tacit collusion were subject to effective sanctions under section 1.

It must be emphasized that tacit collusion is not an unconscious state. If the firm's sales manager recommends that the firm offer a wider variety of products in order to exploit consumer demand more effectively, and the financial vice-president recommends against that course on the ground that it will make it more difficult

but makes nothing of this fact, although as discussed in the text it is suggestive of collusion.

A recent article discusses the extensive utilization of an economic approach to proof of price fixing in a trial in which the plaintiff obtained a jury verdict. Dale R. Funderbunk, "Price Fixing in the Liquid-Asphalt Industry: Economic Analysis Versus the 'Hot Document,'" 7 *Antitrust Law & Econ. Rev.* 61 (1974).

53. See Donald F. Turner, supra note 3, at 669.

54. Id. at 670.

for the industry to maintain "healthy" prices, the president can be in no doubt of the significance of his action if he adopts the financial vice-president's recommendation. Moreover, it is unlikely that there are many cases of purely tacit collusion. What is being proposed here is not so much the alteration of the substantive contours of the law as a change in evidentiary requirements to permit illegal price fixing to be found in circumstances where, although explicit collusion cannot be proved, an actual meeting of the minds on a noncompetitive price can be inferred. In most of these cases there will be explicit although well-concealed collusion that can surely be deterred by threat of punishment.

The only objection to the proposed approach that I consider substantial is the difficulty of proving collusive pricing by economic evidence, given the complex, technical, and often inconclusive character of such evidence. One can imagine a case in which a firm would be subjected to a heavy fine because the economic evidence pointed to the existence of collusion, despite the fact that the firm was not colluding. But the problem of legal error is not limited to the trial of price-fixing cases using economic evidence and can be dealt with in this context by a variety of means, such as by imposing a higher standard of proof on the government in cases where the only evidence of collusion is economic or by eliminating criminal punishments for antitrust violations[55]—the latter being a reform that seems to me attractive, independently of the issue of legal error, for reasons discussed in chapter 10. Moreover, the ambiguity and subjectivity of economic evidence can be exaggerated. In some cases, at least, many different types of evidence will point in the same direction, and where that occurs the probative force of each one considered in isolation is strengthened. Suppose, for example, that all twelve types of evidence discussed in the preceding section of this chapter pointed toward collusion. Each type of evidence might be vulnerable to criticisms of one sort or another that would be persuasive in the absence of other evidence; yet the criticisms might be wholly insufficient to persuade a responsible trier of facts to disregard the *uniform* results of twelve *different* tests of collusive behavior.

---

55. To be sure, this is not a complete answer to the problem of uncertainty. One would still be worried about monetary or injunctive penalties that imposed heavy costs on firms in respect of conduct they weren't actually engaged in. But, as mentioned in the text, legal error is a pervasive problem of legal administration.

I assume that Professor Turner does not believe that economic evidence is so uncertain that it should be deemed inadmissible in a price-fixing case. The issue between us is the narrow one whether some evidence of actual communication among the alleged colluders should be required, as corroboration for the economic evidence. I believe that in some cases the economic evidence of collusion may be sufficiently convincing to enable dispensing with evidence of actual communication. Probably in most such cases there will have been some actual communication among the colluding firms, though it cannot be proved. The absence of such proof is a detail if the economic evidence is sufficiently convincing to stand alone.

I do not want to minimize the objections to the suggested approach; they are substantial. But critics of the approach make the fundamental mistake of comparing it to some ideal of cheap and effective law enforcement, and naturally they find it wanting. The proper comparison is to the real-world alternatives, which include the current "cops-and-robbers" approach to price fixing, the use of structural remedies to break up the leading firms in concentrated markets into smaller units, and the use of the antimerger law to prevent markets from becoming concentrated in the first place. The first alternative is hardly satisfactory and, as we shall see in chapters 5 and 6, neither are the second and third. So, as always in policy matters, the realistic choice is among highly imperfect approaches. This precept should be borne in mind in evaluating the proposal put forth in this chapter.

I do not want to be understood as suggesting that the rule which makes price-fixing conspiracies illegal per se should be abandoned in favor of an economic definition of price fixing. In markets that exhibit the predisposing characteristics toward collusion, proof of an actual conspiracy is convincing evidence of a serious restraint of trade. The rule should be retained for use in such cases. Moreover, some effort should continue to be devoted to preventing price-fixing conspiracies in markets that do not exhibit the predisposing characteristics, but such conspiracies should be punished for what they are—attempts unlikely to succeed—and therefore should be punished less heavily than conspiracies formed in circumstances where a substantial increase in the market price is likely to result from the conspiracy. All I am urging is that the public enforcement agencies also consider proceeding, on the basis of purely economic evidence of collusion, in markets that exhibit the predisposing characteristics but generate no evidence of actual conspiracy. The initial cases brought under such an approach will be protracted, unwieldy, and perhaps inconclusive, but with time economists and lawyers will refine the theoretical and empirical economics of price fixing to the point where the law against price fixing can be administered in accordance with its substantive economic objectives. Considerable progress has already been made in private antitrust cases such as the *Wall Products* case.[56] This experience should embolden the public agencies to experiment with the new approach.

56. See notes 48, 51–52 supra.

5   Breaking Up
Large Firms

In the last chapter I suggested that with the aid of economic science section 1 of the Sherman Act could be used to punish collusive pricing even where the collusive scheme generated no evidence of actual contacts or communications. If this is so, then it should be unnecessary to break up the major sellers in highly concentrated markets in order to prevent them from engaging in tacit collusion; they can be deterred from engaging in such collusion by the same punishments that are used to deter express collusion. Most students of antitrust law take the opposite tack. Convinced that it is impossible to deal with the problem of tacit collusion by punishing it in section 1 proceedings, they urge that highly concentrated markets be forcibly "deconcentrated" in proceedings under either section 2 of the Sherman Act or special new legislation.[1] I disagree with their premise, but I think the conclusion is wrong in any event because the costs of a policy of deconcentration would be disproportionate to any likely gains. My objections apply equally to breaking up a firm found guilty of monopolization in a conventional section 2 proceeding—a single-firm monopolist, as distinct from an oligopolist. "Structural" remedies such as divestiture should be confined to the divestiture of assets recently acquired in an unlawful merger.

1. The legislative proposals are summarized and discussed in a student note, "The Industrial Reorganization Act: An Antitrust Proposal to Restructure the American Economy," 73 *Colum. L. Rev.* 635 (1973). The most thoughtful of the legislative proposals is that of the White House Task Force Report on Antitrust Policy (the "Neal Report") (1968), reprinted in *Small Business and the Robinson-Patman Act, Hearings before the Special Subcomm. on Small Business and the Robinson-Patman Act of the H. Select Comm. on Small Business,* 91st Cong., 1st Sess., vol. 1, at 291 (1969). The case for using section 2 of the Sherman Act to restructure concentrated markets is argued in Donald F. Turner, "The Scope of Antitrust and Other Regulatory Policies," 82 *Harv. L. Rev.* 1207, 1231 (1969).

To indicate the precise character of my objections to drastic structural remedies, let me first make clear my belief that effective deconcentration of oligopolistic (and even more clearly of monopolistic) markets might have some good effects. This belief is based not on the extensive, but ambiguous and in important respects unsatisfactory, statistical evidence demonstrating a positive correlation between concentration and profitability[2] but on the simple theoretical point, by now familiar to the reader, that price fixing, whether tacit or explicit, is facilitated by concentration of the assets of a market in the hands of a few firms. As we saw in the last chapter, other things being equal the costs of reaching agreement are lower with fewer parties to the agreement. The likelihood of cheating—the bane of cartels—is also reduced since it is easier to identify a defector from a small group. To be sure, other factors—such as the elasticity of demand for the industry's product and the speed at which new entry can be effected—also bear importantly on the feasibility and attractiveness of collusion and may in particular cases outweigh the effect of concentration. Still, if concentration were substantially reduced, the costs of collusion would be higher and its incidence therefore lower.

But, although a policy of deconcentration would confer some benefits on society, it would probably not be a wise policy, even if there were no other way to control tacit collusion. It is unlikely to be an effective policy, and if it were effective, its social costs might well exceed its social benefits.

Any proceeding to deconcentrate an industry by reorganizing the major firms into smaller units would probably be cumbersome, protracted, and indeed unmanageable. This would be true, I believe, whatever the precise configuration of the prima facie case and defenses in such a proceeding.

It is not a simple matter to work out a theory on which such a proceeding could be brought under one of the existing antitrust statutes, let alone a streamlined, manageable proceeding. My interpretation of section 1 of the Sherman Act as forbidding tacit collusion requires proof of noncompetitive behavior, and the appropriate relief is an injunction (or, after the principle has become

---

2. The controversy over this evidence is well presented in a recent conference volume. *Industrial Concentration: The New Learning* (Harvey J. Goldschmid, H. Michael Mann & J. Fred Weston eds. 1974).

established, a fine or damages), rather than dismemberment of the leading firms. One could perhaps extend the logic of the *Alcoa* case[3] to the situation where a group of firms, jointly occupying a monopoly position, are acting as if they were a single monopolist. But proof of actual anticompetitive behavior would be necessary (no court would accept the argument that, just because there are only a few firms in a market, they *must* be behaving like a single firm, i.e., charging the monopoly price); and it would be necessary to establish to the court's satisfaction that no less drastic relief than divestiture would restore competition. The most facile route to divestiture would be a proceeding under section 5 of the Federal Trade Commision Act, where it could be argued (though not, in my judgment, persuasively) that the leading firms in a highly concentrated industry should be dismembered because there is some probability that otherwise the industry would behave monopolistically.

Any of these approaches would entail a proceeding of daunting complexity. Not only would the government have to offer evidence of the anticompetitive effect of concentration which the defendants would be free to rebut (even in a section 5 proceeding, the defendants could hardly be prevented from trying to prove that concentration in *their* industry was unlikely to lead to monopoly pricing), a type of inquiry similar to what I have proposed for section 1 tacit-collusion cases, but the issue of possible loss of efficiency from changing the structure of the industry would be fully—and endlessly—litigable.

It is not surprising that most proponents of deconcentration urge passage of new legislation. The thrust of such proposals, for example of the Concentrated Industries Act drafted by the Neal Task Force,[4] is drastically to simplify inquiry by (1) conclusively presuming anticompetitive effect from proof of persistent concentration above a specified level (four or fewer firms with a combined market share of at least 70 percent, in the Neal proposal), and (2) placing on the defendants the burden of proving that deconcentration would reduce the efficiency of the industry.

The Neal Report is the most responsible effort to formulate a program of deconcentration and deserves, but in my opinion does not withstand, careful scrutiny. It is far from clear that the

3. United States v. Aluminum Co. of America, 148 F.2d 416 (2d Cir. 1945); see pp. 214–15 infra.
4. See note 1 supra.

statutory proceeding which it proposes would solve the problem of manageability. While eliminating proof of anticompetitive effect, the proposal introduces a complexity that may no longer be a part of existing antitrust law by requiring that concentration be demonstrated in an economically meaningful market. Moreover, merely shifting the burden of proof on the question of the costs of deconcentration is unlikely to reduce the resources devoted to litigating it. Finally, even in a deconcentration proceeding in which the government had nothing to prove and the defendants were allowed no defenses, the process of reorganizing an industry—deciding what assets to divest and to whom—would be enormously complicated and time-consuming, as any student of corporate reorganizations will appreciate.

Experience with divestiture as an antitrust remedy supports my reservations concerning the manageability of deconcentration proceedings. The two major areas of experience are the enforcement of the Celler-Kefauver Antimerger Act since its enactment in 1950 and the enforcement of section 2 of the Sherman Act against single-firm monopolists since its enactment in 1890. The section 7 experience is less relevant to the deconcentration question; it involves the divestiture of recently acquired firms, and the problems of such divestiture are a good deal less serious than the problems of creating new firms out of an existing firm. Yet two careful studies of relief under section 7 have found that divestiture decrees commonly fail to carry out the objectives of the lawsuit or restore a competitive market structure.[5]

Between 1890 and the end of 1974, the Department of Justice had brought a total of 125 cases involving single-firm monopolization.[6] Some basic data about these cases are presented in tables 5 and 6. The reason for tabulating separately the data on cases

5. See Kenneth G. Elzinga, "The Antimerger Law: Pyrrhic Victories?," 12 *J. Law & Econ.* 43 (1969); Malcolm R. Pfunder, Daniel J. Plaine & Anne Marie G. Whittemore, "Compliance With Divestiture Orders Under Section 7 of the Clayton Act: An Analysis of the Relief Obtained," 17 *Antitrust Bull.* 19 (1972).

6. The source of these statistics is the four-volume set of abstracts of Justice Department antitrust cases published by Commerce Clearing House and known collectively as the "Bluebook." I count as one case multiple cases brought against the same firm in respect of the same conduct (e.g., companion civil and criminal cases). Cases in which a group of independent competitors, acting in concert, is accused of monopolizing a market are excluded since divestiture is almost never decreed in conspiracy cases.

Table 5   Justice Department's Record in Single-Firm Monopolization Cases 1890–1974

Classification	Decided Cases						Relief			Undecided Cases
	Litigated Cases			Consent Decree or Nolo Contendere		Total Decided Cases	% Govt. Obtained Some Relief	Substantial Divestiture		
	Govt. Won	Govt. Lost	% Govt. Won	Number	%			Number	%[1]	
Merger, and merger plus exclusionary practices										
National market	8	8	50.0%	15	48.4%	31	74.2%	11	39.3%	1
Regional or local	5	2	71.4%	11	61.1%	18	88.9%	7	43.8%	2
Total	13	10	56.5%	26	53.1%	49	79.6%	18	40.9%	3
Pure exclusionary practices										
National market	7	7	50.0%	26	65.0%	40	82.5%	3	7.9%	3
Regional or local	6	6	50.0%	16	57.1%	28	78.6%	3	14.3%	1
Total	13	13	50.0%	42	61.8%	68	80.9%	6	10.2%	4
Grand total	26	23	53.1%	69[2]	58.5%	118[2]	80.5%	24	23.3%	7

[1] In computing this percentage, criminal cases—in which divestiture cannot be ordered—are excluded. There are 15 (decided) cases in the criminal category, one of which cannot be classified by type of violation.
[2] Includes one case where nature of market not available.

Table 6   Justice Department's Record in Single-Firm Monopolization Cases 1940–1974

Classification	Decided Cases						Relief			Undecided Cases
	Litigated Cases			Consent Decree or Nolo Contendere		Total Decided Cases	% Govt. Obtained Some Relief	Substantial Divestiture		
	Govt. Won	Govt. Lost	% Govt. Won	Number	%			Number	%[1]	
Merger, and merger plus exclusionary practices										
National market	3	2	60.0	7	35.0	12	83.33	3	27.3	1
Regional or local	3	0	100.0	5	60.0	8	100.00	4	57.1	2
Total	6	2	75.0	12	62.5	20	90.0	7	38.9	3
Pure exclusionary practices										
National market	6	6	50.0	26	68.4	38	84.2	3	8.3	3
Regional or local	4	5	44.4	15	62.5	24	79.2	1	5.6	1
Total	10	11	47.6	41	66.1	62	82.3	4	7.4	4
Grand Total	16	13	55.2	53	64.6	82	84.1	11	15.3	7

[1]See note 1, table 5 supra.

brought since 1940 is that recent experience is presumably more significant in predicting future events (i.e., outcomes of deconcentration proceedings under yet-to-be enacted statutes) than the more remote past; and 1940 is a natural break point in the history of antitrust enforcement.[7] The cases in the tables are divided into two subject-matter groups, "mergers" and "exclusionary practices," the first consisting of cases in which the defendant is accused of having obtained or maintained monopoly power wholly or partly by mergers with competitors, and the second of cases where the defendant was charged only with an exclusionary practice,[8] such as patent abuse, restrictive leasing, vertical integration, or predatory pricing. This distinction is important for our purposes here because divestiture is simpler to effectuate where the firm to be broken up is itself the product of mergers. The mergers suggest the lines along which the firm can be broken up with minimal disruption.

Although the government has obtained some relief in 81 percent of the monopolization cases that had been completed at this writing, in those cases that the defendant chose to contest the government's batting average drops to 53 percent. More relevant is the paucity of cases in which substantial divestiture[9] has been ordered. Of the 118 decided monopolization cases, divestiture has been ordered in only 24, and this figure drops to 14 if cases involving regional or local markets are excluded. Moreover, 13 of the 24 divestitures relate to the earlier (1890–1939) period of antitrust enforcement, when only 36 monopolization cases were brought altogether. In the later period, only 11 out of 82 concluded cases (15 percent) have ended in divestiture.

The reason for the greater frequency of divestiture in the earlier

7. In that year there was a sharp and permanent increase in the volume of Justice Department antitrust cases, and about the same time, too, the Supreme Court became markedly more friendly to antitrust enforcement.

8. This term is defined at p. 28 supra. Exclusionary practices are considered at length in chapter 8, infra.

9. I exclude cases where divestiture seems (one is not always sure) to have been trivial—e.g., where it involves a few machines, a minor subsidiary (such as Alcoa's Canadian affiliate, ordered divested in the *Alcoa* monopolization case). Thus I exclude, for example, the divestiture of plant yielding $8.5 million in annual sales in the reopened *United Shoe Machinery* case in 1969, sixteen years after the entry of the final judgment in the case. I also exclude "dedication" (i.e., divestiture) of patents.

period appears to be the greater number of merger-to-monopoly cases in that period. Divestiture is the natural and normal remedy in a merger case, and 14 pure merger-to-monopoly cases were brought in the 1890–1939 period and only 7 in the later period. Of the 68 pure exclusionary-practice cases that have been decided, substantial divestiture has been decreed in only 6, and in only 4 of the 62 cases brought in the modern period. One of the 4 was a local newspaper case. The other 3 involved national markets. In all 4 cases divestiture was pursuant to a consent decree. I have found no contested case involving exclusionary practices only in which substantial divestiture was ordered. But it is unclear whether this is due to the greater difficulty of divestiture in a case not involving mergers or to the fact that in pure exclusionary-practice cases divestiture, far from being the natural and normal remedy, is extraordinary. If the alleged misconduct consists of exclusionary practices rather than completed acquisitions, an injunction against continuation of the practices will normally be an adequate remedy (although it may be possible to argue in some cases that an injunction would take too long to eliminate a monopoly position obtained by exclusionary practices).

I have been able to obtain information on the consequences of divestiture in 11 out of the 14 national-market monopolization cases in which substantial divestiture was decreed.[10] The picture that emerges of what antitrust divestiture has meant in practice is not an edifying one:

1. In the first of these cases, the suit against John D. Rockefeller's Standard Oil monopoly, the final decree (1911) simply dissolved the holding company that had owned the various operating companies. The result was to spin off the operating companies to the shareholders of the holding company—Rockefeller and his associates. Not only did the Rockefellers retain control (eventually dissipated by normal turnover of stock ownership) of the operating companies, but since the companies were organized along regional lines and each had exclusive rights to the Standard

10. My sources were the antitrust "Bluebook" (see note 6 supra); George C. Hale, "Trust Dissolution: 'Atomizing' Business Units of Monopolistic Size," 40 *Colum. L. Rev.* 615 (1940); Simon N. Whitney, *Antitrust Policies: American Experience in Twenty Industries* (1958); and, with respect to the more recent cases, information kindly supplied me by Donaldson, Lufkin & Jenrette Securities Corporation.

Oil trademark within its assigned territory, there was at first little competition among the companies. The decree had substituted a series of regional monopolies for a national monopoly.

2. In the *American Tobacco* case (also 1911), a company that controlled most of the tobacco-products industry was broken up into three companies, the largest of which retained 37 percent of the cigarette market. Apparently these companies continued to collude for a number of years. They were eventually convicted in a criminal case of having conspired to monopolize the tobacco industry during the 1930s.[11]

3. In another early case, this one against du Pont's monopoly of explosives, the divestiture decree (1912) succeeded in reducing du Pont's market share from 64–72 percent to about 32 percent. The decree had little effect on du Pont, since explosives had become only a very small part of its business, or indeed on the explosive industry, since many of the plants that were ordered divested produced black powder, which became obsolete shortly afterward.

4. *The International Harvester* decree (1918) required a firm having a virtual monopoly of the production of agricultural machinery to divest some of its assets. However, after divestiture International Harvester still had about two-thirds of the market. So dissatisfied was the government with the results of the decree that it sought to reopen the case and obtain additional divestiture. The court refused to modify the decree.

5. In the *Corn Products* case (1919), a glucose monopolist was ordered to divest itself of six plants. Evidently the plants were of little value or competitive significance: two ended up in the bankruptcy court, and the other four were sold outside of the industry. Contemporary observers believed that Corn Products had been strengthened by the divestiture.

6. The *Eastman Kodak* case involved a challenge to a monopolist of photographic supplies. Some plants were ordered divested (1920), but it appears that the decree had little impact on the industry or on the defendant, which to this day continues to dominate the photography industry in this country.

7. In the first post-1940 national-market monopolization case which was litigated and in which divestiture was ordered, the Pullman Company, a manufacturer and operator of sleeping cars,

11. The *American Tobacco* case mentioned in chapter 4.

was required to elect whether to retain its manufacturing or its operating division. It chose to retain the former, and sold the operating division to a consortium of railroads. By 1947, when the decree was entered, the sleeping-car business was in decline and already losing money. The president of Pullman has been quoted as saying that he was glad Pullman lost the case! The decree spurred Pullman to unload a dying business.

8. The last litigated national-market divestiture case involved Grinnell's monopoly of the central-station protection business. Grinnell had acquired Holmes Electric Protective Company in 1950 and most of the stock of American District Telegraph Company (ADT) in 1953, ADT being the principal source of the monopoly. These subsidiaries, along with Grinnell's investment in Automatic Fire Alarm Company, were divested in 1968. This purely vertical divestiture would not in itself have broken up the monopoly, but, in addition, ADT was forced to divest itself of service contracts and equipment in twenty-seven cities which brought in revenues of $3.7 million annually. This seems not to have eliminated ADT's monopoly for, during the period 1967–73, while making most of the required divestitures, ADT increased its revenues from $87.4 million to $148.3 million and its profits from $6.2 million to $10.7 million; apparently the divested assets represented only a small fraction of ADT's total business.

9. In a case settled by consent decree in 1956, IBM was required to divest itself of its tabulating-card productive capacity in excess of 50 percent of the nation's total capacity. Tabulating cards were an unimportant part of IBM's business.

10. United Fruit (now United Brands) had a monopoly position in the production and importation of bananas. A consent decree entered in 1958 required United to divest itself of 35 percent of its productive capacity. But, when divestiture finally occurred in 1972, the divested operations generated only 12.7 percent of United's banana output.

11. MCA, Inc., a producer of filmed television shows and other entertainment services, was required to dissolve its talent agency. When the dissolution occurred in 1962, television production was already MCA's main business, accounting for 85 percent of its sales, and MCA had previously agreed with the Screen Actors Guild to get out of the talent-agency business. As part of the consent settlement, MCA was permitted to acquire Decca Records.

Why has divestiture such a poor record as either a Clayton Act section 7 or a Sherman Act section 2 remedy? The characteristic delay of antitrust proceedings is at least part of the reason. Often by the time the divestiture decree is entered or can be carried out the industry has so changed as to make such a decree an irrelevance. A striking example is the *Alcoa* case, brought in 1937 but not finally decided until after World War II. The enormous increase in the demand for aluminum during the war resulted in the creation and rapid expansion of competing aluminum producers, so that by the late 1940s Alcoa no longer had a monopoly market share and a divestiture decree was rightly judged unnecessary and inappropriate.

The average length of all of the single-firm monopolization cases in which substantial divestiture has been decreed is 63 months, and of the litigated national-market cases, 83 months. These averages not only conceal a substantial variance but systematically understate the true length of the average case, since the statistics generally measure duration only to the entry of the final judgment rather than to the completion of divestiture. The lapse between final judgment and divestiture is often considerable. The final judgment in the *United Fruit* case was entered 167 months after the case was first filed, but another 54 months elapsed before final approval of United's plan of divestiture. It is hardly surprising that the conditions of an industry should often alter markedly while the divestiture proceeding is wending its leisurely way toward completion. We can expect the same problem to arise in deconcentration proceedings,[12] for any responsible proposal for deconcentration (such as the model statute of the Neal Report) is bound to furnish numerous opportunities for complicating and protracting a deconcentration proceeding.

Another reason for the poor record of divestiture as an antitrust remedy is that the government's lawyers tend to lose interest in a case at the relief stage. They derive both personal satisfaction and career advancement from the trial of an antitrust case, but gain neither from the post-trial relief negotiations and proceedings,

---

12. And this regardless of whether such proceedings are assigned to the federal district courts or to some special tribunal. Experience with administrative agencies and other specialized tribunals suggests that they conduct their proceedings no more expeditiously than the courts. For some evidence in the antitrust field see Richard A. Posner, "A Statistical Study of Antitrust Enforcement," 13 *J. Law & Econ.* 365, 377–81 (1970) (FTC statistics).

which they tend consequently to scant. In principle, it should be possible to alter the incentive structure of government legal service to correct this imbalance; but the problem has persisted stubbornly and may continue to defy solution.

Suppose that I am being too pessimistic and a deconcentration proceeding would in fact prove manageable and effective. My objections would change but not disappear. I would now be concerned that deconcentration might impose heavy costs on society by requiring industries to operate with higher costs than before they had been deconcentrated. This possibility led the authors of the Neal Report to include in their model act a provision relating to economies of scale which they explained in the following words:

> A decree cannot require a firm to take steps which would result in substantial loss of economies of scale. This provision would, for example, preclude divestiture reducing a firm below minimum efficient size or creating new entities below minimum efficient size. The burden of proof is on the firm, and the possible loss of economies is not a defense to the issuance of a judgment. . . . Division of a single plant would ordinarily result in substantial loss of economies of scale, and the Act permits a firm to establish that a decree would result in a net loss of economies of scale beyond the plant level. Net loss of economies of scale beyond the plant level might be established directly or by considering the minimum size of viable competitors in an industry. Thus, the court would not ordinarily divide an oligopoly firm into firms smaller than that indicated by experience to be necessary to survival in the industry. We are not unaware of efficiencies other than economies of scale; other efficiencies will generally reflect scarce resources such as unique management talent. These resources may be transferred pursuant to a deconcentration decree without significant loss.[13]

This discussion is unsatisfactory. There is no accepted method of establishing "directly" the existence of economies of scale at either the plant or the firm level. The methods that have been used (mostly engineering cost studies) suffer from grave conceptual shortcomings[14] and are, in any event, probably insufficiently

13. "Neal Report," supra note 1, at 311–12.
14. See Caleb A. Smith, "Survey of the Empirical Evidence on Economies of Scale," in *Business Concentration and Price Policy* 213 (Universities-Nat'l Bur. Comm. for Econ. Res. 1955); John S. McGee, "Ef-

developed to generate evidence assimilable in a legal proceeding. The indirect method suggested by the Neal Report, which is to consider the minimum size of viable competitors, is inappropriate in the context of a deconcentration proceeding. By assumption, the industry under scrutiny in such a proceeding is one in which the major firms are charging higher than competitive prices; that is the fundamental premise of a policy of deconcentration. Such prices will attract into the industry firms that may have higher costs than the existing firms and may be "viable" only because of the umbrella of the monopoly price. The method proposed by the Neal Report thus consists of observing a fringe of possibly inefficient small firms and inferring from their existence that the reorganization of the major firms in the industry into firms of that size would not raise the total cost of the industry.

The passage from the Neal Report quoted above states that the only proper concern in a deconcentration proceeding is with economies of scale. This is incorrect also. The reason offered for dismissing sources of efficiency besides scale, such as managerial skill, is that such resources can be transferred pursuant to a deconcentration decree without significant loss. A simple example will show that this cannot be assumed. Suppose that one firm has a 50-percent market share because of its very talented president (or a management team that would be less efficient if split up), who has reduced the firm's costs and thereby enabled it to undercut its competitors. If the industry is deconcentrated, and the firm's market share reduced, say to 12 percent, the industry's costs will rise, because by hypothesis the cost of production is now higher for the 38 percent of the industry's output that has been shifted to the firms having inferior management. The larger the market share that is controlled by "unique management talent" (the Neal Report's expression), up to the point where the economies resulting from managerial superiority are completely offset by diseconomies of scale, the lower the costs of the industry will be. And this is true regardless of how much of the increased revenues of the firm due to the president's special abilities are captured by him in the form of higher salary or other compensation. That question relates solely to the distribution of the social gains from lower costs. Those gains are reduced if his ability to lower the industry's

ficiency and Economies of Scale," in *Industrial Concentration: The New Learning,* supra note 2, at 55.

costs is limited by a measure that withdraws from his control a large portion of the assets over which he had previously exercised his talent for cost reduction.

Nor can the problem of reducing concentration without sacrificing possible efficiencies, scale and otherwise, with which concentration might be associated be swept under the rug by positing that efficiency is not an important factor in concentration. Economic theory (and common sense!) suggest that it is quite important in explaining *persistently* high concentration—the only kind the Concentrated Industries Act would affect.[15] Ask yourself how it is that an industry becomes, and remains, highly concentrated, notwithstanding that it is presumed to be charging supracompetitive prices (that presumption is the foundation of a deconcentration policy). It could become concentrated as a result of mergers designed to facilitate monopoly pricing; this was the basis of the dominant position once enjoyed by U.S. Steel in the steel industry. Over time, however, we would expect concentration so achieved to erode as the monopoly price charged by the leading firms induced the entry of new competitors and the resulting expansion of the industry's output and reduction of the market shares of the existing firms. That is precisely what occurred in the steel industry, albeit gradually (but we don't know at what point in its long decline U.S. Steel ceased to have substantial monopoly power).[16] If concentration persists, where are we to seek an explanation? One possibility—but an unlikely one, as we shall see in chapter 8—is in exclusionary practices. And if they are the explanation deconcentration is unlikely to be a necessary or suitable remedy. The practices can be enjoined or punished. To be sure, it *might* take longer for competition to be restored through the entry of new firms than if the monopolist were broken up, but this is speculation, given the likely length of a deconcentration proceeding.

Another possible reason for persistent concentration is an unexpired patent or some other governmental grant of monopoly power which prevents new competition; but this would provide

15. The act is limited to markets in which high levels of concentration have persisted for at least ten years. Allowing for time to bring suit, prosecute it to a successful conclusion, and complete the actual divestiture, one can expect that any state of concentration altered by the act would be in the neighborhood of twenty years old.

16. See p. 29 supra.

no basis for deconcentration either except in the special case where the members of an industry obtained patents by acquisitions that were not scrutinized under appropriate legal standards designed to prevent monopolization by the acquisition of competing patents. Still another possibility is that there are (nongovernmental) barriers to entry, so that new firms would have higher costs than existing firms. That this is an unlikely explanation can be seen by considering, as a type of prospective entrant, an existing but very small firm in an industry (almost every industry, however concentrated, has a fringe of small firms). If the leading firms are charging a monopoly price, one or more small firms will have an incentive to expand their output by shading the monopoly price. If a "barrier" prevents the small firm from expanding, it must be something that makes the small firm's marginal costs as high as the monopoly price charged by the leading firms so that the small firm cannot make money by shading that price. But why should its costs be higher than those of the leading firms unless there are economies of scale that it is too small to exploit or unless the leading firms are protected by valid patents, engage in exclusionary practices, or have superior management?

By viewing the existing small firms in the market as the equivalent of potential entrants, which they are, and asking what "barriers" they face to growing, we can legitimately elide the question of nonrecurring costs of entry. Those costs are irrelevant if there are small firms in the market that can grow to be large firms, for they will do so if the leading firms charge a price above the competitive level. In any event, there is grave doubt whether there are important nonrecurring costs of entry—barriers to entry in the true sense. Economies of scale do not create a barrier to entry; they only dictate the level of output that the new entrant must achieve in order to minimize his costs. The amount of capital required for entry is not a barrier to entry either; presumably it is no greater for the new entrant than for the firms in the market. Control of an essential input could be used to block entry, but this is not an important case, and it can be dealt with as an abuse of the input monopoly.

Advertising is frequently considered a barrier to entry. The argument is that massive advertising creates a consumer preference for existing brands which the new entrant can overcome only with still more massive advertising. This is implausible, however. Massive advertising of the existing brands will raise the cost and hence the price of those brands, and thus give the more moderately advertised or nonadvertised new brand a price advantage. The new entrant needn't advertise as heavily as the existing firms. He needn't advertise at all, but can market his brand through retail chains that affix their own brand names to the manufacturer's product and assume the entire burden of marketing the product. The argument is also contrary to the evidence, which shows that heavily advertised brands are associated with unstable brand preferences; massive advertising induces customer switching back and forth among brands, not the customer loyalty to a single brand that is posited by those who argue that advertising creates a barrier to entry.[17]

Oliver Williamson is one of the most forceful exponents of the view that there are nonrecurring costs of entry,[18] but he has been able to offer only one moderately persuasive example: the cost of capital. That cost includes a premium for risk, and if new ventures are characteristically riskier than established businesses the existing firms in the market may be able to raise money at lower cost than a new entrant. But this argument overlooks the point that many potential entrants are diversified firms that can raise money cheaply; and its empirical significance is unknown.

Williamson has also argued that if a firm once achieved a dominant position in a market by luck or skill, its position would tend to persist by sheer inertia. This would be true, however, only in the unlikely event that the managers of the firm did nothing to exploit their dominant position. If the firm raised its price above the competitive level its market share would decline unless it was so much more efficient than the other firms in the market (or new entrants) that its profit-maximizing monopoly price was below the costs of these other firms.

In short, it takes a good deal of strained and ad hoc argumentation to explain persistent monopoly or concentration without assuming unlawful exclusionary practices, lawful patent protection, economies of scale, superior management, competitive pricing, or other factors that would not normally justify dissolution proceedings.

17. See Lester G. Telser, "Advertising and Competition," 72 *J. Pol. Econ.* 537, 550 (1964).

18. See his "Dominant Firms and the Monopoly Problem: Market Failure Considerations," 85 *Harv. L. Rev.* 1512 (1972); Book Review, 83 *Yale L. J.* 647 (1974).

I would like to point out another respect in which a policy of deconcentration could impose substantial costs on society. As a firm's market share approaches the level at which the commencement of a deconcentration proceeding becomes likely, the firm will have an incentive to reduce its market share, or stabilize it, or retard the rate of its increase. The logical way to do this is by increasing price. The result is to bring about the very thing that a policy of deconcentration is intended to prevent—pricing above the competitive level. The Neal Report dismissed this problem with the remark that the remedies provided for in the Concentrated Industries Act are not punitive. But the question is not how the legal system characterizes the proceeding. It is whether a deconcentration proceeding would impose costs on the defendants. If so, firms will be willing to incur some costs to avoid being subjected to the proceeding. Obviously it *would* impose costs, if for no other reason than that the Neal Report's proposal assumes that the leading firms in concentrated industries enjoy supracompetitive profits before, but not after, deconcentration; the loss of such profits are costs to the firms involved.

It is true that the application of the proposed Concentrated Industries Act is triggered by industry, rather than firm, concentration levels. But it does not follow that a firm will take no steps to prevent its market share from growing, reasoning that its growth is unlikely to affect significantly whether the industry will reach the forbidden level. If it is a large firm, its market share *will* significantly affect the four-firm concentration ratio on which the application of the act turns. Moreover, under the terms of the act no firm can be the target of a deconcentration proceeding unless its market share is at least 15 percent. Therefore, even if the industry's concentration ratio is at or above the triggering level, the firm will have an incentive to prevent its market share from reaching 15 percent, quite apart from the effect of its market share on that of the leading firms as a group. Most important, the basic premise of the Neal Report is that leading firms in highly concentrated markets are capable of a form of undetectable collusion. If so, they will collude to avoid market-share increases that bring them to the forbidden level.

To summarize: the costs of a deconcentration policy, even one so carefully formulated as the Neal Report's model act, probably outweigh the benefits, which are conjectural. We do not know how much or how little the probability of collusive pricing is altered by marginal changes in concentration ratios, but we know that the administrative costs of deconcentration proceedings will be great, and we have theoretical grounds for concern that a policy of deconcentration will lead to higher costs in a significant fraction of concentrated industries.

Although I have focused on the appropriateness of divestiture in the deconcentration context, the analysis would be unchanged if the focus were shifted to single-firm monopoly cases. The possibility that breaking up a monopoly would sacrifice economies of scale and other efficiencies, the probability that persistent monopoly reflects factors that make dissolution either an unnecessary or an inappropriate remedy, and the perverse incentive effects of establishing a market-share threshold above which a firm becomes subject to divestiture are exactly parallel to the problems that I have been discussing in the deconcentration context.

6   Horizontal Mergers, Potential Competition, and Market Definition

Thus far I have discussed three approaches to the problem—fundamental to antitrust policy—of collusive pricing. The first is the conventional rule against price fixing, which punishes the *attempt* to fix prices rather than *effective* price fixing as such. The second is the use of economic evidence to prove the existence of price fixing whether or not there are detectable acts of collusion. The third is the deconcentration of highly concentrated markets in order to increase the costs of collusion. Still another approach, which resembles the third but is more limited in impact, and a good deal more practical, is to forbid mergers that, by creating high levels of concentration in a market, facilitate collusive pricing. This has been, in fact, the principal method by which the law has sought to deal with the problem of collusive pricing that is believed not to be effectively punishable by means of conventional price-fixing proceedings.

The Place of Merger Law in the Scheme of Antitrust

Now an antimerger law is distinctly a second-best solution to the problem of collusion; the best solution would be to deter it. An antimerger law is bound to be a very costly method of dealing with collusion, not only because divestiture is such a costly remedy[1] but also because mergers that may be held to violate the law may serve to exploit economies of scale sooner than by internal expansion, to concentrate assets in the hands of superior managers, and (where merger occurs pursuant to a takeover bid) to punish inefficient or corrupt managers. Moreover, an antimerger law is a crude instrument for coping with collusion, because the linkage between concentration and collusion is so complicated and so poorly understood. Since concentration is only one of the factors

---

1. To be sure, often an unlawful merger can be enjoined in advance of consummation, thus rendering divestiture unnecessary.

that predispose a market to collusion, one cannot specify a "dangerous" level of concentration without knowing a good deal about a particular market; and even then, the theory of collusion is not so well developed that one can say at precisely what point a rising level of concentration will markedly increase the danger of collusive pricing of a sort difficult to punish directly under the Sherman Act.

Had the law of section 1 of the Sherman Act developed along the lines suggested in chapter 4 and become an effective deterrent against tacit collusion, the only need for an antimerger policy would be to prevent competing sellers from getting around the prohibition against collusion by merging into a single firm having monopoly power—the kind of merger that one encounters in the *U.S. Steel* and other early trust cases.[2] But that is not the way the law has developed. Since 1950, when the Celler-Kefauver Antimerger Act was passed, the prevention of mergers that increase concentration without creating monopoly has been a principal focus of antitrust policy—and I regard the entire antimerger program since that time as an unfortunate by-product of the failure to have dealt directly with the problem of collusive pricing.

This chapter discusses the evolution of legal policy with respect to mergers between competing, or potentially competing, firms that do not create an actual monopoly and also with respect to the important subsidiary question of defining the market in which to compute the market shares that so often play a decisive role in the decision of merger cases. I shall not attempt to conceal my dismay at the intellectual confusion that has characterized the Supreme Court's efforts to fashion antitrust policy in the merger field.

Horizontal Mergers

The modern development of horizontal-merger law begins in 1948 with *United States* v. *Columbia Steel Co.*[3] The case involved the acquisition by U.S. Steel of Consolidated Steel Corporation,

---

2. Of course, given omniscience, it would not be necessary to forbid even such mergers, but only to forbid monopoly pricing by the firm resulting from the merger. However, experience with public-utility regulation suggests that the direct control of monopoly pricing is extraordinarily difficult, much more so even than inferring tacit collusion by the methods suggested in chapter 4.

3. 334 U.S. 495 (1948).

a competitor in steel fabrication. The market shares of the merging firms were (at most) 13 and 11 percent respectively. The Court held that the merger did not violate section 1 of the Sherman Act, as construed in accordance with the following standard:

> In determining what constitutes unreasonable restraint, we do not think the dollar volume is in itself of compelling significance; we look rather to the percentage of business controlled, the strength of the remaining competition, whether the action springs from business requirements or purpose to monopolize, the probable development of the industry, consumer demands, and other characteristics of the market. We do not undertake to prescribe any set of percentage figures by which to measure the reasonableness of a corporation's enlargement of its activities by the purchase of the assets of a competitor. The relative effect of percentage command of a market varies with the setting in which that factor is placed.[4]

The striking thing about this standard is the lack of any theory behind the inclusion of the enumerated items. The Court says that the dollar volume involved in the merger is not "of compelling significance" but fails to explain why it has any significance at all. The percentage of business controlled is mentioned, but as a factor apparently of no greater weight than several others, including "the strength of the remaining competition." Why is the strength of the remaining competition not simply the market share of the firms in the market that are not parties to the merger? Why are the market shares of the merging firms and of the remaining firms considered different factors rather than alternative ways of looking at the same factor? Why is intent important? Why must attention be given to "the probable development of the industry" and to "consumer demands"? What do these expressions mean, anyway?

Now we know that a firm that has 100 percent of a properly defined market, or even somewhat less,[5] will charge a price higher than the competitive level and that this price may persist for quite a long time, notwithstanding the incentive it creates for new firms to enter the market and existing firms to expand their output. But it is highly improbable that a firm having 24 percent of a market could maintain a higher than competitive price in this fashion. I think the Court sensed this and had no alternative theory of how such a merger might affect competition but was not suffi-

4. Id. at 527–28 (citations omitted).
5. See pp. 29, 49 supra.

ciently confident of its premises to announce a clearly permissive standard for nonmonopolistic mergers.

Columbia Steel was decided at a time when Congress was considering whether to amend section 7 of the Clayton Act to plug the "asset loophole." As originally enacted in 1914, section 7 had been limited to stock acquisitions, and since a merger is an asset acquisition the statute was held to be inapplicable to mergers.[6] As a result, cases like *Columbia Steel* had to be brought under section 1 of the Sherman Act, and the decision in that case suggested that section 1 was not effective in dealing with nonmonopolistic mergers: either they were permissible, or the statutory standard was too vague and multifactored to be workable.

Section 7 was amended in 1950 by the Celler-Kefauver Antimerger Act to include asset acquisitions, but the original section 7 standard (which forbade an acquisition if its effect might be to lessen competition substantially) was retained, and its meaning was unclear. No rules had evolved out of the few cases brought under the original statute. The utility of cases decided under other sections of the Clayton Act as precedents under the amended statute was limited: as we shall see in chapter 8, tying, exclusive dealing, price discrimination, and the other practices regulated by the Clayton Act are quite unlike horizontal mergers.

About all that emerges clearly from the legislative history of the 1950 amendments is Congress's concern with an allegedly "rising tide of economic concentration" in the American economy. There are two senses in which concentration might be thought relevant to public policy. First, of course, it might result in a higher than competitive price level by facilitating a kind of collusion among the sellers in the market that might be so difficult to detect as to be unreachable under the Sherman Act; second, and somewhat less clearly, the reduction in the number of firms implied by rising concentration[7] could be thought to endanger social values associated with the preservation of small firms. While both of these concerns with concentration are reflected in the legislative history,[8] they do not have the same significance in the

6. This history is recounted in United States v. Philadelphia National Bank, 374 U.S. 321, 337–40 (1963).

7. But notice that an increase in concentration could be associated with an increase in the dispersion of the size of firms rather than with a decrease in their absolute number.

8. See, e.g., S. Rep. No. 1775, 81st Cong., 2d Sess. 3, 5 (1950).

interpretation of the statute. The economic concern is inescapably relevant to the competitive effects of a horizontal merger; it furnishes the theory, which eluded the Court in *Columbia Steel*, of how a merger that does not create a monopoly market share may nonetheless result in a substantial lessening of competition. But the social concern with concentration is more plausibly viewed as a reason why some members of Congress may have wanted horizontal mergers to be tested by a stricter standard than that of the Sherman Act as interpreted in *Columbia Steel* than as a component of the standard itself. It seems unlikeiy that Congress, if it had intended the social concern to enter into the actual decision of cases, would have retained the standard of illegality of the original section 7 and the other Clayton Act provisions, since that was a standard of competitive effect rather than of small-business protection. Rather, it would have modified the standard, just as it did in the Robinson-Patman Act amendments to section 2 of the Clayton Act.[9]

The Supreme Court first interpreted the amended section 7 in *Brown Shoe Co.* v. *United States*.[10] The part of the Court's opinion that discusses the statutory standard emphasizes Congress's concern with the "rising tide of economic concentration" and states that the "keystone" of that concern was the "provision of authority for arresting mergers at a time when the trend to a lessening of competition in a line of commerce was still in its incipiency."[11] This remark has given currency to the dubious notion that a merger is more dangerous in a market where concentration has been rising. Suppose it has been rising because of changes in the conditions of supply or demand that have increased the minimum efficient firm size. In such a case forbidding mergers will not prevent, but will only postpone, higher concentration, which will occur as some firms expand to take advantage of the economies of scale and squeeze others out of the market. Nor is it at all clear that one wants to prevent concentration in these circumstances. Prices may be higher with less concentration, due to the greater costs of operating at an inefficient scale of production. Now suppose that, although there is no underlying economic trend toward concentration, we somehow know that the firms in the market want to make acquisitions that will eventually

9. See 15 U.S.C. § 13 (1974).
10. 370 U.S. 294 (1962).
11. Id. at 317.

result in a high level of concentration—perhaps because they want to fix prices, but more likely because of tax or other reasons unrelated to the efficient organization of the market. In this case we can intervene and stop the merger trend whenever we think that another merger will carry the market across the threshold that separates acceptable from unacceptable levels of concentration.[12] In neither case, nor in the intermediate cases, is it tenable to regard the mere existence of a trend toward concentration as evidence that a merger should be forbidden that does not in itself create an unacceptable level of concentration.

Another consideration stressed in *Brown Shoe*'s formulation of a standard of illegality under the new section 7 is that Congress wanted to prevent only mergers "having demonstrable anticompetitive effects"; for "the legislative history illuminates congressional concern with the protection of *competition*, not *competitors*, and its desire to restrain mergers only to the extent that such combinations may tend to lessen competition."[13] This appears to be a decisive rejection of the social concern with excessive concentration, and a ringing endorsement of the use of economic criteria. But no standard for implementing an economic approach is proposed. According to the Court, Congress did not "adopt a definition of the word 'substantially,' whether in quantitative terms of sales or assets or market shares or in designated qualitative terms, by which a merger's effects on competition were to be measured."[14] The congressional deliberations reflect "a conscious avoidance of exclusively mathematical tests."[15]

> Congress indicated plainly that a merger had to be functionally viewed, in the context of its particular industry. That is, whether the consolidation was to take place in an industry that was fragmented rather than concentrated, that had seen a recent trend toward domination by a few leaders or had remained fairly consistent in its distribution of market shares among the participating companies, that had experienced easy

12. There may, of course, be great difficulty in deciding what that threshold is, and any choice will inevitably be arbitrary to some extent. My point is only that there is no reason to make the threshold vary according to whether there has been a trend toward concentration in the market prior to the merger.

13. 370 U.S. at 319–20 (emphasis in original).

14. Id. at 321.

15. Id. at 321, n. 36.

access to markets by suppliers and easy access to suppliers by buyers or had witnessed foreclosure of business, that had witnessed the ready entry of new competition or the erection of barriers to prospective entrants, all were aspects, varying in importance with the merger under consideration, which would properly be taken into account.[16]

The theme is elaborated in a footnote:

Subsequent to the adoption of the 1950 amendments, both the Federal Trade Commission and the courts have, in the light of Congress' expressed intent, recognized the relevance and importance of economic data that places [sic] any given merger under consideration within an industry framework almost inevitably unique in every case. Statistics reflecting the shares of the market controlled by the industry leaders and the parties to the merger are, of course, the primary index of market power; but only a further examination of the particular market —its structure, history and probable future—can provide the appropriate setting for judging the probable anticompetitive effect of the merger.[17]

In *Brown Shoe*, as in *Columbia Steel*, one has no sense that the Court had any notion of how a nonmonopolistic merger might affect competition. A clue to the Court's confusion is its reference to "market power" in the last quoted passage. Clearly, the Court thinks that the possession of "market power" is highly relevant, perhaps crucial, to finding a violation of section 7. But it is unclear what the term means to the Court. If it means monopoly power, the Court has backed into the (implicit) standard of *Columbia Steel*. Is "market power" perhaps some debased form of monopoly power—the power of a single firm, not acting in cooperation with competing sellers, to maintain a price slightly above the competitive level? Yet it is unlikely that a firm lacking a monopoly market share (not necessarily 100 percent, but much more than involved in the usual section 7 case) could *unilaterally* keep its price substantially above the competitive level. The real significance of concentration, which is obscured by the term "market power" and which seems to have eluded the Court's understanding in *Brown Shoe*, is that it facilitates collusion, explicit or tacit, among the firms in the market by reducing the costs of collusion and of detecting cheating. Once this point is grasped, inquiry can

16. Id. at 321–22.
17. Id. at 322, n. 38.

proceed to the critical question: at what level of concentration does the danger of undetectable collusion become substantial? The point was not grasped in *Brown Shoe*.

This is further shown by the Court's application of the legal standard to the facts of the case (I confine my attention to the horizontal aspect). In some cities, the Court found,[18] the combined share of the retail shoe sales of Brown and Kinney (the acquired firm) was very large—as much as 57 percent. The Court seems not to have cared, however, how large the market shares were, so long as they exceeded 5 percent. Thus, after noting that the combined market share of the merging firms exceeded that level in 118 cities, the Court states: "[if] a merger achieving 5% control were now approved, we might be required to approve future merger efforts by Brown's competitors seeking similar market shares."[19] The implication that the difference between a 5-percent and a 57-percent market share is not crucial in the application of section 7 is a clue that the Court's real concern is not with competition, despite its earlier statement to that effect. A 57-percent market share might give a firm power over price, regardless of the number or size distribution of its competitors. But without knowing something about the over-all concentration of the market, one cannot attach any significance to a 5-percent market share. If the largest firm had 5 percent, it would mean there were at least 20 competitors in the market, and possibly a great many more. The probability of the sort of collusion that cannot be effectively reached under the Sherman Act would not be great in an industry of 20 sellers of roughly equal size.

The Court's confusion is underscored by the weight it attaches to the *absence* of concentration in shoe retailing. "In an industry as fragmented as shoe retailing," the Court states, "the control of substantial shares of the trade in a city may have important effects on competition."[20] The Court has gotten the point backward: the less concentrated a market is, the *less* significance should be attached to the market share of the merging firms. If a market has 100 firms, all of equal size, the fact that 5 of them consolidate, creating a single firm having 5 percent of the market, has virtually no competitive significance. The difficulty of colluding will not

18. Incorrectly, as pointed out in John L. Peterman's useful article, "The Brown Shoe Case," 18 *J. Law. & Econ.* 81 (1975).
19. 370 U.S. at 343–44.
20. Id. at 343.

be reduced appreciably; the leading firm must still collude with a large number of other firms in order to be able to maintain a price significantly above the competitive level. In contrast, in a market of only 5 firms the merger of the 2 smallest to create a new firm having 5 percent of the market might conceivably have some adverse effect, by reducing from 5 to 4 the number of firms that must collude in order to monopolize the market completely.

We soon discover that the objection to the merger of Brown and Kinney has nothing to do with the probability of collusion between the resulting firm and competing shoe retailers. The Court's concern is not that Brown-Kinney might charge a higher price as a result of the merger but that it might charge a lower price and thereby hurt its competitors—which is bad, in the Court's view, even if the lower price is made possible by genuine social cost savings due to integrated operation:

> Of course, some of the results of large integrated or chain operations are beneficial to consumers. Their expansion is not rendered unlawful by the mere fact that small independent stores may be adversely affected. It is competition, not competitors, which the Act protects. But we cannot fail to recognize Congress' desire to promote competition through the protection of viable, small, locally owned businesses. Congress appreciated that occasional higher costs and prices might result from the maintenance of fragmented industries and markets. It resolved these competing considerations in favor of decentralization. We must give effect to that decision.[21]

First the Court says that the act protects competition, not individual competitors; in the next breath it says that the act protects higher-cost from lower-cost competitors.

A decision that seeks to prevent a competitor from realizing opportunities for cost savings is inconsistent with the economic objection to concentration. In the end, then, *Brown Shoe* is seen to rest on the social objection, which is that concentration involves the elimination of small firms that the Supreme Court values although the consumer does not. I suggested earlier why I think it is improper to view the amended section 7 as enacting the social theory of concentration. And it is peculiar, to say the least, that the Court should not have mentioned that theory in discussing the factors that Congress supposedly wanted it to consider in applying

21. Id. at 344.

section 7. More important, the decision in *Brown Shoe* does not really further the ultimate objectives of the social theory. If an integrated firm like Brown has lower costs than nonintegrated retailers, it will expand its share of the retail shoe market whether or not it acquires Kinney. The principal effect of a very strict rule against horizontal mergers is not to retard economic progress; it is to reduce the sale value of small firms by making it difficult for their large competitors—an important class of potential purchasers of small firms—to buy them.

The next major merger case to be decided by the Court was *United States* v. *Philadelphia National Bank.*[22] Although it follows *Brown Shoe* by only a year, the opinion in *Philadelphia Bank* reflects a radically different conception of section 7. Whereas the Court in *Brown Shoe* rejected any simple, quantitative test of illegality, the Court in *Philadelphia Bank* warns of "the danger of subverting congressional intent by permitting a too-broad economic investigation," and declares that "in any case in which it is possible . . . to simplify the test of illegality, the courts ought to do so in the interest of sound and practical judicial administration."[23] Whereas the Court in *Brown Shoe* lacks a clear idea of why concentration is a bad thing, the Court in *Philadelphia Bank* assumes that the objection to concentration is the economic one, and uses the economic literature on oligopoly pricing as the source of a specific test of illegality. The test is that a merger which (1) creates a firm having 30 percent of the market and (2) thereby increases concentration among the leading firms by at least 33 percent is presumptively unlawful.[24]

The rule declared in the *Philadelphia Bank* decision has the virtues of being precise and objective, and thus workable, and of being derived from the fundamental purpose of the statute, which is to encourage competitive pricing by preventing high levels of concentration. Yet just three years later, in *United States* v. *Von's Grocery Co.,*[25] the Court veered sharply away from the path of *Philadelphia Bank.* The market shares involved in *Von's* were smaller than in *Philadelphia Bank,* but the Court in the earlier case had not suggested that the particular percentages specified in

22. 374 U.S. 321 (1963).
23. Id. at 362.
24. The purpose of the second part of the test is to exclude mergers where the acquired firm is a trivial factor in the market.
25. 384 U.S. 270 (1966).

its rule were the minimum that would trigger the presumption of illegality, and the government in its brief in *Von's* remained within the intellectual framework of the *Philadelphia Bank* opinion. It pointed out that with the three largest sellers in the relevant market (retail grocery sales in Los Angeles) accounting on the eve of the merger for about 19 percent of the total sales of the market and the eight largest for about 39 percent, the market was sufficiently concentrated to be classified as a "loose oligopoly." After the merger the three largest firms had 23 percent of the market and the eight largest 42 percent. Thus, the merger involved a perceptible if modest increase in concentration in a market that, in the government's view, for which some economic support could be marshaled, was already dangerously concentrated.

The most glaring deficiency in the government's case was the fact that it ignored the ease and rapidity of entry into the retail grocery business. The record indicated that a modern supermarket able to compete on terms of substantial equality with the leading firms in the market could be started with a capital investment of only $700,000. The grocery chains in Los Angeles could not have fixed prices without inducing such rapid and widespread entry by new firms as to force price back to a competitive level before the cartel could obtain substantial monopoly profits. In such circumstances, price fixing is not very attractive, even if it can be done with impunity.

The government's theory of illegality was completely ignored by the Court, in an opinion given over largely to an eccentric history of the antitrust laws. We learn that their original purpose was not to protect consumers from having to pay prices in excess of competitive levels but, on the contrary, to prevent "powerful business combinations" from " 'driving out of business the small dealers and worthy men whose lives have been spent therein, and who might be unable to readjust themselves to their altered surroundings.' "[26] The Court's quotation is from an entirely gratuitous passage in an early cartel case (cartelization, by raising prices above the competitive level, makes it easier rather than more difficult for smaller and less efficient firms to prosper).

The *Von's* history lesson continues with the observation that because "the Sherman Act failed to protect the smaller business-

26. Id. at 274, quoting United States v. Trans-Missouri Freight Ass'n, 166 U.S. 290, 323 (1897).

man from elimination through the monopolistic pressures of large combinations which used mergers to grow ever more powerful,"[27] Congress passed the original section 7. When that failed to stop mergers (not that it had been intended to apply to mergers), Congress amended the statute in 1950, and thereby enacted the social objection to concentration: "the basic purpose of the 1950 . . . Act was to prevent concentration in the American economy by keeping a large number of small competitors in business."[28] There is nothing here about competition; the Court does not suggest that "a large number of small competitors" is a necessary condition of competitive pricing.

In applying the social theory of concentration to the facts of the case, the Court emphasizes that the number of single-store grocery companies in Los Angeles had declined from 5,365 in 1950 to 3,818 in 1961. The relevance of this observation is unclear. Shopping Bag, the acquired firm, was not a single-store grocery company but a substantial chain. The government had argued that the merger had increased the likelihood of supracompetitive pricing in the relevant market. Such prices would help the single-owner stores—which are presumably less efficient than the chains (why else has their number declined steadily over time?)—to cover their costs. The Court, however, thought the merger would make the merging firms "even more powerful" than they had been before the merger.[29] We are back in the world of the *Brown Shoe* opinion. Mergers are bad because they enable the merging firms to injure their small competitors by underpricing them. (As a detail, I point out that the Court in *Von's* cited no evidence, and the record contained no evidence that it could have cited, to support the proposition that the merger would reduce the costs of the

27. 384 U.S. at 274–75.
28. Id. at 278.
29. Ibid. The Court in *Brown Shoe* had recognized that the way in which the merged firm would harm its small competitors was by passing on to the consumer the cost savings made possible by the merger (or a portion of them), that is, by reducing price. See 370 U.S. at 344. The mode of injury is not specified in *Von's* but is presumably the same. Conceivably, a more efficient competitor might injure a less efficient one without underpricing him (for example, by paying a higher rent for choice locations); but this is unlikely, especially if the more efficient competitor confronts equally or more efficient competitors who constrain his prices to his costs and thus force him to pass on his cost savings to the consumer in the form of lower prices.

merging firms or otherwise increase their "power" vis-à-vis single-owner stores.) The Court decided the *Von's* case for the government on the theory that the firm resulting from the merger would charge *lower* prices than before the merger, when the government had argued that the firm resulting from the merger would charge *higher* prices.

Even if the protection of small business, rather than the protection of the competitive process, were the controlling policy in the interpretation and application of section 7, it is difficult to see how that policy would be served by making virtually any nontrivial horizontal merger illegal, the apparent rule of the *Von's* case.[30] If large grocery chains have lower costs than single-store or other small grocery companies, they can increase their output relative to that of the small companies even if forbidden to make any mergers at all, and will do so if competitive. The only hope for the small, less efficient groceries is that the large chains will collude and charge higher than competitive prices, which will reduce the chain's output and enable more small grocers to survive despite their higher costs. Thus a permissive policy toward horizontal mergers would by facilitating collusion help the small grocer. Indeed, the interests of small business would probably best be served by a rule permitting *all* horizontal mergers, including plainly monopolistic ones. To be sure, some monopolistic mergers might harm small competitors, either by enabling economies of scale to be exploited a little earlier or, less often, by facilitating predatory practices. But these adverse effects on small competitors would be almost certainly dominated by the tendency of monopolistic firms operating without legal constraint to charge prices higher than their costs and thus place an umbrella over less efficient competitors.

A related question, ignored by the Court in *Von's,* is: what constitutes a small business entitled to legal protection? Shopping Bag, with its 36 stores, was not a corporate giant, its $90 million annual sales being insignificant in comparison to the sales of A&P, Safeway, and the other national food chains. It was a family firm (as was Von's), and the merger with Von's was motivated by the usual considerations that induce family firms to seek to be acquired, such as desire to have a more readily marketable security than the stock of a family firm. Companies in the size range of Shopping Bag are clearly hurt by the Court's rule, yet from the

30. Some room for maneuver was left, perhaps, by the Court's emphasis on the merging firms being "powerful." 384 U.S. at 278.

standpoint of fostering an economy of numerous, relatively small firms they are probably entitled to more judicial solicitude than the Mom-and-Pop stores—whose progressive demise cannot possibly be halted by judicial fiat.

The rule of the *Von's* case may have been impaired by the later decision in *United States* v. *General Dynamics Corp.*[31] The Court's opinion, which upheld the challenged merger, was written by Justice Stewart, a frequent dissenter from the Warren Court's merger decisions (including *Von's*); and although it is carefully written to preserve a façade of continuity with *Von's,* one is again conscious of a grinding shift of mental gears. The case involved a merger of leading coal producers and resulted in increasing the market share of the two largest firms in the two geographical markets involved from 45 to 49 percent, and from 44 to 53 percent, respectively; and the merger took place against a background of a rapid and steep decline in the number of coal producers (from 144 to 39 between 1957 and 1967, in one of the markets). Given *Von's,* one might have thought that these facts established a clear-cut violation of section 7. But the Court reached back to *Brown Shoe* for the proposition that while market-share percentages are " 'the primary index of market power . . . only a further examination of the particular market—its structure, history and probable future—can provide the appropriate setting for judging the probable anticompetitive effect of the merger.' "[32] This requirement of "further examination" had, of course, been dropped in *Philadelphia Bank,* and the whole approach had been utterly rejected in *Von's.* Examining further, the Court in *General Dynamics* found that the acquired firm's market share overstated its competitive position. Virtually all of the firm's coal reserves were already committed under long-term contracts, and no other reserves were available for it to acquire—they also were committed under long-term contracts. Thus the acquired firm's ability to compete for new business was so limited that it could not be considered an important potential source of supply for new customers; its disappearance as an independent firm would not be noticed.

The Court was saying in effect that since the acquired firm was incapable of making any significant new sales it ought to be discounted as a competitive factor in the market, like a firm that had gone out of business but was still receiving income from earlier

31. 415 U.S. 486 (1974).
32. Id. at 498, quoting 370 U.S. at 322, n. 38.

installment sales. Conceivably, even the *Von's* Court might have considered the acquired firm in this case sufficiently powerless not to fall within the ban on mergers between "powerful" firms. But one doubts it.[33] If the Court's quotation from *Brown Shoe* is taken at face value, the rule is now to be that market shares are just the starting point for analysis; some effort to assess their significance in the particular economic setting of the merger must also be made. This would seem to imply that a firm in Von's position could now argue that the exceptional ease and rapidity of entry into the retail grocery business greatly diminished the significance to be attached to large market shares—shares that would be significant in a market like steel where the creation of new competition is at best a gradual process. The new dispensation of the *General Dynamics* case cannot in logic be—and has not been—limited to the special case of a firm that can no longer obtain an essential input.[34]

At this writing, the Court's direction in the merger area is unclear. Is it returning to the *Columbia Steel* era of freewheeling inquiry into all relevant aspects of the merger, with little guidance as to what is relevant since the purpose of the law being applied is not clearly grasped? Is any evidence now to be admissible that tends to show that a merger does (or does not) offend either the social or the economic objections to concentration? It would be depressing to think that one had to choose between *Von's* and *Columbia Steel*. A third alternative is a return to the approach of the *Philadelphia Bank* case, which involves deducing a simple rule from the economic objection to concentration. Perhaps this is what the Court intends.[35]

33. The two justices who had been in the majority in *Von's* and were still members of the Court when *General Dynamics* was decided (Douglas and Brennan) dissented.

34. A few months later, in United States v. Marine Bancorporation, 418 U.S. 602 (1974), the Court held that market-share percentages do not have their ordinary significance in a case where state-law limitations on branch banking confined a bank to a single office in the relevant market. And a year later, in United States v. Citizens & Southern National Bank, 422 U.S. 86 (1975), the Court again discounted the significance of market-share statistics in a bank-merger case, this time because prior to merger the parties were not competing with each other, due to a network of informal relationships amounting to a de facto union of the firms.

35. In both *Marine Bancorporation* and *Citizens & Southern* (see supra n. 34), the Court described its *General Dynamics* decision as holding that

On the assumption that my preferred solution to the problem of tacit collusion, which would imply a broadly permissive policy toward horizontal mergers,[36] is not about to be adopted, I shall now consider how the rule of the *Philadelphia Bank* case might be brought into closer conformity with current economic knowledge. When that case was decided, most students of industrial organization believed that if one seller had as much as 20 to 25 percent of the sales in his market there was a serious danger that the market price would be above the competitive level.[37] This scholarly consensus has been shattered. There is increasing evidence and conviction that considerably higher levels of concentration may be necessary in order to create a substantial danger of tacit collusion, given the many difficulties of purely tacit formation and implementation of a collusive pricing scheme.[38] Scholarly thinking has also changed with respect to the costs of preventing mergers between competing firms. There is less confidence than formerly that economies of scale are likely to be exhausted at levels of concentration well below the point at which the prohibitions of section 7 might come into play.[39] It is true that blocking a merger or series of mergers aimed at attaining efficient firm size will delay rather than prevent attainment of that goal, since firms will expand internally to take advantage of the available economies of scale. But, by the same token, legal rules that forbid mergers designed to exploit economies of scale can have no durable impact on levels of concentration. We are also more sensitive today to the importance of mergers as a method for displacing less efficient corporate managements, a social value that is distinct from economies of scale and impaired by rules severely restricting horizontal mergers.[40]

market-share statistics establish a rebuttable presumption of illegality. This was the formulation employed in *Philadelphia Bank*.

36. See pp. 96–97 supra.

37. See references in 374 U.S. at 363, n. 38, and 364–65, n. 41.

38. See p. 56 supra, and references cited there.

39. See, e.g., Harold Demsetz, "Two Systems of Belief About Monopoly," in *Industrial Concentration: The New Learning* 164 (Harvey J. Goldschmid, H. Michael Mann & J. Fred Weston eds. 1974); John S. McGee, "Efficiency and Economies of Scale," in id. at 55.

40. To be sure, even a complete ban on horizontal mergers would not eliminate all possibility of corporate takeover by the merger route, assuming that broad scope was allowed for vertical, or at least conglomerate, mergers. However, frequently a firm in the same market will have a much

The revisions in our thinking about mergers call for conservative rules of liability. There is little basis in current thinking for automatic intervention in markets in which the four largest firms have a combined market share of less than 60 percent.[41] But, in my opinion at least, mergers that either (1) carry a market across that threshold, or (2) significantly increase concentration in a market that exhibits other predisposing characteristics to collusive pricing (as discussed in chapter 4), should be presumed to be illegal; and the grounds for rebutting the presumption should be limited to factors that establish a specific competitive incapacity of the acquiring or acquired firm (as in *General Dynamics*) which deprives the market-share statistics or other predisposing characteristics in the particular case of their ordinary significance. I would not allow a generalized defense of efficiency. Not only is the measurement of efficiency (whether based on economies of scale, superior management, or whatever) an intractable subject for litigation;[42] but an estimate of a challenged merger's cost savings could not be utilized in determining the total economic effect of the merger unless an estimate was also made of the monopoly costs of the merger—and we simply do not know enough about the effect of marginal increases in the concentration ratio under different market conditions to predict the price effects, and hence monopoly costs, of a challenged merger, against which to compare the projected cost savings of the merger. A further point is that the cost savings made possible by an anticompetitive merger may be dissipated by expenditures on measures for engrossing the expected monopoly profits, made larger by those savings—expenditures, for example, on persuading the courts to permit the merger

better idea of whether another firm's management is maximizing its opportunities than a firm in another market. Also, managerial complementaries are likely to be greater between firms in the same market than between firms in different markets.

41. Thus, an important study of underwriting costs found that an increase beyond eight in the number of bids submitted did not reduce those costs substantially. Reuben Kessel, "A Study of the Effects of Competition in the Tax-Exempt Bond Market," 79 *J. Pol. Econ.* 706, 723 (1971). An industry where the four largest firms have less than 60 percent of the market is likely to contain at least eight significant competitors.

42. Especially since for purposes of defense in a merger case it would also be necessary to determine how soon the efficiencies might have been realized without a merger, e.g., by internal growth or managerial changes.

to take place. Finally, if the less encompassing prohibition of horizontal mergers that I have proposed were adopted, there would be less need to worry about the adverse consequences of ignoring most of the efficiency justifications of challenged mergers, for most mergers would not be subject to challenge.

Mergers between Potential Competitors

The idea that eliminating a potential competitor might be the basis of an antitrust violation is old—it appears briefly in *Columbia Steel*—but its modern development begins with *United States v. Penn-Olin Chem. Co.*[43] The government challenged under section 7 a joint venture between Pennsalt and Olin Mathieson to build a sodium-chlorate plant to serve the Southeastern United States, a growing market served by only two firms. Both joint venturers were chemical companies. Pennsalt had manufactured sodium chlorate prior to the joint venture but its market was in the West; Olin had not. Each firm had considered, and according to the district court neither had completely rejected, the possibility of building its own plant in the Southeast, before deciding on the joint venture.

The district court assumed that if, but for the joint venture, both Pennsalt and Olin would have built plants in the Southeast, the joint venture would violate section 7 by reducing the number of competing firms from four to three. But the court found it highly unlikely that both would have built plants. It made no finding as to the probability that but for the joint venture one would have built a plant "while the other continued to ponder,"[44] since it could see no significant competitive difference between that situation and the joint venture.

The Supreme Court did not disturb the district court's finding that both firms would not have built plants. But it remanded the case for a finding as to whether if the joint venture had been blocked and only one of the firms had built a plant the other "would have remained a significant potential competitor"[45] whose threat to enter the market would have constrained the pricing decisions of the firms in the market. The following "standard" was proposed to guide the district court on remand:

43. 378 U.S. 158 (1964).
44. Id. at 173.
45. Id. at 175–76.

We note generally the following criteria which the trial court might take into account in assessing the probability of a substantial lessening of competition: the number and power of the competitors in the relevant market; the background of their growth; the power of the joint venturers; the relationship of their lines of commerce; the competition existing between them and the power of each in dealing with the competitors of the other; the setting in which the joint venture was created; the reasons and necessities for its existence; the joint venture's line of commerce and the relationship thereof to that of its parents; the adaptability of its line of commerce to noncompetitive practices; the potential power of the joint venture in the relevant market; an appraisal of what the competition in the relevant market would have been if one of the joint venturers had entered it alone instead of through Penn-Olin; the effect, in the event of this occurrence, of the other joint venturer's potential competition; and such other factors as might indicate potential risk to competition in the relevant market.[46]

No one who reads this laundry list can believe that the Court had a clear understanding of either the problem of potential competition or the practical limitations of judicial fact-finding.

To grasp the role of potential competition in the scheme of section 7, it is useful—as always in the antitrust field—to go back to fundamentals. The purpose of section 7, viewed economically (the only view taken in *Penn-Olin*), is to prevent the emergence of conditions that substantially increase the probability of effective collusion. As was explained in chapter 4, collusion is more likely the less elastic is the demand for the output of the potentially colluding firms at the competitive price and the lower are the costs of collusion. Thus, anything that increases the elasticity of demand without reducing the costs of collusion reduces monopoly power. The existence of potential competitors increases the elasticity of the demand facing the existing sellers in the market by providing a source of supply to which consumers will be able to turn if prices rise above the competitive level. Hence we must ask whether the joint venture challenged in *Penn-Olin* reduced the elasticity of demand for sodium chlorate in the southeastern market. The Court's (implicit) view is that it probably did, because, had it not been for the joint venture, either Pennsalt or Olin Mathieson would

46. Id. at 176–77.

have built a plant in the Southeast and the other would have continued to pose a threat of doing so. But the Court seems wrong in this, especially since it accepted the district court's finding that both firms would not have entered the market on their own.[47]

Before the joint venture there were only two firms in the southeastern sodium-chlorate market.[48] This probably made the conditions for effective collusion propitious except for the possibility that an increase in price would lead to an early collapse in the demand for the output of these firms as new firms, attracted by cartel profits, entered the market. We do not know the extent to which the existing firms' pricing was in fact constrained by the existence of potential competition, but it is at least conceivable that the prospect of new entry so reduced the expected gains from collusive pricing—so increased the elasticity of demand for the existing firms' product in the medium to long run[49]—as to discourage those firms from attempting to collude.[50] If so, the elimination of potential competition would have fostered collusion. But the joint venture did not simply eliminate a potential competitor in the southeastern market; it also added a new competitor in that market, which must have reduced the probability and effectiveness of collusion by increasing the number of firms (from two to three) whose pricing would have to be coordinated. The Court discounted the procompetitive effect of the joint venture by remarking that, if the joint-venture route had been barred, one of the joint venturers would probably have entered the Southeast on its own. But even if the district court had found that it was overwhelmingly probable

47. On remand from the Supreme Court's decision, the district court found that *neither* firm would have entered the market by itself, and on this ground once again dismissed the complaint. 246 F. Supp. 917 (D. Del. 1965), aff'd by an equally divided Court, 389 U.S. 308 (1967).

48. Ignoring, as the Court did, the very slight sales that Pennsalt had made in the Southeast.

49. See supra note 30, at 57.

50. This is *not* the argument that colluding firms will set a price equal to the cost of any new entrant in order to forestall entry, a foolish policy since, if the long-run marginal costs of the new entrant are no higher than those of the existing firms, the usual case as we have seen, the effect of such a policy will be to constrain price to the competitive level, resulting in zero monopoly profits. The rational strategy for colluding sellers is to set a price higher than the cost of the new entrant, since as long as substantial entry takes some time to materialize this policy will enable some monopoly profits to be obtained.

that one (but not both) of the joint venturers would have entered the market, the Court would have erred seriously in discounting the joint venture's procompetitive effect to zero. Entry by means of the joint venture was, we know ex post, a certainty. Although a court can try to estimate the likelihood that in the absence of the joint venture at least one of the firms would have entered on its own, it cannot be certain that this would have happened. The fact that the firms adopted the joint-venture method of entry suggests at the very least that entry by this method was more attractive to the firms and therefore occurred earlier than it would have by another method.

Another doubtful feature of the Court's analysis is the suggestion that, once one firm had entered the market (assuming now that the joint venture had been blocked), the remaining firm would have continued to pose a threat of new entry and thus constrained pricing in the southeastern market. This possibility was small given the district court's finding, which the Supreme Court accepted, that both firms would not have entered the market on their own. The likelihood of collusive pricing in that market was presumably greater when there were only two firms—that is, before the hypothesized entry of either Pennsalt or Olin—than it was afterward, when there were three. At the earlier stage, therefore, the ratio of market price to cost was likely to be higher, and hence entry more attractive, than after a third firm (Penn-Olin) appeared in the market. But if both firms would not have entered the southeastern market when there were only two firms in that market, as the district court found and the Supreme Court agreed—if, in other words, the joint venturers believed that the market could support only three sellers—there is no reason to expect that after one of them had entered, the remaining firm would still have considered entering on its own.[51] Knowing this, the firms in the southeastern market would have drastically discounted the significance of this firm as a possible future competitor.

The most questionable feature of the *Penn-Olin* decision is the

---

51. A more extreme example may help to clarify this point. Suppose that a market contains only one firm; there are twenty firms that could enter it; and we know, somehow, that only ten—we do not know which ten—will do so. Ten firms enter the market and the market price falls. Should we expect the remaining firms to enter? No. When prices were higher, and entry therefore more attractive, they did not enter, and the entry of their ten fellows has now made entry less attractive than before.

implicit assumption that the only four firms in the world that are relevant to the analysis of the competitive effect of the joint venture are the two firms selling sodium chlorate in the Southeast plus Pennsalt and Olin Mathieson, two firms mulling entry into that market by one method or another. Suppose that after the joint venture Penn-Olin colludes with the existing firms in the Southeast. Pennsalt and Olin Mathieson are no longer potential competitors, but what of the remaining chemical firms in the country? Will they not be attracted to the southeastern sodium-chlorate market by the monopoly profits being generated there? The Court's list of factors to be considered by the district court on remand omits the effect on the strength of potential competition of eliminating one potential competitor. Yet economic theory suggests that charging monopoly prices in a market will create attractive opportunities for a significant number of firms whose long-run costs of operating in the market will not be substantially higher than those of the firms already in it. The possibility that the ranks of potential competitors might be so depleted that a reduction in their number by one would be perceived by the firms in the market as the elimination of a significant constraint on collusive pricing seems sufficiently remote to require that it be proved.

To recapitulate, the existence of potential competition may constrain collusive pricing in a market by increasing the perceived elasticity of demand facing the sellers in the market, and so in principle the elimination of potential competition could have anticompetitive consequences. But it does not follow that eliminating *a* potential competitor is likely to have an appreciable effect. The number of potential competitors is a function of the ratio of price to cost in the market in question, and any increase in price above cost will make entry attractive to a number of firms by giving them an opportunity to obtain monopoly profits. At prices substantially above cost—the sorts of prices with which the antitrust laws are properly concerned—the number of potential competitors will normally be very large. Moreover, the fact that Pennsalt and Olin Mathieson chose to enter by means of a joint venture rather than individually, coupled with the district court's finding (accepted by the Supreme Court) that both firms would not have entered individually, is strong evidence that the procompetitive effect of the joint venture in injecting a third firm into the southeastern market outweighed its anticompetitive effect (a very tenuous one, as we have seen) in removing the potential competition of the firm that would not have entered individually once the other firm did so.

The potential-competition doctrine was next applied by the Supreme Court in *Federal Trade Commission v. Procter & Gamble Co.*[52] The case involved the acquisition by Procter of the Clorox Company, which produces roughly half of all of the household liquid bleach sold in this country. The illegality of the acquisition was placed on two mutually inconsistent grounds, the first being that it enhanced Clorox's already dominant position in the liquid-bleach industry and the second that it eliminated Procter as a potential competitor of Clorox.

The first ground strongly implies that Procter had both the ability and the desire, if the merger had been blocked, to enter the market by internal expansion and underprice the existing producers there—including Clorox.[53] But, if this is true, what is the point of forbidding the acquisition? Procter, given its capability and disposition, will enter the market internally and destroy its feeble competitors. The end result of the acquisition and of forbidding the acquisition will be the same, a monopoly position for Procter & Gamble.[54] Evidently the ideal situation from the Court's point of view would have been for Procter never in fact to enter the bleach market but always to be thought by Clorox to be about to enter. However, the Court's analysis of Procter's great strengths (an incorrect analysis, as we shall see) and aggressive purposes implies that this is an unlikely outcome.

To isolate the potential-competition issue in the case, let us for the moment disregard the first ground of decision and assume that

52. 386 U.S. 568 (1967).

53. The Court believed, though incorrectly (see John L. Peterman, "The Clorox Case and the Television Rate Structures," 11 *J. Law & Econ.* 321, 389, 396 [1968]) that Procter could buy advertising time on television at lower cost than Clorox; and Procter had, of course, a much deeper pocket than Clorox. See 386 U.S. at 575, 579, n. 3.

54. There is a paradox here unremarked by the Court. If Procter is simply more efficient than any firm in the liquid-bleach market, then, as stated in the text, it will obtain a monopoly of that market regardless of whether the acquisition of Clorox is blocked. If, however, Procter is not more efficient but simply more powerful, which seems to have been the Court's view, then its obtaining a monopoly of the liquid-bleach market by the exercise of that power would violate section 2 of the Sherman Act. And if *that* is the case, it is unclear why the Court should have regarded Procter as a formidable potential competitor; Procter would be "formidable" only because of power that it could not employ without being punished for violating the Sherman Act.

Procter had no decisive cost or other competitive advantage over Clorox or other bleach producers. The question is then whether Procter's situation prior to the merger as a potential competitor of Clorox is likely to have affected Clorox's pricing decisions. The answer is no. If Clorox charged a monopoly price, entry into the liquid-bleach market would become attractive to a great many firms, for monopoly profits are not that widely available in the economy, and no patents, raw-material scarcities, heavy capital requirements, or large economies of scale complicate entry into the bleach market. Even expertise in the marketing of consumer goods is not required for entry into this market since liquid bleach can be sold through large retail chains that affix their own brand names to the bleach and assume complete responsibility for its promotion and marketing.[55] Indeed, it is difficult to imagine an easier market to enter than household liquid bleach (unless it is shoe retailing or retail groceries). Thus, this seems to have been a case in which the number of potential competitors was legion and the elimination of a single one could have had no perceptive effect on the behavior of the firms in the market.

The Court emphasized Proctor & Gamble's tremendous reputation as a producer of consumer goods similar to liquid bleach, partly to support the first ground of the decision but also to support the second ground by distinguishing Procter from the faceless horde of potential competitors. The point, however, proves too much. To identify Procter as a uniquely effective producer of the class of products that includes liquid bleach is to establish the futility of preventing it from acquiring Clorox—a firm in no position to compete on equal terms with the Procter & Gamble of the Court's imagination.

55. The Court seems to have believed that because a retailer's house-brand bleach sold at a lower price than Clorox, such brands did not provide effective competition for Clorox. But, so far as appears, the difference in price between national-brand and house-brand bleach is fully explained by the higher cost of advertising and promotion incurred by the manufacturer when he sells under his own brand name, and if so the price difference need not connote monopoly power. The price of Clorox bleach may well be held to the competitive level (where price equals marginal cost) by the lower-priced house-brand bleaches, since any attempt by Clorox to enlarge the price difference by increasing its price might cause such massive substitution in favor of the house brands as to make the higher price unprofitable. (For some evidence in support of this proposition see John L. Peterman, supra note 53, at 324.)

Actually, it seems unlikely that Procter had any special advantages as a potential producer of liquid bleach. The very high price that it paid for Clorox is suggestive.[56] If Procter really had been a serious prospect to enter the bleach market on its own, and if once in the market it would have been a more effective competitor than Clorox, as the Court apparently believed, it could have bought Clorox quite cheaply; the latter's prospects as an independent firm would have been dim. Indeed, it could be argued that Procter was less likely than one or more other firms to have entered the bleach market by internal growth rather than merger. It is unlikely that the highest bidder for Clorox would be a firm that thought itself well able to enter the market internally and thereby reduce Clorox's profitability, should Clorox refuse to sell out to it on attractive terms. The highest bidder for Clorox would probably be a firm that had no other way of entering the bleach market and thus could not chisel down the purchase price by credibly threatening to enter the market internally should negotiations fail. Since Clorox was unable to get a better offer from anyone other than Procter, presumably Procter was such a firm. If so, it was not in the forefront of potential competitors.

Alternatively, Procter & Gamble may have been the high bidder because there were managerial or other complementarities between Procter and Clorox that made Clorox's assets more productive in Procter's hands than in anyone else's. But if so, the merger would increase efficiency and should presumably be allowed. There seems to be no theory under which Procter's purchase of Clorox identifies Procter as a most likely potential entrant whose elimination by merger should be actionable under section 7.

In *Penn-Olin* the Court had remanded for an assessment of the significance, as a potential competitor, of the firm that would not have entered the relevant market on its own had the joint venture been blocked. The question whether a firm that will definitely not enter the relevant market on its own can be a potential competitor was considered by the Supreme Court in *United States* v. *Falstaff Brewing Corp.*[57] Falstaff had acquired Narragansett, a

---

56. Procter bought Clorox in exchange for stock having a market value of more than $30 million. In the year prior to the merger, Clorox had net income of $2.6 million. The puchase price indicates that Procter thought Clorox's earnings would continue to increase whether or not Proctor entered the market.

57. 410 U.S. 526 (1973).

leading seller of beer in New England, where Falstaff had not previously done business. Relying heavily on testimony of Falstaff officers, the district court found that the company had no intention of entering the New England market except through acquisition, and concluded that therefore Falstaff could not be considered a potential competitor in that market. The Supreme Court reversed. It held that the district court's conclusion did not follow from its premise: even if it were certain that Falstaff would not have entered the market except via the challenge merger, Falstaff might have posed a threat of entry that would have constrained the pricing of the firms in the market.

At first blush this result seems to depend on a difference between what Falstaff knew (and the courts now know) about its intentions and what the brewers selling in the Northeast thought about those intentions—a difference that vanishes once the testimony of Falstaff's officers comes to the attention of the brewers in the Northeast. But I think the Court was correct (although for the wrong reasons),[58] in *Falstaff* though not in *Penn-Olin,* in refusing to give controlling weight to evidence, however convincing, that the acquiring firm had no intention of entering the relevant market on its own. Intentions alter with circumstances. Suppose that the brewers in the Northeast decide that if they colluded on price, entry would occur so rapidly as to make their collusion unprofitable, and as a result they charge the competitive price for beer. A Falstaff may have no interest in building a brewery in the Northeast to sell beer at a price that would yield only the competitive rate of return. But it does not follow that Falstaff is not a significant potential competitor of the brewers in the Northeast. The fact that a somewhat higher price in the Northeast would cause it to change its mind about not entering may be one of the

58. The Court seemed intent on making the logical distinction between Falstaff's *knowledge* of its own intentions and its competitors' *perceptions* of those intentions. There is a distinction, but it is a fragile reed on which to build antitrust doctrine. Would firms considering collusion be long deterred by mistaken perceptions concerning the intentions of some firm outside of the market? And if they did persistently exaggerate the likelihood of one firm's entry into the market, would they not tend to magnify the strength of *all* potential competitors, in which event eliminating a single potential competitor would have little significance for their behavior? (Incidentally, on remand the district court found that Falstaff was not perceived as a likely entrant, and again dismissed the complaint. 383 F. Supp. 1020 [D.R.I. 1974].)

reasons why the higher price is not charged. The difference between *Falstaff* and *Penn-Olin* is that in *Falstaff* the merger did not alter the structure of the relevant market except insofar as it eliminated one potential competitor, whereas in *Penn-Olin* the joint venture made a highly monopolistic market somewhat less so, and the potential competitor eliminated, given its assumed inability or unwillingness to enter the market when the market had been a duopoly, was a firm unlikely to be a significant factor in the thinking of the firms in the market.

The Court did not reach the hard question in *Falstaff*—whether eliminating Falstaff as a potential competitor was likely to make a significant difference in the thinking of the firms in the market—but seems to have alluded to the issue in noting that Falstaff was one of only three brewers among the nation's ten largest that were not selling in New England. But why cut off the class of most likely potential competitors at number ten? Narragansett was not one of the nation's ten largest brewers yet had 20 percent of the New England market. If a monopoly price were to be charged in New England, that market would become highly attractive to any number of brewers not already selling there. There is no reason to think that Falstaff would enter sooner or on a larger scale than others. Indeed, as in *Procter & Gamble,* the fact that Falstaff chose to enter the New England market by purchasing the leading firm in the market, presumably at the best price which that firm could command for its assets, is some evidence that Falstaff would not have been the first brewer to enter the market on its own if the price of beer in New England had risen above the competitive level.

The potential-competition doctrine is unsatisfactory, although the problem is less one of deep confusion as to fundamental policies, as has afflicted the Court in dealing with horizontal mergers, than one of inability to develop objective and workable standards. In dealing with potential competition the Court has based policy squarely on the economic view of section 7. And concern with potential competition is in principle a reasonable corollary of the concern with collusive pricing that underlies the economic theory of section 7. To be sure, the Court has not applied the concept of potential competition very well, but that is almost a detail. The essential problem is the impossibility of developing workable rules of illegality in this area. There is no practical method of ranking, even crudely, the potential competitors in a market for the purpose of identifying a set of most likely or most feared entrants.[59] And even if one could identify such a set through the methods of litigation, one would not know how to evaluate the elimination of one of its members. There is no theory or evidence that tells us that if the number of equally potential competitors in a market falls from ten to nine or four to three or two to one the pricing decisions of the firms in the market will be affected.

The doctrine of potential competition was introduced into antitrust law by the Supreme Court, and the Court can abandon it—and should do so. In theory, as I have suggested, the elimination of a potential competitor could affect the price level in a market by reducing the elasticity of demand as perceived by the firms that are already in the market, assuming that conditions were otherwise favorable to collusion. But there appears to be no way of translating this theoretical insight into an objective standard of illegality. As a first approximation, the elimination of an individual potential competitor can be expected to have no competitive significance at all, since there are presumably a number of other equally potential competitors—firms that could enter the market at a cost no higher than that of the eliminated firm and would do so if the market price were appreciably higher than the competitive level. There may be cases in which this presumption could be rebutted if only we knew how to measure the entry costs of different firms or to determine reliably the perceptions of the firms in the market. We can do neither of these things, so that if the government were required to prove as a matter of fact that the elimination of a given potential competitor altered the structure of competition in the relevant market it would always fail. The alternative to requiring proof on these questions is to adopt presumptions based on theoretical or commonsensical probabilities. The government, of course, prefers this approach, but the only presumption it has been able to suggest is that the fact of acquiring a firm shows that the acquirer was more likely than other firms to have entered (or have been perceived as likely to enter) the market by internal expansion (or, what amounts to the same thing, by a "toehold" acquisition). We have seen that the opposite presump-

---

59. Asking the firms in the market to testify about their perceptions regarding potential competition is a peculiarly futile mode of inquiry. They can hardly be expected to testify that they refrained from colluding because of fear that firm A or B or . . . Z would have entered the market.

tion would be more reasonable; the acquiring firm is *less* likely than at least some other firms to have entered the market by internal expansion. If this presumption were accepted, the chances of the government's prevailing in a potential competition suit would fall very nearly to zero. And so what? After years of trying, neither the government nor any other proponent of the potential-competition doctrine has been able to come up with either a theoretical or an empirical basis for believing that the elimination of a specific potential competitor has ever affected the price level of a market.

The reader may be troubled by the implications of this analysis for the problem of defining the "market" in which to calculate market-share statistics in a conventional horizontal-merger case. As we are about to see, the definition of market is also an exercise in the appraisal of potential competition. We ask whether a firm that at present has no sales of Product X, or in Region Y, should nonetheless be included in that product or geographical market because it is potentially able to sell there. What makes this sort of inquiry manageable, however, is the existence in the market-definition context of simple, if very crude, proxies for the underlying quantitative measures. We ask whether two products are virtually indistinguishable in production or consumption, and if they are we place them in the same product market. We ask whether two firms that sell the identical product but in different regions would have to incur substantial transportation costs in order to ship into each other's regions, and if not we collapse the regions into a single geographical market. These are awfully rough, but serviceable and not entirely arbitrary, methods of identifying a group of potential competitors whose ability to enter a market is so great that they are competitively equivalent to the firms already in the market.[60] No similar proxies are available for determining which if any members of a group of more remote potential competitors have such good prospects for entry that they influence price levels in the market. On the basis of present knowledge it would seem best simply to ignore potential competitors who cannot be regarded as equivalent to the firms already in the market.

60. See United States v. El Paso Natural Gas Co., 376 U.S. 651 (1964), which I read as holding simply that two firms do not have to be selling to the same customer at the same time in order to be in competition for the customer's business, especially where the product in question is bought infrequently.

Given the relative unimportance of transportation costs in the beer industry, it might have been appropriate to treat it as a single national market. In that event, Falstaff and Narragansett would have been actual competitors and their merger a horizontal one to be tested under whatever rule of thumb is used for deciding the legality of such mergers. So viewed, the merger would have seemed competitively insignificant; the combined market share of Falstaff and Narragansett is very small when the relevant market is the entire nation, because there are so many substantial brewers. But we have seen that there is no objective basis for singling out Falstaff among them as especially important in the thinking of the New England brewers. If Falstaff can fairly be deemed a part of the New England market before it bought Narragansett, so should the rest of the nation's brewers.

The Problem of Market Definition

Even if the Supreme Court were to adopt the suggestions in the preceding sections of this chapter, and abolish the potential-competition doctrine and raise substantially the threshold beyond which a horizontal merger is deemed presumptively unlawful because of its effect on concentration, the merger law might still be excessively stringent. The definition of the market in which to measure the market shares of the merging parties and their competitors is critical; given enough flexibility in market definition a surprising number of innocuous mergers can be made to appear dangerously monopolistic.

The importance attached to defining a market in which to appraise the competitive effects of a challenged merger is one more example of the law's failure to have developed a genuinely economic approach to the problem of monopoly. If we knew the elasticity of demand facing a group of sellers, it would be redundant to ask whether the group constituted an economically meaningful market. The effect of other sellers on the ability of the members of the group to collude effectively would be automatically registered, together with all other facts relevant to the potential gains from collusion which our ignorance compels us to exclude from antitrust analysis, in the measured elasticity.[61] It is only because we lack confidence in our ability to measure elasticities, or perhaps because we do not think of adopting so explicitly economic an approach, that we have to define markets instead.

61. See Appendix, infra pp. 246–47.

But the concept of elasticity remains indispensable in giving meaning to the concept of market. The potential gains from collusion will almost certainly be small if a slight increase above the competitive price would result in a proportionately much greater reduction in the quantity demanded of the product, resulting in sharply lower total revenues at the higher price.[62] In these circumstances sellers are unlikely to collude anyway so we needn't worry very much about a merger or series of mergers that reduces their number and thereby lowers the costs of collusion.

If we ask *why* a slight increase in the price of a product might result in a substantial drop in the quantity demanded from the sellers—why, in other words, demand is elastic at the current price—two possibilities come to mind. The first is that the product has good substitutes at that price, so that even a slight increase in price would deflect many consumers to them. The second possibility is that the makers of some other product (which need not be a good substitute in consumption) can readily switch to producing this product and would do so if its price rose any further, because at the new price they could earn a higher return by making this product instead of whatever they are making now. In short, the ability of a group of sellers to collude is limited by the existence of sellers of products that are good substitutes either in consumption or in production, and we have to include these additional sellers to delimit a group of sellers that can be assumed to be facing a relatively inelastic demand. The expanded group is a market in the sense, which is the only one relevant to an economic analysis of competition and monopoly, of a group of sellers who have the power to increase their profits by merging or colluding. A merger that significantly reduced the costs of collusion to such a group would be a cause for concern.

Producers of poor substitutes in consumption or production also constrain monopoly pricing. A sufficiently large price increase will make poor substitutes at the competitive price look good to consumers, will induce producers of other products to make even costly adaptations in their production processes in order to pro-

62. It is possible, but in general unlikely, that the loss of revenue would be offset by the reduction in total costs resulting from the lower output. In the limit, of course, where demand is perfectly elastic, any price increase would result in a reduction of the quantity demanded to zero, and the seller would have no revenues or profits.

duce the monopolized product, and may even induce the creation of entirely new firms to produce it. But in a market so broadly defined as to include poor substitutes, the large number and small market shares of individual sellers will understate the feasibility of collusive or monopolistic pricing, so it seems better to use the narrower definition, one which includes only sellers of *good* substitutes in either consumption or production.

Observe that market definition is a two-step process. The first is to identify a group of purchasers entitled to the protection of the antitrust statute in question (e.g., consumers of corned beef in New York City). The second is to identify the group of sellers who are serving those purchasers, or could do so if those sellers increased their price markedly because they sell a product that is a good substitute in either consumption or production. The output of the product together with its good substitutes constitutes the output of the relevant market; it is the denominator, and the output of each of the producers the numerator, in calculating each producer's market share.

Market definition is thus conceptually straightforward, but it has been badly handled by the courts. In the leading case of *United States* v. *E. I. du Pont de Nemours & Co.* (the cellophane monopolization case), the Supreme Court stated that the "market is composed of products that have reasonable interchangeability for the purposes for which they are produced—price, use and qualities considered."[63] This formulation is deficient in two respects. First, it ignores substitution in production. A folding carton produced for one soap company is not interchangeable with a folding carton produced for another company, due to differences in the advertising copy printed on the carton and to other minor design and production differences stemming from the carton manufacturer's efforts to custom-design his cartons for each user; an air-conditioner designed for a Volkswagen "Beetle" will not fit into a Mercedes (or for that matter another Volkswagen model); a computer terminal designed to plug into an IBM computer won't plug into a Burroughs. Yet in all of these examples the two products are made with the same components, facilities, equipment, workers, etc., and an increase in the price of one product above the

63. 351 U.S. 377, 404 (1956).

competitive level would result in a prompt switch into its production by firms producing the other product.[64]

Second, the cellophane formulation fails to specify the price level at which the products alleged to comprise the relevant market are reasonably interchangeable. As mentioned earlier, at a high enough price even poor substitutes look good to the consumer. This is simply a corollary of the proposition stated in chapter 2 that a monopolist always tries to sell in the elastic portion of his demand curve. In *du Pont* the issue was whether the defendant had monopoly power, and in that setting it was vital to specify whether cellophane and other flexible wrapping materials were reasonably interchangeable at the *current* price of cellophane, which might be a monopoly price, or at the *competitive* price (i.e., cost) of cellophane. Reasonable interchangeability at the current price but not at a competitive price level, far from demonstrating absence of monopoly power, might well be a symptom of that power; this elementary point was completely overlooked by the Court.

In principle what the Court should have done was to compare the quality and cost of the different flexible wrapping materials, with a view to determining whether materials comparable in quality to cellophane could be produced at a cost no higher than the cost of producing cellophane or, if no materials of the same quality existed, whether the quality differences between cellophane and its substitutes were offset by differences in cost.[65] If such comparisons are deemed beyond the capacity of courts to make, about the only alternative is to assume that products whose design, physical composition, and other technical characteristics are substantially different are not good substitutes in consumption. This is a crude generalization, but it makes a good deal more sense than the cellophane approach, under which the higher the monopoly price, and therefore the greater the substitution of other products, the less likely it is that the court will find that the defendant has monopoly power.

This problem does not arise in a merger case, where the issue is not whether the current price exceeds the competitive level but whether the merger might result in a further deterioration of

---

64. As recognized in the important recent decision in Telex Corp. v. International Business Machine Corp., 510 F.2d 894 (10th Cir. 1975).

65. See Donald F. Turner, "Antitrust Policy and the Cellophane Case," 70 *Harv. L. Rev.* 281, 302, 309 (1956).

competitive conditions. If there are good substitutes in consumption or production at the current price, it is a detail whether that price is competitive or monopolistic; the important point is that a merger is unlikely to lead to a further price increase. Thus the criteria of relevant market should be different in monopolization and merger cases, although the Supreme Court has said that they are the same.[66]

The Supreme Court addressed the issue of defining the market in merger cases in *Brown Shoe*, discussed earlier in this chapter, stating that the test of the cellophane case (reasonable interchangeability) was applicable in merger cases,[67] but only for determining the "outer boundaries" of the market:

> within this broad market, well-defined submarkets may exist which, in themselves, constitute product markets for antitrust purposes. The boundaries of such a submarket may be determined by examining such practical indicia as industry or public recognition of the submarket as a separate economic entity, the product's peculiar characteristics and uses, unique production facilities, distinct customers, distinct prices, sensitivity to price changes, and specialized vendors.[68]

The "submarket" approach is unsound. If the "outer boundaries" of the market include only the product's good substitutes in both consumption and production—which seems a fair reading of *Brown Shoe*'s reformulation of the cellophane test—then a submarket would be a group of sellers from which sellers of good substitutes in consumption or production had been excluded, and these exclusions would deprive any market-share statistics of their economic significance. To be sure, some of the criteria listed in the quoted passage are relevant to market definition, such as the product's peculiar characteristics, sensitivity to price changes (presumably changes in the prices of substitute products), and unique production facilities (implying that there are no good substitutes in production), although others do not seem particularly relevant

66. United States v. Grinnell Corp., 384 U.S. 563, 579 (1966).

67. The Court stated, however, that "cross-elasticity of production facilities may also be an important factor in defining a product market within which a vertical merger is to be viewed." 370 U.S. at 325, n. 42. The Court was right to add a production-substitutability test to the test of the cellophane case but wrong to limit it to vertical-merger cases; it is equally applicable in a horizontal case.

68. 370 U.S. at 325 (citation omitted).

or helpful, at least without explanation, which the Court did not offer. But the relevant criteria should already have been considered in defining the "outer boundaries"; they are implicit in the reformulated cellophane test.

I shall not burden the reader with a detailed examination of the many aberrant market-definition cases since *Brown Shoe*. In *United States* v. *Aluminum Co. of America*[69] the Court placed insulated copper and insulated aluminum conductor in separate markets without referring to either footnote 42 in the *Brown Shoe* opinion of two years before[70] or the district court's finding that manufacturers of conductor could run either copper or aluminum through their machines—that they were, in short, excellent substitutes in production. In *United States* v. *Continental Can Co.*[71] the Court placed cans and glass jars within the same market, the "container market," on the theory that a merger between poor substitutes might still lessen competition,[72] but arbitrarily excluded from the market a no-poorer substitute, plastic containers. In *United States* v. *Pabst Brewing Co.* the Court, in a fit of nonsense, said that there is no requirement of proving that regional market shares are meaningful because of transportation costs or other factors that prevent sellers in other regions from competing on equal terms with the sellers in the region in question, since section 7 proscribes mergers which may lessen competition substantially in any section of the country.[73] Similar atrocities may be found in the decisions of the lower federal courts.

I shall focus instead on the effort of the Department of Justice, in its Merger Guidelines promulgated in 1968, to formulate a coherent set of criteria for the definition of the market. The crucial language of the Guidelines is as follows:[74]

> A market is any grouping of sales . . . in which each of the firms whose sales are included enjoys some advantage in competing with those firms whose sales are not included. The

69. 377 U.S. 271 (1964).
70. See note 67 supra.
71. 378 U.S. 441 (1964).
72. A theory analytically indistinguishable from that of potential competition, discussed in the preceding section of this chapter.
73. 384 U.S. 546 (1966).
74. Department of Justice Merger Guidelines, 1 CCH Trade Reg. Rep. ¶ 4510 (1968).

advantage need not be great, for so long as it is significant it
defines an area of effective competition among the included
sellers in which the competition of the excluded sellers is,
ex hypothesi, less effective. . . .

The sales of any product or service which is distinguishable
as a matter of commercial practice from other products or
services will ordinarily constitute a relevant product market,
even though, from the standpoint of most purchasers, other
products may be reasonably, but not perfectly, interchangeable
with it in terms of price, quality and use. . . .

The total sales of a product or service in any commercially
significant section of the country . . . will ordinarily constitute
a geographic market if firms engaged in selling the product
make significant sales of the product to purchasers in the
section. . . . The market need not be enlarged beyond any
section meeting the foregoing test unless it clearly appears that
there is no economic barrier (*e.g.*, significant transportation
costs, lack of distribution facilities, customer inconvenience, or
established customer preference for existing products) that
hinders the sale from outside the section to purchasers within
the section. . . .

This is a responsible effort to devise standards for market definition, but not a particularly successful one. To begin with, the
proposition that any seller who is at a "significant" although not
"great" disadvantage in competing with the merging firms should
be excluded from the market is a dubious one. Suppose the difference in costs between the included and excluded sellers (holding
quality constant) is only a few percentage points—"significant,"
since it is large enough to prevent the excluded sellers from getting any business away from the included sellers so long as the
latter sell at a competitive price, i.e., a price equal to their cost.
Then, even if all of the included sellers merged together, the
resulting price increase could be no greater than the cost spread
between the included and excluded sellers; in the more common
case of a merger between two of the firms, the price effect would
be even smaller. The antitrust enforcers have more serious things
to worry about than trivial departures from competitive pricing.

On much the same ground I find untenable the notion, again
suggestive of a misplaced concern with trivial departures from
competitive pricing, that only producers of *perfect* substitutes must
be included in the market. A better criterion would be whether
the substitutes in question are "good" substitutes. The application

of either criterion is of course difficult in practice, and I am sympathetic to the desire of the Guidelines' authors for a simple proxy such as whether the product is distinguishable as a matter of commercial practice. But this particular proxy seems an especially, and unnecessarily, poor one, since it does not indicate the respects in which or the purpose for which the product is distinguished by the trade, while suggesting that very small distinctions place products in different markets. As suggested earlier, a better formulation is one that treats products as different if they are substantially different in design, physical composition, and other technical characteristics.

The most glaring omission from the Guidelines' product-market standard is any reference to substitutes in production. Evidently, even perfect substitutes in production need not be included in the relevant market. The omission is particularly surprising because the Guidelines discuss the geographical dimension of market definition in some detail, and that dimension is implicitly a matter of substitution in supply. Cement sold in California is obviously not interchangeable from the consumer's standpoint with cement sold in Nevada. But the California cement producer may be able to shift some of his output to Nevada if the Nevada cement producer tries to charge a higher than competitive price, and if so the California producer is included in the Nevada market.

The provisions in the Guidelines with respect to the geographical dimension of the market have their own problems. The basic criterion of a separate geographical market under the Guidelines is whether there are any transportation costs or other barriers to sales in a particular area of the country by firms not currently selling there. This criterion is unsound. The existence of economic barriers confronting sellers not active in a particular local area does not make that area a market. To illustrate, if widgets sell for 25 cents in Kansas City and 20 cents in Pittsburgh, and the cost of transporting widgets from Pittsburgh to Kansas City is five cents, the Pittsburgh sellers may make no sales in Kansas City. But a slight price rise in the Kansas City market would draw the Pittsburgh sellers in, and they are therefore a part of the Kansas City market so far as predicting the possible price consequences of a merger is concerned. The Guidelines create the unfortunate impression (perhaps unintended) that it is proper to exclude from the relevant market sellers who are barred by transportation or other costs from selling there *at the existing price* but who would not be barred if that price were to rise, even slightly, as a result of price fixing.

The Guidelines' geographical-market criteria could be improved by two additions designed to impart greater precision to the criteria. The first would be an explicit statement that *all* sales of plants that have (or at some time during the recent past had) *some* (nontrivial) sales in the relevant market should be included in the market. Such a plant should be able quite easily to shift additional output to the area if a differential price rise makes such a shift attractive. Since this assumption will not always be correct, the rule should allow for an exception. For example, where sales from distant plants had been made only in periods of shortage when prices in the local area were very high, the rule would not apply.

The second desirable addition to the Guidelines' geographical-market criteria would be a provision that other firms that do not now sell, and have not recently sold, any part of their output in the relevant market should be excluded from it if (1) the price (or prices) they charge in their own market (or markets), plus the common-carrier charges for shipping the product from their markets to the one in question, appreciably exceed (say, by 5 or more percent, depending on the absolute size of the market in question) the market price in the latter market; or (2) they are forbidden by law to sell in that market. This is an easily applied test for excluding from the relevant market firms that would be barred by transportation costs or legal restrictions even if the market price rose appreciably. Again, an exception is necessary. It may sometimes be possible for outside sellers to overcome apparently formidable transport problems quite inexpensively by establishing a local production or distribution point.

This chapter has advocated a substantial retrenchment in antimerger policy. The concentration thresholds beyond which the danger of undetectable collusion is regarded as substantial would be raised considerably, and horizontal mergers that do not carry a market across these thresholds left in peace. Moreover, markets would be defined more carefully than heretofore and the result of correct definitions would in most cases be to reduce the measured concentration of the market. Mergers that merely eliminate potential competition should be considered lawful per se. In a later chapter I shall advocate an even more drastic retrenchment of policy toward vertical mergers. Yet all of the reforms that I urge in the merger area flow directly from an economic analysis of the proper scope of an antimerger law, can be implemented without any amendment of the antitrust statutes, and should be adopted in the interest of rational antitrust policy.

7   Collusion: Two Problems of Characterization

A recurrent problem in the administration of the antitrust laws has been to decide when a practice amounts to price fixing, or is sufficiently like it to be forbidden for the same reasons that we forbid price fixing. Because price fixing is a per se offense, meaning that the only issue to be decided is whether the defendant in fact engaged in the practice, the government and other antitrust plaintiffs are constantly pressing the courts to place practices in the per se category on the ground that they are the equivalent of price fixing. This pressure has resulted in some serious deformities in antitrust policy. The two most important of these[1]—and the subject matter of this chapter—are the rules governing (1) the exchange of price and other information among competing firms and (2) the imposition of restrictions on competition in the distribution of a manufacturer's goods. In seeking an explanation for the poor showing of the courts in these areas, we shall be led back once again to the fundamental, and fundamentally unsound, tendency in the design and enforcement of the price-fixing rule to ignore economics.

Exchanges of Information among Competitors

Confronting a price-fixing rule that attaches conclusive significance to proof of an "actual" agreement to fix prices, competitors have an incentive to engage in all of the preliminary steps required to coordinate their pricing but to stop just short of "agreeing" on what price to charge. The most important step is the exchange of information as to what prices each is charging, or charged in the recent past, or intends to charge in the future. Such exchanges foster collusive pricing both by enabling convergence on a single (supracompetitive) price and by facilitating detection of, and

1. Outside of the patent field, which I do not discuss in this book. See Ward S. Bowman, Jr., *Patent and Antitrust Law: A Legal and Economic Appraisal* (1973).

thereby discouraging, sales below that price. But it does not follow that exchanges of price and related information should be forbidden in order to reduce the amount of collusive pricing. Unlike collusive pricing itself, such exchanges may yield significant social benefits as well as costs.

In general, the more information sellers have about the prices and output of their competitors the more efficiently the market will operate. A firm cannot decide how much to produce, or indeed whether to produce at all, without knowing what the market price is. Nor can it make an intelligent decision about whether to expand productive capacity without knowing something about the plans of competitors to expand their capacity. Yet such information could also be useful in enabling a cartel to restrict its output by limiting the expansion of productive capacity. Information is thus a two-edged sword: it is necessary if the competitive process is to work properly, but it can also facilitate collusion. And one cannot make the dilemma go away by observing that a seller can obtain all of the information that he wants about the prices of his competitors by asking his customers, or theirs, about those prices. Since information is costly to acquire, customers do not always have good information about the competitive alternatives facing them, and they may not honestly disclose the information that they do have; a customer might try to get a better price from one seller by misrepresenting another seller's offer.

Nor is is enough to answer that a seller need not know *anything* about his competitors' prices because in a competitive market price is equal to cost and each seller knows what his own costs are. This oversimplifies the competitive process in two important respects. First, it ignores the possibility that the sellers in the market have different costs. In that event, the correct (market-clearing) price will be equal to the cost of the marginal seller and above the costs of the other sellers; if any of the intramarginal sellers reduce their price to their costs, the market would fail to clear and a shortage of the product would develop. Second, equality of price and (long-run marginal) cost is efficient only when the market is in an equilibrium, or stable, condition. It is not the efficient solution when the market is in disequilibrium—which is very often, since any change in cost or in demand will alter a market's equilibrium price and output. If, for example, there is an unexpected increase in the demand for a product, then until supply catches up with the new demand price will be bid up above the cost of production as a method of rationing the existing supply so that the consumers who value it the most can be sure to obtain it. Constraining price to cost in these circumstances would result in an inefficient allocation of resources.[2]

Let us now examine how the courts have fared in attempting to distinguish between the legitimate role of information exchanges among competitors and their role in facilitating collusion. Again I shall limit my attention to the leading Supreme Court decisions. In the *Hardwood case*,[3] a trade association of hardwood manufacturers had adopted an "open-competition plan," to which 365 of its members, accounting in the aggregate for about a third of the total hardwood production in the United States, subscribed. As described by the association, the purpose of the plan was to provide a "central clearing house for information on prices, trade statistics and practices," and it was fulfilled by requiring each member to furnish the trade association with daily reports showing in great detail all the sales made by the member, with price, purchaser's name, and other information, plus monthly reports containing the member's current price lists, monthly production, and sold and unsold inventory. All of the information was broken down by lumber grade, size, quality, etc., according to uniform classifications established by the association. The plan also involved submission to the association of members' estimates of their future production plans and general market conditions. The voluminous information collected by the administrator of the plan was distributed in a series of detailed reports to the members of the association, who also met to discuss competitive problems in the industry, such as "overproduction." There was no agreement to charge the same prices or to limit production, but members were exhorted to "follow their most intelligent competitors."

The Supreme Court held that the "open competition plan" violated section 1 of the Sherman Act. While taking too seriously defendant's argument that "reporting to one another past transactions cannot fix prices for the future,"[4] the Court at the same time attached sinister significance to precisely the items of infor-

2. Similarly, an unexpected fall in demand might require the firms to sell below their full costs in order to avoid a glut.
3. As American Column & Lumber Co. v. United States, 257 U.S. 377 (1921), is known.
4. Id. at 398.

mation involved in the plan that seem both relatively innocuous from an antitrust standpoint and clearly relevant to intelligent forward planning by the association's members. Each member was asked (1) to estimate his production for the next two months, (2) to indicate whether he expected to shut down his plant during that period, and (3) to state his view of market conditions and the general outlook for business. According to the Court, these three questions "plainly invited an estimate and discussion of future market conditions by each member, and a coordination of them by an expert analyst could readily evolve an attractive basis for cooperative, even if unexpressed, 'harmony' with respect to future prices."[5] But this seems to be a pretty far-fetched conjecture.

Next the Court stated:

> It is plain that the only element lacking in this scheme to make it a familiar type of the competition suppressing organization is a definite agreement as to production and prices. But this is supplied: By the disposition of men "to follow their most intelligent competitors," especially when powerful; by the inherent disposition to make all the money possible, joined with the steady cultivation of the value of "harmony" of action; and by the system of reports, which makes the discovery of price reductions inevitable and immediate. The sanctions of the plan obviously are financial interest, intimate personal contact, and business honor, all operating under the restraint of exposure of what be deemed bad faith and of trade punishment by powerful rivals.[6]

The Court's point about the effect of the reports on the detection of price reductions is well taken, but the rest of the passage is a muddle. To say that the only element lacking in the plan is the only thing the law forbids—an agreement to fix prices—is an odd point to make in *support* of liability. And the disposition of people to follow their most intelligent competitors cannot bridge the gap between information and collusion unless it is believed that *any* market in which the sellers are well informed about transaction prices is bound to be cartelized. The "inherent disposition to make all the money possible" is, of course, the "invisible hand" of competition as well as of monopoly. And the existence of sanctions

5. Ibid.
6. Id. at 399.

for violating the plan is irrelevant to the question whether the plan amounts to price fixing: if it does not, why object to its being enforced by appropriate sanctions? The Court also stated that the members of the association "began actively to cöoperate through the meetings, to suppress competition by restricting production,"[7] but the only evidence cited was some general exhortations to avoid overproduction, such as " *'No man is safe in increasing production.' "*[8]

A few months after the "open-competition plan" was launched, the plan administrator wrote to members asking for their experience with the plan and "any incidents showing benefits derived from it."[9] The Court described the replies he received as "significant confessions,"[10] of which the following is representative: " 'From the first report we received under this plan we were enabled to increase our price $6 per thousand on a special item of oak. We had just taken a small order at what we thought a satisfactory price, but discovered immediately that others were getting more money. Since then we have booked orders for a number of special items at the increase of $6 per thousand.' "[11] It did not occur to the Court that the old price might have been below the market-clearing level, or that the large price increases during the year in which the plan was in effect, which the Court attributed largely to the plan (while conceding that it "was a year of high and increasing prices generally and that wet weather may have restricted production to some extent),"[12] might have brought the industry nearer to the level of prices that would have prevailed under conditions of perfect information and perfect competition.

The Court skirted the key issue whether there was collusive pricing by pronouncing the behavior of the members of the plan "abnormal," since "genuine competitors do not make daily, weekly, and monthly reports of the minute details of their business to their rivals. . . ."[13] But perhaps the reason for this "abnormal" conduct was that the hardwood manufacturers found themselves in an abnormal situation or that sellers in other industries obtain the same

7. Id. at 402.
8. Ibid (emphasis in original).
9. Id. at 408.
10. Ibid.
11. Ibid.
12. Id. at 409.
13. Id. at 410.

information in other ways. The latter point gave the Court brief pause:

> In the presence of this record it is futile to argue that the purpose of the Plan was simply to furnish those engaged in this industry, with widely scattered units, the equivalent of such information as is contained in the newspaper and government publications with respect to the market for commodities sold on boards of trade or stock exchanges. One distinguishing and sufficient difference is that the published reports go to both seller and buyer, but these reports go to the seller only; and another is that there is no skilled interpreter of the published reports, such as we have in this case, to insistently recommend harmony of action likely to prove profitable in proportion as it is unitedly pursued.[14]

The exchange of information about selling prices has indeed been carried furthest in the organized markets for commodities and securities—and these are the markets assumed to approximate most nearly the economist's model of perfect competition rather than to foster that undesirable "harmony" which results from following one's "most intelligent competitors." The hardwood trade association was trying to do on a modest scale what the organized markets do more thoroughly. The Court's attempted distinctions are unpersuasive. Even if information exchanged through the association was withheld from buyers (Justice Brandeis in his dissenting opinion stated that it was freely available to buyers), the Court offered no reason, and none appears, why this fact alone converted an effort to increase market information into a cartel. As for the "skilled interpreter," i.e., the plan's administrator, again no reason was offered or appears why his general exhortations to avoid overproduction should be expected to result in cartel pricing.

The first thing to note about the *Hardwood* case—now approaching it from an economic standpoint—is that there was no evidence of an explicit price-fixing agreement. If there was collusive pricing, it was tacit. So the first question the Court should have asked was whether the facts of the case disclosed conditions so propitious to collusion as to enable effective price fixing without a detectable conspiracy. The answer is no. The plan had 365

14. Id. at 411.

members, who controlled only a third of the nation's hardwood production. It does not appear that there were significant local or regional markets in which the number of effective competitors might have been much smaller,[15] or that the number 365 conceals a few large sellers who dominated the industry. Moreover, the buying side of the industry probably included a number of large and knowledgeable buyers. The circumstances were in fact extraordinarily unpropitious for collusion, and it strains credulity to imagine the hardwood manufacturers colluding effectively without explicit price fixing. That is not to deny that the members of the industry and the administrator of the open-competition plan would have liked the market price to rise above the competitive level. But it seems unlikely that the plan could have achieved that goal, and since the members of the association were presumably rational we should look for an alternative explanation for its adoption.

Such an explanation is suggested in Justice Brandeis's dissenting opinion. He notes that the "hardwood lumber mills are widely scattered," with most being "located near the sources of supply; isolated, remote from the larger cities and from the principal markets."[16] Evidently no one, public or private, collected or published data concerning production, inventories, and market prices, as was and is done for other goods by government agencies, organized markets, trade journals, etc. In these circumstances, there was substantial value, social as well as private, in the kind of information-collection and dissemination program organized by the association, though not in every detail of the plan (such as purchasers' names). The same circumstance that makes an inference of collusion implausible—the low level of concentration in the industry—underscores the need for some system of centralized information exchange. With such a large number of firms it must have been difficult for each one to discover the prices, outputs, and production plans of the others. Overproduction would be a matter of legitimate concern in such an industry, rather than simply a code word for competitive output, for a seller might very

15. Cf. id. at 415 (Mr. Justice Brandeis, dissenting). It should be noted that the leading economic study of the lumber industry found the industry to be highly competitive on the selling side. Walter J. Mead, *Competition and Oligopsony in the Douglas Fir Lumber Industry* (1966).

16. 257 U.S. at 415.

well expand his productive capacity not realizing that the added capacity would be redundant in light of additions to capacity being made by other sellers.

The next major case in which the Court attempted to distinguish between legitimate information exchanges among competitors and their role in facilitating collusion was *Maple Flooring Mfrs.' Ass'n* v. *United States*.[17] This time, the defendant association had only 22 members rather than 365, and their aggregate market share was 70 percent rather than 33 percent. A predecessor association had formed an explicit price-fixing agreement but had abandoned it after failing to obtain the approval of the Federal Trade Commission. The practices of its successor challenged by the government were (1) the collection and distribution of price information similar to that in *Hardwood*, but without the names of the purchasers and with wide publicity accorded to the published information; (2) the compilation and distribution of a booklet showing freight rates between Cadillac, Michigan (the basing point used in fixing prices under the earlier, discontinued association agreement); (3) the computation and distribution to the members of the association of the average cost of the various types of maple flooring; and (4) meetings of the association at which the statistics were discussed.

The defendant association had been organized the year following the Supreme Court's *Hardwood* decision and was a fairly transparent attempt to do what the hardwood association had done, and more, while avoiding the details that had seemed to disturb the Court the most, such as the fact that the information collected by the hardwood association had not been widely publicized among buyers and the exhortations to avoid overproduction, cutthroat competition, etc. This trimming was enough to convince a Court now dominated by the justices who had dissented in *Hardwood* to uphold the association's activities on the basis of general, and generally valid, observations about the importance of information to competition that were not, however, carefully related to the activities in issue. An inference of collusion fairly leaps out of the facts recited in the Court's opinion. Although the industry was not highly concentrated, it was a good deal more concentrated than the hardwood industry, and its history suggested that the current association was simply an underground version of the explicit cartel that its predecessor association had auda-

17. 268 U.S. 563 (1925).

ciously asked the Federal Trade Commission to approve. Two of the major activities of the association—the freight book and the average-cost compilation—are difficult to explain on any ground other than facilitation of collusion. The only purpose of disseminating in such detail freight rates from Cadillac, and Cadillac only, could have been to encourage its use as a basing point; and as explained in chapter 4, basing-point pricing is a method of collusion. And the only apparent purpose of the average-cost compilation was to provide a basis for continuing the price agreement of the predecessor association (which had pegged price at cost plus 10-percent profit plus freight from Cadillac). An industry's average cost is a pretty useless statistic except for purposes of establishing a basis for converging to a collusive price, since it provides little information with respect to the conditions of supply (and none with respect to demand). The important question to the individual seller is the difference between the market price and *his* costs, together with future levels of demand and supply. Knowing the average industry cost does not help him to answer this question.

The *Hardwood* and *Maple Flooring* decisions illustrate the pitfalls of an approach to collusion that treats the attempt to fix price rather than the completed act as the violation. The government won *Hardwood* because of the plan manager's self-promoting efforts to convince the members of the association that he had enabled them to get higher prices, and it lost *Maple Flooring* because the association in that case did not admit that it was trying to affect the price level. Yet the likelihood of an actual effect on the long-run market-price level was greater in *Maple Flooring*, and the likelihood that the exchange of information increased efficiency was greater in *Hardwood*.

Maple Flooring established a broad area within which the exchange of information among competitors acting through a trade association was permitted regardless of the structure of the market in which the exchange took place or the nature of the information exchanged; more than forty years later, in *United States* v. *Container Corp. of America*,[18] the Supreme Court analyzed an exchange of information in a manner at least superficially promising in terms of reorienting the law in an economic direction. The case involved the sale of corrugated shipping containers in the southeastern United States. Containers are produced to the special

18. 393 U.S. 333 (1969).

order of the customer, who usually solicits bids from several suppliers. Before submitting a bid a supplier would sometimes ask another supplier what he had bid. The Court found an "agreement" to exchange price information in this manner (though not an agreement to fix prices) and held that the agreement violated section 1 of the Sherman Act.

The Court stated that the exchange of price information "seemed to have the effect of keeping prices within a fairly narrow ambit,"[19] although the only evidence cited in support of this finding was that during the relevant period capacity exceeded demand and prices fell, yet a number of new manufacturers entered the southeastern market. The Court did not explain why these facts indicated that prices had been "stabilized."

The heart of the opinion is the following passage:

> Interference with the setting of price by free market forces is unlawful *per se*. Price information exchanged in some markets may have no effect on a truly competitive price. But the corrugated container industry is dominated by relatively few sellers. The product is fungible and the competition is price. The demand is inelastic, as buyers place orders only for immediate, short-run needs. The exchange of price data tends toward price uniformity. For a lower price does not mean a larger share of the available business but a sharing of the existing business at a lower return. . . . The inferences are irresistible that the exchange of price information has had an anti-competitive effect in the industry, chilling the vigor of price competition.[20]

This passage is seared with ambiguity. If it is the law that "interference with the setting of price by free market forces" is a per se violation, then it would seem that exchanges of price information are unlawful regardless of purpose, character, or consequences, since the exchange "interferes" with the market-price determination that would exist in the absence of the exchange. But if that is the Court's point, the rest of the discussion, with its emphasis on concentration, elasticity of demand, and other market conditions, is purely decorative. An alternative reading of the "interference" sentence is possible and is clearly preferable in terms both of policy and of explaining the other language in the opinion.

19. Id. at 336.
20. Id. at 337.

It is that the idea of a "free market" does not exclude all information sharing among competitors; such sharing is forbidden only where its character and circumstances are such as to facilitate collusion rather than improve the workings of the competitive process.

This interpretation allows us to assign some meaning to the Court's discussion of the conditions in the southeastern market. As we have seen, the more highly concentrated a market is, the likelier it is that an exchange of information will foster collusion rather than simply help to equilibrate demand and supply; an inelastic demand at the competitive price indicates that a collusive price would be a much more profitable price to set; the more important the role of price is in the competition among sellers, the less likely it is that the gains from price fixing will be dissipated in increased expenditures on nonprice competition; the more fungible or uniform the product, the lower will be the costs of collusion; and a combination of excess capacity with frequent new entry is a symptom of collusive pricing. Thus the Court seems to have been looking at the correct factors from an economic standpoint. To be sure, one can criticize—indeed, quite harshly—the details of the Court's discussion. The only evidence of concentration remarked by the Court is that the eighteen defendants accounted for 90 percent of the corrugated containers shipped from plants in the Southeast. If these firms were of roughly equal size (their relative size is not indicated), it would imply that the largest firm in the market had only 5 percent of the market and the four largest 20 percent, by no means a high level of concentration. Moreover, the opinion makes no effort to establish that plants located in the Southeast constitute in fact a relevant market. And the very low cost of new entry ($50,000–$75,000), inexplicably emphasized by the Court, would greatly reduce the prospects for collusive pricing. Also, the discussion of elasticity is obscure, in part because of a failure to distinguish between elasticity at the competitive price and at the current, "stabilized" price. Nor is it clear that the Court understood the significance of excess capacity combined with frequent new entry. Finally, corrugated containers are not really fungible —they are produced to the customer's specifications. But one must be grateful for small things. The general thrust of the Court's analysis is broadly consistent with an economic approach to the question of the permissible scope of information exchanges in a way that *Hardwood* and *Maple Flooring* are not. The Court appears to have recognized that the propriety of the exchange depends on whether or not the market in which it occurs exhibits the predisposing characteristics to collusion.

The economic approach to the question of the permissible scope of information exchanges can be summarized in the following propositions:

1. An agreement to exchange information is harmful to competition only when it is ancillary to an express or tacit price-fixing scheme. In the absence of collusive pricing, practices that increase the amount of information sellers have about the conditions of demand and supply may be presumed to increase the efficiency of the market.

2. If there is collusive pricing, any ancillary information exchange should also be punished, since the exchange of information may be an effective method of deterring sales below the agreed-upon price by facilitating their detection.

3. The difficult case is where explicit collusion is not provable. There are two possible approaches. If tacit collusion can be proved by other evidence, of the kinds discussed in chapter 4, the analysis of the information exchange is the same as in point 2 above; this is one approach. The other is to treat the information exchange as itself evidence of tacit collusion, and is appropriate where the structure of the market (1) strongly predisposes it to collusion while at the same time (2) affording no legitimate basis for an exchange of information. Both conditions would presumably be satisfied in a highly concentrated market, where it could not be argued persuasively that an exchange of information was necessary to enable demand and supply to be equilibrated.

4. The nature of the information exchanged will sometimes provide a clue to the proper legal treatment of the exchange. The freight-rate and average-cost information distributed by the maple-flooring association was virtually useless from the standpoint of fostering competitive pricing but quite useful in facilitating cartel pricing.

5. However, the *form* of the exchange—whether through a trade association, through private exchange as in *Container*, or through public announcements of price changes—should not be determinative of its legality. The form of the exchange depends on factors irrelevant to its effects on competition. Price lists are rare in the corrugated-container industry because containers are pro-

duced to each customer's specifications. Therefore, an exchange of information virtually had to take the form of exchanging price quotations in person or over the phone. This did not make the exchange more (or less) sinister than if it had occurred by publication of prices in a trade journal. Conversely, the fact that in a particular market it may be feasible to communicate price information by issuing price lists which are published or otherwise circulated widely should not immunize the exchange of price information from legal sanction if the conditions of the market suggest that the exchange promotes collusive rather than competitive pricing.

The foregoing propositions have not been adopted by any court as the law of section 1 applicable to the exchange of information by competitors. But they have at least some support in the *Container* opinion, and as in the case of my proposal to bring tacit collusion within the reach of section 1 no judicial precedent stands in their way. Indeed, it should be plain that the approach to information exchanges proposed here is but a specific application of the general approach to collusion proposed in chapter 4, though it could be implemented without having to adopt the general approach.

Restrictions on Competition in Distribution

I turn now to the line of cases in which the Supreme Court has wrestled with the question as to when a restriction on competition imposed by a manufacturer in the distribution of his goods should be treated as equivalent to a cartel agreement among the distributors. A preliminary question is why in the absence of an antitrust prohibition it is common for manufacturers to restrict competition among the dealers (or other distributors) of their products. At first blush such behavior seems irrational. The difference between the price at which the manufacturer sells to the dealer and the dealer's price to the consumer is the manufacturer's cost of distribution,[21] and any seller (even a monopolist) wants to minimize that cost. Put differently, since a higher retail price reduces the demand for the manufacturer's good and hence his sales revenues, one might expect the manufacturer always to encourage rather than restrict competition among his

---

21. For the sake of simplicity, I assume a simple two-tiered distribution system in which the manufacturer sells directly to the retail dealer.

dealers in order to minimize the retail price of his product. Economic analysis suggests two possible reasons why manufacturers nonetheless often restrict competition in the distribution of their goods when the law permits such restrictions. First, the manufacturer may be the cat's paw of cartelizing dealers: the dealers want to fix prices and somehow coerce, or otherwise enlist, the manufacturer (perhaps they pay him) to act as their agent in administering a cartel, which he does either by fixing a uniform retail price for his goods or by assigning nonoverlapping sales territories to the dealers. It is not enough, however, for the dealers to enlist only a single manufacturer in their scheme. They must also enlist all (or at least most) of his competitors. Otherwise the only effect of the cartel may be to induce consumers to substitute other manufacturers' brands of the product in question.

Second, the manufacturer may want to increase the amount of nonprice competition among the dealers in order to stimulate the provision of point-of-sale services.[22] Perhaps the product cannot be marketed effectively unless the dealer maintains a large, well-stocked showroom, deploys a highly trained and motivated sales force, advertises the product extensively, or provides other costly presale services. If the manufacturer fixes a minimum resale price that exceeds the cost of reselling his product without any such services, but nonprice (i.e., service) competition among the dealers is not constrained, the dealers will step up such competition among themselves—i.e., increase the provision of services—in an effort to engross as much as possible of the difference between the retail price (which is fixed) and the (old) cost of distribution. They will continue to increase their outlays on service competition until the marginal cost of distribution has risen to meet the resale price. When that point is reached the dealers will not be receiving any monopoly profits but will instead be furnishing the level of services desired by the manufacturer. Given effective nonprice competition among the dealers, the level at which the manufacturer pegs the retail price above the cost of distribution without services will automatically determine the level of dealer services provided.

This process is simply a special case of the fundamental tendency, discussed in chapter 2, whereby competition to *become* a monopolist transforms expected monopoly profits into costs. The

22. See Lester G. Telser, "Why Should Manufacturers Want Fair Trade?," 3 *J. Law & Econ.* 86 (1960).

expected profits from being able to sell the manufacturer's product at a price above the existing cost of distribution induce the dealers to increase their expenditures on distribution until those profits are competed away; monopoly profit is transformed into service competition. The reader may be wondering, however, why, if the consumer demands such services, the retailers do not provide them without prompting and raise their prices to cover the higher costs of distribution. The reason is that some retailers will prefer to provide no services and instead take a "free ride" on those retailers who do. Let dealer A provide the elaborate showroom, demonstration, and other services that consumers demand and raise his price to cover the costs of the services. Dealer B, rather than provide any services, can suggest to his customers that they first utilize A's services to pick the model they want and then return to B for the purchase. B can offer a lower price than A since he does not incur the expenses that A incurs in providing services. Faced with B's lower-priced competition, A will eventually stop providing services (or provide fewer of them), and the manufacturer's desire for point-of-sale services will be frustrated. Although the free-riding problem could be eliminated by A's charging separately for point-of-sale services, it should be obvious why the manufacturer might not consider an admission fee to a dealer's showroom a satisfactory alternative to a minimum retail price, which eliminates the incentive for free riding by preventing B from undercutting A.

Superficially, it might appear that this dealer-service theory of resale price maintenance presupposes either that the manufacturer enjoys monopoly power or that there is collusion among competing manufacturers to impose resale price maintenance on their dealers. Imagine in the example in the preceding paragraph that another dealer, C, sells a product that is a perfect substitute for the product sold by A and B. C can tell his customers to shop at A and B, taking advantage of the presale services that those dealers provide, and then return to C to buy the identical product (albeit made by a different manufacturer) at the lower price that C is able to offer since he does not bear the expense of providing such services.

However, C's attempt to take a "free ride" on the services provided by the dealers in another manufacturer's product will succeed only if that product has the identical characteristics of the product that he sells. A and B may be Ford dealers, and C a

Chevrolet dealer. Fords and Chevrolets may be good substitutes for one another, yet have sufficiently different design and performance characteristics so that a demonstration ride or other presale service offered by a Ford dealer may not be an adequate substitute for presale services offered by a Chevrolet dealer, in which event the latter may not be able to take a free side on the former after all. A purist might insist that competition implies the complete identity of the competing products' characteristics. If a Ford has a somewhat different configuration of characteristics from a Chevrolet, at least some consumers may prefer one to the other even at a slightly higher relative price, and this means that the demand for each brand will not be perfectly elastic. It is not, however, the negligible "monopoly power" resulting from brand differences that enables a manufacturer to impose resale price maintenance without worrying about free riding by dealers of competing brands; it is the differences themselves that prevent free riding by making presale services for different brands of the same product noninterchangeable. Thus, resale price maintenance is consistent with effective competition at the manufacturer level.

I have thus far assumed that restrictions on dealer competition designed solely to get around a free-rider problem are unobjectionable from the standpoint of antitrust policy. This assumption may be challenged. Professor Comanor, for example, while admitting the existence of the free-riding problem, opposes restrictions in distribution on the ground that they enable the manufacturer to increase consumer preference for his brand, thus giving him monopoly power.[23] It is difficult, however, to understand how giving the consumer presale services that he must want (otherwise he would switch to brands sold, at a lower price, without services) is a form of monopolizing in some invidious sense. Comanor considers one presale service—advertising—to be a source of spurious consumer preferences. This is a popular though unsubstantiated view which in any event ignores the other presale services, besides advertising, that resale price maintenance or equivalent restrictions encourage (display, demonstration, convenient hours, etc.) and that can hardly be criticized as tending to bamboozle consumers. If advertising is misleading or otherwise objectionable there must be better ways of dealing with the problem than by frustrating

23. William S. Comanor, "Vertical Territorial and Customer Restrictions: White Motor and Its Aftermath," 81 *Harv. L. Rev.* 1419, 1425–33 (1968).

manufacturers' efforts to assure a range of presale services, not limited to advertising, to the consumers of their products.

Neither the "dealer-cartel" nor the "dealer-services" theories of restricted distribution have yet been tested empirically. And it is not entirely clear how one would go about doing so;[24] nor can certain other explanations be ruled out.[25] Consequently, the task of the courts in resolving antitrust challenges to restricted-distribution schemes is inevitably a difficult one—but this cannot explain why for several generations now the Supreme Court has been deciding restricted-distribution cases without any theory *at all* as to why manufacturers restrict distribution.

In the earliest case, *Dr. Miles Medical Co.* v. *John D. Park & Sons Co.,*[26] a manufacturer of patent medicines had agreed with its dealers on minimum retail prices. The Supreme Court held the agreement unenforceable on the ground that it was contrary to the public policy declared in the Sherman Act. The relevant portion of the opinion begins with the following statement, which is not

24. It might appear that the dealer-services theory would be supported if one found resale price maintenance imposed on products that are customarily provided together with presale services. The problem, however, as mentioned in chapter 4, is that a pure dealers' cartel might generate such services too, as the members of the cartel stepped up their expenditures on service competition in an effort to engross the lion's share of the monopoly profits generated by the cartel price. The difference between the services induced by dealer cartelization and those induced by the manufacturer's voluntary imposition of resale price maintenance—a difference analytically crucial but hard to identify in an empirical study—is that in the former case the services are provided beyond the point at which their marginal value to the consumer is equal to their marginal cost to the dealer.

A more promising method of empirically studying the competing theories of restricted distribution would be to inquire whether output had increased or decreased in a market following the imposition of resale price maintenance. The dealer-cartel theory implies that it would decrease, as with any other cartel. The dealer-services theory implies that it would increase, because the provision of presale services should increase the demand for the product—otherwise the manufacturer would not have imposed resale price maintenance. Note, however, that after its initial dip output in the dealer-cartel case should also begin to increase, as the dealers step up service competition among themselves in an effort to engross as large a part as possible of the cartel profits.

25. See Robert H. Bork, "The Rule of Reason and the Per Se Concept: Price Fixing and Market Division, II," 75 *Yale L.J.* 373, 453–64 (1966).

26. 220 U.S. 373 (1911).

further explained: "that these agreements restrain trade is obvious."[27] This bare assertion is used by the Court to shift to Dr. Miles the burden of proving that it is "entitled" to restrict price competition among its dealers.[28] Various places (such as the patent law) are searched but no source of such an "entitlement" is found.

In dealing with Dr. Miles's argument that it has been damaged by price cutting, the Court gets to the point:

> The bill asserts the importance of a standard retail price and alleges generally that confusion and damage have resulted from sales at less than the prices fixed. But the advantage of established retail prices primarily concerns the dealers. The enlarged profits which would result from adherence to the established rates would go to them and not to the complainant [Dr. Miles]. It is through the inability of the favored dealers to realize these profits, on account of the described competition, that the complainant works out its alleged injury. If there be an advantage to a manufacturer in the maintenance of fixed retail prices, the question remains whether it is one which he is entitled to secure by agreements restricting the freedom of trade on the part of dealers who own what they sell. As to this, the complainant can fare no better with its plan of identical contracts than could the dealers themselves if they formed a combination and endeavored to establish the same restrictions, and thus to achieve the same result, by agreement with each other. If the immediate advantage they would thus obtain would not be sufficient to sustain such a direct agreement, the asserted ulterior benefit to the compainant cannot be regarded as sufficient to support its system.[29]

The Court here begins by saying that the profits generated by the minimum retail price inure to the dealers rather than to Dr. Miles. This should have made it wonder why Dr. Miles was in court defending the agreements. As we have seen, if the only effect of resale price maintenance is to increase dealers' profits, not only is the manufacturer not benefitting but he is losing since he is paying more for distribution than the competitive price. At this point in the passage the Court seems assailed by misgivings and admits the possibility that there may be some advantage to Dr. Miles from minimum retail prices after all. But the implications of this con-

27. Id. at 400.
28. Ibid.
29. Id. at 407–8.

cession are not pursued. The only issue in the Court's view is whether Dr. Miles is "entitled" to whatever advantage it derives from resale price maintenance, and the Court holds that it is not because it may not impose a restriction that if created by agreement among the dealers would amount to a dealers' cartel. But the Court does not suggest that the case in fact involves a dealers' cartel, with Dr. Miles as its agent.

Because the Court had in fact no view as to why the challenged agreements were made, it naturally failed to grasp the importance of the source of the restraint. It makes all the difference whether minimum retail prices are imposed by the manufacturer in order to evoke point-of-sale services or by the dealers in order to obtain monopoly profits. The same restraint has in the first case nothing to do with cartelization or other anticompetitive conduct, and in the second is a garden-variety violation of the Sherman Act's prohibition against price-fixing agreements between competitors.

Having decided in *Dr. Miles* that resale price maintenance was illegal per se, the Court in *United States* v. *Colgate & Co.*[30] and *United States* v. *General Electric Co.*[31] inexplicably condoned two methods by which sellers could circumvent the rule of *Dr. Miles.* Under *Colgate*, a manufacturer is free (1) to announce a policy of refusing to sell to dealers who fail to charge the manufacturer's suggested retail price, and (2) to terminate nonadhering dealers. The usual criticism of the *Colgate* rule is that the permitted conduct amounts to an agreement between the manufacturer and the adhering retailers to fix retail prices in violation of the principle established in *Dr. Miles.* I accept this characterization of the conduct permitted by *Colgate*, yet is seems to me that *Colgate*, viewed apart from *Dr. Miles*, is not an unreasonable decision, and had the order of the cases been reversed one could have argued forcefully that *Dr. Miles* was erroneously decided because it departed from the *Colgate* rule.

The key passage in *Colgate* is the following:

> In the absence of any purpose to create or maintain a monopoly, the [Sherman] act does not restrict the long recognized right of trader or manufacturer engaged in an entirely private business, freely to exercise his own independent discretion as to parties with whom he will deal. And, of

30. 250 U.S. 300 (1919).
31. 272 U.S. 476 (1926).

course, he may announce in advance the circumstances under which he will refuse to sell.[32]

In other words, since the manufacturer is presumptively the one in the best position to know whether or not it is efficient to distribute his product through price cutters, his decision (whether or not viewed as creating an agreement) should be honored in the absence of evidence of monopolistic purpose (his or, presumably, the dealers'). This presumption could easily have been used to decide *Dr. Miles* the other way. The weakness of the *Colgate* opinion, as of *Dr. Miles* (including Holmes's dissent in *Dr. Miles*, which the *Colgate* opinion resembles), is the lack of any theory of *why* a manufacturer might prefer not to deal with price cutters.

In the *General Electric* case the Court approved resale price maintenance where the dealer was a consignee of the manufacturer and therefore the manufacturer's agent rather than a purchaser. No reason was suggested why a contract of agency should be treated differently from a sales contract. Finding the element of agreement required by section 1 of the Sherman Act was not the problem. There was an explicit contract between the manufacturer and the dealers, which since it fixed the dealers' prices was a contract in restraint of trade under *Dr. Miles*. There was not, as in *Dr. Miles*, a technical "restraint on alienation," since title had not passed to the dealers, but *Dr. Miles* does not seem to require proof of a restraint on alienation.[33] The principle of that case is, rather, that a manufacturer may not impose a restraint that the dealers would be forbidden to impose by agreement among themselves. The principle is clearly violated by the uniform resale price resulting from the consignment agreements in the *General Electric* case.

Distinguishing between sale and agency may sometimes be helpful in avoiding the absurdity of interpreting the Sherman Act to forbid a firm's sales manager to tell his salesmen what prices to charge. But there was no danger of mistaking intrafirm for interfirm transactions in *General Electric*. The retail dealers were not owned or controlled by the manufacturer. They were independent drugstores and hardware stores which carried many items besides GE light bulbs. The fact that they sold General Electric's light

32. 250 U.S. at 307.

33. The Court had mentioned in *Dr. Miles* that the resale price agreement imposed a restraint on alienation, but in the context of replying to Dr. Miles's claim that it had a common-law right to fix the resale price of its products. See 220 U.S. at 404–05.

bulbs on consignment did not make them branches of General Electric.

It is difficult to believe that *Colgate* and *General Electric* would have been decided the way they were if the Court had had a definite opinion as to what is wrong (or right) with resale price maintenance. If the objection was to cartelization by dealers, why suggest two methods by which dealers could continue to cartelize with the assistance of their suppliers? If resale price maintenance was thought sometimes to serve the legitimate interests of manufacturers, why require them to use the *Colgate* privilege or consignment in order to control their dealers' prices, rather than explicit sales contracts?

Although *Colgate* and *General Electric* have never been explicitly overruled, their vitality has been sapped by later decisions. Two in particular stand out. In *United States* v. *Parke, Davis & Co.*,[34] the Court held that a manufacturer may not threaten to cut off wholesalers for selling to retailers who fail to adhere to the manufacturer's suggested retail price. The practical consequence is that the *Colgate* privilege is available only to manufacturers who sell directly to their retail dealers. This result was said to follow from the fact that the *Colgate* privilege is limited to the "mere announcement of . . . [the manufacturer's] policy [of not dealing with price cutters] and the simple refusal to deal."[35] But the Court did not explain why the *Colgate* privilege must be defined so narrowly as to be unavailable to manufacturers who happen to use wholesalers in the distribution of their product though it remains usable by manufacturers who deal directly with retailers. Surely not to give a competitive advantage to manufacturers large enough to do their own wholesaling!

It has been suggested that the implicit theory of *Parke, Davis* is that the combination between Parke, Davis and its wholesalers to cut off price-cutting retailers smacked of boycott, which is a per se violation of the Sherman Act.[36] This is not a satisfactory explanation. Resale price maintenance is also a per se violation of

34. 362 U.S. 29 (1960).
35. Id. at 44.
36. See Donald F. Turner, "The Definition of Agreement Under the Sherman Act: Conscious Parallelism and Refusals to Deal," 75 *Harv. L. Rev.* 655, 686 (1962); Edward H. Levi, "The Parke, Davis-Colgate Doctrine: The Ban on Resale Price Maintenance," 1960 *Sup. Ct. Rev.* 258, 325 (Philip B. Kurland ed.).

the Sherman Act, but it is permitted by *Colgate* when the method there prescribed is used. Therefore, why shouldn't boycotts also be permitted when effectuated by exercise of the method approved in *Colgate*?

In *Simpson* v. *Union Oil Co.*[37] the Court held that a producer of gasoline could not lawfully fix retail prices in consignment agreements with service stations. The Court noted various differences between the terms of the consignment agreement involved in *Simpson* and those in *General Electric*—which provoked a stinging dissent from Justice Stewart, who pointed out that the agreements in the two cases were virtually indistinguishable. But Justice Stewart was allowing himself to be deflected to a side issue —whether the Court was overruling *General Electric* (the Court coyly refused to admit that it was). Given *Dr. Miles*, which the Court was not about to overrule, *General Electric* was untenable and might as well have been overruled.

What is interesting, indeed scandalous (yet unremarked by the dissent), is the reason the Court in *Simpson* offered for holding that resale price maintenance imposed through consignment agreements was unlawful after all. It is that *Parke, Davis* forbids a seller to use *coercion* to achieve his dealers' adherence to a resale price-maintenance scheme, and the consignment agreement in *Simpson* was coercive given the disparity in economic power between producer and dealer. The agreement took away from the service stations—who are "small struggling competitors"—"the only power they have to be wholly independent businessmen."[38] Resale price maintenance is bad, in short, because it unfairly oppresses dealers.

This rationale for the rule against resale price maintenance stands *Dr. Miles* on its head. According to the Court in *Dr. Miles,* resale price maintenance benefits dealers (at least "primarily") and is bad because it has the same effect as a dealers' cartel. According to the Court in *Simpson*, resale price maintenance is bad because it benefits the manufacturer and oppresses the dealer by taking from the latter the power to price competitively. The two grounds for outlawing resale price maintenance cannot be reconciled.

The second ground is plainly untenable. Simpson must have believed that he would enjoy greater profits (or smaller losses) at a price lower than that fixed by Union Oil, but it does not fol-

37. 377 U.S. 13 (1964).
38. Id. at 20–21.

low that placing a floor under retail dealers' prices is a device that manufacturers use with the purpose, or usual effect, of depressing their dealers' earnings. Although a manufacturer *might* set a retail price so high that the resulting reduction in the quantity demanded of his product decreased the retailer's earnings by a greater amount than the higher price increased them, he has no incentive to do such a thing (it would reduce his own profits), and such mistakes must be relatively rare. The possibility of the manufacturer's misconceiving his self-interest is a weak foundation for a per se rule against resale price maintenance.

The submerged conflict between *Dr. Miles* and *Simpson* came to the surface in *Albrecht* v. *Herald Co.*,[39] where a newspaper publisher (Herald) terminated a distributor (Albrecht) for exceeding the retail price set by the publisher. The Herald Company was in effect buying distribution from Albrecht. The price it was paying was the difference between what it charged Albrecht and what Albrecht charged the retail customer.[40] Albrecht raised the price he was charging the Herald Company for distribution by increasing his retail price and thus enlarging the spread between the wholesale and retail prices. The Herald Company reacted by terminating Albrecht and substituting a distributor willing to adhere to the old spread—i.e., willing to charge the Herald Company a lower price for distributing its newspaper. It is difficult to understand what proper antitrust question is raised by such conduct. It amounts to searching out the lowest bidder—just the sort of conduct the antitrust laws are intended to foster.

But I am concerned here with a different matter—the Court's extraordinary treatment of the basis for the rule forbidding resale price maintenance. Justice Harlan, in dissent, pointed out that the imposition of a ceiling on the dealer's price to the consumer could hardly be viewed as equivalent in purpose or effect to a cartel among the dealers, and hence that the rule of *Dr. Miles* was inapposite. To this the Court replied:

> Our Brother HARLAN seems to state that suppliers have no interest in programs of minimum resale price maintenance, and hence that such programs are "essentially" horizontal

---

39. 390 U.S. 145 (1968).

40. To illustrate, if Herald charged Albrecht 10 cents a paper and Albrecht charged his customers 15 cents, Herald would in effect be paying 5 cents for the retail distribution of the paper.

agreements between dealers even when they appear to be imposed unilaterally and individually by a supplier on each of his dealers. Although the empirical basis for determining whether or not manufacturers benefit from minimum resale price programs appears to be inconclusive, it seems beyond dispute that a substantial number of manufacturers formulate and enforce complicated plans to maintain resale prices because they deem them advantageous. As a theoretical matter, it is not difficult to conceive of situations in which manufacturers would rightly regard minimum resale price maintenance to be in their interest. Maintaining minimum resale prices would benefit manufacturers when the total demand for their product would not be increased as much by the lower prices brought about by dealer competition as by some other nonprice, demand-creating activity.[41]

This is a competent statement of the dealer-services theory of resale price maintenance. But it demolishes the intellectual foundations of the *Dr. Miles* rule, forbidding resale price maintenance per se. The quoted passage both acknowledges that a dealer-cartel rationale for outlawing resale price maintenance is inadequate because in many cases the manufacturer in imposing resale price maintenance will be pursuing his own interests rather than the dealers' and implicitly rejects the dealer-exploitation rationale of *Simpson*, for the dealer-services argument does not imply any exploitation of dealers. What, then, is the rationale for the rule against resale price maintenance?

The Court in *Albrecht* does not say, except insofar as the reasons that it gives as to why fixing *maximum* resale prices is illegal per se might possibly suggest an answer. These reasons are that the maximum price (1) may be too low for the dealer to provide services demanded by the consumer, (2) may channel distribution through large dealers who might otherwise have to face significant nonprice competition, and (3) may become the minimum price. The first reason implies that manufacturers misconceive their self-interest and is hardly an adequate basis for a per se prohibition. It also undermines the case for forbidding the setting of *minimum* resale prices, by emphasizing the importance of presale services, which, as the Court recognizes, are encouraged by setting minimum resale prices. The second and third reasons are ingenious rather than substantial, and taken together the three reasons

41. Id. at 151, n. 7 (citations omitted).

do not so clearly outweigh the manufacturer's interest in minimizing his distribution costs as to justify a per se rule against terminating a high-priced dealer. And they provide no basis at all for a per se rule against setting minimum resale prices once the dealer-cartel rationale of *Dr. Miles* is discarded.

In the same general period in which *Simpson* and *Albrecht* were decided, the rationale of *Dr. Miles* was being undermined from another direction. In *White Motor Co. v. United States*[42] the Court was asked to hold illegal per se the practice of a manufacturer in assigning exclusive sales territories to his distributors. It refused to do so, though as Justice Clark pointed out in dissent the case was clearly governed by the statement in *Dr. Miles* that "the complainant can fare no better with its plan of identical contracts than could the dealers themselves if they formed a combination and endeavored to establish the same restrictions, and thus to achieve the same result, by agreement with each other."[43] An agreement to divide markets is a classic method of cartelization. Its advantages compared to price fixing are that the parties do not have to negotiate a common price and do not have to worry about dissipating cartel profits in nonprice competition. If consumers are highly mobile, however, market division may not be an effective method of cartelization; adherence to the agreement will be difficult to police, and a supplementary price-fixing agreement may be necessary to maintain an "equitable" division of the cartel's profits among its members. Price fixing and market division are thus alternative methods for achieving the same thing—monopoly pricing and profits—with the choice governed by the circumstances facing the cartel. There is no basis for choosing between the methods on social grounds. If resale price maintenance is like dealer price fixing, and therefore bad, a manufacturer's assignment of exclusive sales territories is like market division and therefore bad too, if *Dr. Miles* is to be followed.

The Court's holding in *White Motor* was a very narrow one. Territorial restrictions were not endorsed. The Court did not even hold that they were to be tested by the Rule of Reason. It held that the appropriate rule of law, whatever it might be, was not to be formulated until after trial (the district court had granted the government's motion for summary judgment). The Court did, however, suggest that territorial restrictions "may be allowable pro-

42. 372 U.S. 253 (1963).
43. Id. at 282, quoting 220 U.S. at 408.

tections against aggressive competitors or the only practicable means a small company has for breaking into or staying in business."[44] This formulation seems to be a variant of the dealer-services argument. If the manufacturer of a new product wants to induce a dealer to make a large initial investment that will be lost if the product fails to gain consumer acceptance, he must compensate the dealer for the substantial risk involved. One way of doing this is to assure the dealer freedom from competition in the distribution of the product, as by giving him an exclusive territory. Without such protection the dealer might be unwilling to carry the untried product. If it failed to win consumer acceptance he would lose his investment in promoting it; and if it gained consumer acceptance, the manufacturer might begin distributing it through other dealers who, not having either made the initial promotional investment or incurred the same risk as the first dealer, would compete the retail price down to a level that would prevent the first dealer from recouping his investment with a return commensurate with the risk he had borne. The subsequent dealers would be free riders, much as in the standard dealer-services cases discussed earlier.

But if this is a good justification for exclusive territories, it is an equally good justification for resale price maintenance, which as we have seen is simply another method of dealing with the free-rider problem. Indeed, *any* argument that can be made on behalf of exclusive territories can also be made on behalf of resale price maintenance,[45] for just as they are alternative methods of dealer cartelization, so they are alternative methods of buying services in distribution, and the choice turns on considerations irrelevant to any proper concern of the antitrust laws.

In the case of a very expensive item such as a truck (the product in *White Motor*), where consumers will invest significant travel time in making their purchase, a manufacturer can reach the consuming public through relatively few, relatively dispersed dealers, whom he can induce to provide the level of services he wants by assigning them exclusive territories. Competition among potential dealers to obtain an exclusive franchise will lead them to offer successively more extensive presale services until, at the margin, the cost of these services will equal the price increment

44. 372 U.S. at 263.
45. See Robert H. Bork, supra note 25, at 429–64.

that the dealer can command for the manufacturer's product by virtue of being free from the competition of other dealers. But if the product in question is not an expensive one, so that consumers are unwilling to invest substantial travel time in purchasing it, the dealers will have to be more numerous and proximate to one another, and a system of exclusive territories will be unmanageable. In this situation resale price maintenance is the more efficient method of evoking the desired services; and it may be more efficient in general because of its greater flexibility. The manufacturer can choose any level of presale services that he desires his dealers to provide and then, by setting the minimum resale price appropriately, assure that precisely that level of services is provided. Exclusive territories do not lend themselves to this sort of fine tuning. The level of services evoked by the territorial method will be that level—no more, no less—which reduces the expected monopoly profits of the dealer to zero when he charges the monopoly price.[46] If the manufacturer prefers a lower retail price and fewer services, he will have to place a ceiling on the dealer's price[47]—as was done, in fact, by the defendant in *Albrecht*.

Justice Douglas, writing for the majority in *White Motor*, did not reply to Justice Clark's argument that price fixing and market division are the same animal. In a concurring opinion Justice Brennan did, and in the course of doing so he offered still another rationale for the rule of *Dr. Miles*:

> The analogy to resale price maintenance agreements is also appealing, but is no less deceptive. Resale price maintenance is not only designed to, but almost invariably does in fact, reduce price competition not only *among* sellers of the affected product but quite as much *between* that product and competing brands.[48]

While it is true that industry-wide resale price maintenance might

---

46. This assumes, of course, that there is competition to become a dealer and that the manufacturer has some means of enforcing the dealer's express or implied commitment to provide a particular level of service. Enforcement of the dealer's service commitment is ordinarily unnecessary where the inducement to provide dealer services is provided by resale price maintenance, since (nonprice) competition among the dealers will assure that each provides the desired level of services.

47. Or alternatively reduce the size of the territories or the duration of the exclusive right.

48. 372 U.S. at 268 (emphasis in original).

facilitate cartelizing,[49] it is improper to leap from this point (not even mentioned by the justice) to the conclusion that resale price maintenance "almost invariably" reduces competition among manufacturers practicing it. To see why, assume that manufacturers, being prevented from inducing retailers to provide presale services through resale price maintenance, take over the retailing function themselves, provide the services, and set a retail price that covers the costs of those services, a price equal to the price they would have required their retailers to set had they been permitted to use resale price maintenance. Clearly, there could still be price competition among the manufacturers, albeit it would now occur at the retail rather than at the wholesale level.

Another practice at issue in the *White Motor* case was the reservation by White Motor to itself of certain large accounts. The Court did not discuss this practice separately, although Justice Brennan in his concurring opinion suggested that it was probably illegal because he could imagine no compelling justification for its use. That the Court should have considered this "customer limitation" a practice so similar to exclusive territories as not to warrant separate discussion shows how far it had gone toward abandoning the rationale of *Dr. Miles*. The customer limitation could not be likened in its purpose or effect to a dealer cartel; it cannot promote dealers' interests to be prevented from bidding on large accounts.

The customer limitation not only undermines the dealer-cartel explanation of the exclusive territories; it also provides affirmative evidence that White Motor's purpose in creating such territories was to induce the provision of dealer services. There may be a class of customers who, because of size, sophistication, or special needs, do not require dealer services. The manufacturer may be in a better position than any dealer to provide these customers with whatever presale services they do require. If so, the manufacturer who allows his dealers to compete with him for such an account is inviting them to take a free ride on his services. He provides the services at a cost that he hopes to recoup in the price charged these customers; the dealers then offer the customers a lower price, which they can do since they do not incur any services expense with respect to these customers. In such a case, forbidding dealers to compete for these accounts is just like limiting competition among dealers in order to prevent some of them from taking a free ride on presale services provided by others.

49. See pp. 67–68 supra.

The limbo created by *White Motor* existed for four years, until in *United States v. Arnold Schwinn & Co.*[50] the Court decided that both the territorial and customer restrictions involved in *White Motor*, and all other restrictions placed on the resale of a manufacturer's goods,[51] were illegal per se because they violate "the ancient rule against restraints on alienation and open the door to exclusivity of outlets and limitations of territory further than prudence permits."[52] These are feeble grounds. The "ancient rule" against restraints on alienation, although mentioned in *Dr. Miles,* was not the ground of decision in that case,[53] and in any event would not have been violated by the kind of restriction that White Motor or Schwinn imposed on its dealers.[54] More important, as we saw in chapter 3, the common law of restraint of trade was neither based on a policy of promoting competition nor enacted into federal law by the Sherman Act, and there is no occasion, therefore, to consider what a nineteenth-century judge interpreting a confusing body of English precedents would have done if confronted by methods of distribution unknown in his time. As for the dictates of "prudence," cited by the Court as reinforcing the teachings of the "ancient rule," nowhere does the Court explain why authorizing restrictions on distribution would be "imprudent."

The second part of the opinion holds that while restrictions on distribution may not be imposed in a contract of sale, they may be imposed in a consignment agreement. We are back in the world of the *General Electric* case. *Simpson* is cited but distinguished, without further explanation, as involving "culpable price fixing."[55] The Court states that restricting distribution in contracts of consignment is justified "by the demonstrated need of the franchise system to meet [the] competition" of "mass merchandisers."[56]

50. 388 U.S. 365 (1967).
51. The manufacturer in *Schwinn*, besides assigning territories, forbade both its wholesalers and its franchises to sell to nonfranchised retail outlets—presumably in order to protect the franchised outlets against free riding.
52. 388 U.S. at 380.
53. See p. 154 supra.
54. See Milton Handler, *The Twentieth Annual Antitrust Review* 1967, 53 *Va. L. Rev.* 1667, 1684–86 (1967).
55. 388 U.S. at 380. One could just as appropriately describe the various nonprice restrictions imposed by Schwinn's consignment agreements as "culpable market division."
56. Id. at 381.

But if this is so, why should not Schwinn be allowed to restrict distribution in a contract of sale as well as in one of consignment? And if, as the Court states, the "net effect" of the challenged restrictions "is to preserve and not to damage competition in the bicycle market,"[57] on what theory would a resale price restriction "damage competition in the bicycle market"?

The distribution cases are an intellectual failure of imposing dimensions. Not only is there no economic difference between imposing restrictions by sales contract and by agency contract, and between price fixing and market division; there appears to be no difference related to *anyone*'s notion of the purposes of the Sherman Act. The Court is not protecting small business by these distinctions; it has traditionally been the small retailers who have most wanted to enter into resale price-maintenance agreements and the small manufacturers, like White Motor and Schwinn, that were particularly desirous of imposing restrictions on distribution. The distribution cases are legalistic in the worst sense: they turn on legal distinctions that are unrelated to the purposes or policies of the statute being applied.

A legalistic mode of analysis is perhaps inevitable when the practice in question, here restricted distribution, is not understood; but it may also retard understanding of the practice. It was that favorite method of legal reasoning, reasoning by analogy,[58] which, employed in the *Dr. Miles* opinion, got the Court off on the wrong foot in analyzing restricted distribution. The Court reasoned that resale price maintenance was bad because it was like a dealers' cartel (which was surely bad) in that it eliminated price competition among dealers. But the antitrust laws were surely not intended to forbid all transactions that eliminate some competition merely because a cartel eliminates competition; that would make every merger between competing firms illegal regardless of the market shares of the merging firms. Rather than searching for analogies, the Court in *Dr. Miles* should have sought guidance in the purposes of the Sherman Act. It should have asked itself whether it was really an aim of the act to compel price competition among dealers in a particular manufacturer's brand. Posing that question might have led the Court to consider *why* a manufacturer might

57. Id. at 382.
58. See Edward H. Levi, *An Introduction to Legal Reasoning* (1948).

not desire price competition among his dealers and then to see how resale price maintenance, when imposed voluntarily by the manufacturer, might (like some mergers) have an additional effect that was not present in a cartel—the provision of an optimum level of presale services.

The reader is entitled to insist that, having criticized the Court's approach to restricted distribution, I propose a better one, and I shall. I believe that the law should treat price and nonprice restrictions the same and should make no distinction between the imposition of restrictions in a contract of sale and their imposition in an agency contract. The difficult question is whether the law should permit or prohibit price and nonprice restrictions in distribution, however imposed. The answer is not an easy one to give because, as mentioned earlier, restricted distribution can be a method either of increasing the efficiency of distribution, or of monopolizing. However, economic theory suggests that it will more commonly be manufacturer imposed and efficiency enhancing than dealer imposed and monopolizing. The number of firms in and the ease of entry into most branches of distribution militate strongly against effective cartelization of distribution. Effective dealer cartels are probably rare and this ought to rule out a per se rule against restricted distribution.

But we don't yet know enough about restricted distribution to adopt a rule of per se legality either, and consequently I believe that the Justice Department (and other antitrust plaintiffs) should be permitted to continue to bring cases challenging restrictions in distribution. But they should be required to *prove* that the challenged restriction is, in fact, a dealer cartel. Nor is it an appropriate shortcut to predicate legality on whether the restriction is "horizontal" or "vertical." That was the mistake the Court made in *United States* v. *Sealy, Inc.*[59] Like the manufacturers in *Sealy*, who divided territories not in order to charge monopoly prices but in order to encourage the advertising of their joint trademark, dealers have a legitimate, nonmonopolistic interest in seeking to overcome through joint action serious free-rider problems. Therefore, distribution cases cannot be decided simply by identifying the *source* of the restriction (i.e., whether the manufacturer or the

59. 388 U.S. 350 (1967); see p. 50 supra. See also United States v. Topco Associates, Inc., 405 U.S. 596 (1972).

dealer)—even if that were an easy thing to do. It is necessary in every case to determine whether the objective of the challenged restriction is to increase the provision of presale services or to generate monopoly profits. In *Sealy* itself the defendant sellers' combined share of the mattress market was too small to permit an inference of monopolistic purpose or effect (less than 20 per cent), and this suggests a possible rule for deciding some restricted-distribution cases: the lawfulness of the restriction should be conclusively presumed if the aggregate share of the relevant market possessed by the firms whose competition is restricted is not of monopoly proportions.[60] I can think of no other shortcuts to the decision of these cases that can be justified on the basis of our present knowledge of the purposes and effects of restricted distribution. That is another way of saying that we will not have a rational body of antimonopoly rules until we learn how to determine the economic effects of challenged business practices.

Conclusion

Having now completed the examination, begun in chapter 4, of collusion (in the broadest sense of the term), I would like to pause briefly for a summary reflection on Part Two. The entire thicket of problems and failures examined in these chapters—the criminalization of the price-fixing rule, the inability to deal with tacit collusion, the deconcentration proposals, the overextension of the merger law, the confusion over market definition, the inept legal treatment of information exchanges among competitors, and the crowning fiasco of the restricted-distribution decisions—has a single source: the failure of the courts and the enforcement agencies, and ultimately of the antitrust lawyers and economists, academic and practicing, to develop tools for determining when a group of sellers is maintaining a price that is above the competitive level. If the law had such tools, it could deal with tacit collusion, or oligopoly pricing, simply as another form of culpable price fixing. There would be no need for deconcentration programs or stringent antimerger rules, whose only justification is as second-

60. Of course a manufacturer always has 100 per cent of the market if his brand is deemed a relevant market—and of course it should not be, since other brands are a good substitute. Thus under the proposed rule resale price maintenance would not be actionable unless the dealers' prices of all, or at least most, of the brands of a product were fixed by agreements with their suppliers.

best methods of dealing with tacit collusion. There would be no need for any special doctrines with respect to resale price maintenance or other restrictions on distribution, and the problem of the permissible scope of information exchanges among competitors would be easily solved. The need for defining the relevant market would probably remain but the function of market definition would be clearer and confusion in the application of the market concept less. What may at first glance appear to be the desirable simplicity and freedom from reliance on economic analysis of the per se rule against price fixing is thus seen, on closer analysis, to be the cause of a far-reaching doctrinal shambles.

III   Exclusionary Practices

8   Exclusionary Practices, Real and Imagined

    I suggested in chapter 3 that anticompetitive practices could be divided into three groups: practices that result in or facilitate collusive pricing; exclusionary practices; and practices that are monopolistic in the sense of increasing the gains from and hence incentives to engage in monopoly pricing but are neither collusive nor exclusionary ("unilateral noncoercive monopolizing"). The focus of the book up to this point has been on the first category, reflecting my conviction that, of the three, collusion poses the most serious danger to the maintenance of a competitive economy. The present chapter discusses the second and third categories. It discusses them together because the practices that I denote by the term "unilateral coercive monopolizing" have, in traditional antitrust analysis, been regarded as a species of exclusionary practice. The principal practices that will be discussed are tying, predatory price cutting, vertical mergers, exclusive dealing, and boycotts.

    Some economists believe that it is virtually impossible for a firm or group of firms ever to exclude competitors or potential competitors from the market unless they have lower costs or obtain the aid of the government in the form of a patent or other exclusive right.[1] I do not share this view, but I do think that the number and severity of the exclusionary practices have been greatly exaggerated.

Tying Arrangements

    I begin with a practice that has been incorrectly classified as exclusionary. This is the tying arrangement, whereby as a condition of the sale of one product the seller requires the buyer to purchase a second product from him. The traditional objection to

1. For representative expressions of this view see Ward S. Bowman, Jr., *Patent and Antitrust Law: A Legal and Economic Appraisal* (1973); Robert Bork, "Vertical Integration and the Sherman Act: The Legal History of an Economic Misconception," 22 *U. Chi. L. Rev.* 157 (1954).

tying arrangements is that they enable a firm having a monopoly in one market to obtain a monopoly in a second market. Thus, a firm having monopoly power in the market for business machines could obtain a monopoly of punch cards as well simply by refusing to sell or lease its machines unless the purchaser or lessee agreed to use only its punch cards in the machines.[2] Accordingly, the early cases required proof of monopoly power, or of some proxy therefor such as a patent,[3] in the market for the tying product. Later the requirement of proving monopoly power was attenuated, to the point where now only a minimal, and in some cases no, showing is required;[4] once the courts became accustomed to thinking of the tie-in as a device by which a monopolist of one market levered his way into a position of dominance in other markets, it must have seemed to them redundant to require proof of monopoly in the first market, since how could a tie-in be imposed unless such power existed?

One striking deficiency of the traditional, "leverage" theory of tie-ins, as the courts have applied it, is the failure to require any proof that a monopoly of the tied product is even a remotely plausible consequence of the tie-in. In the *A. B. Dick* case,[5] for example, the defendant had tied ink to its mimeograph machines. It is hardly credible that A. B. Dick was attempting to monopolize the ink industry; only a small fraction of the ink sold in this coun-

2. See International Business Machines Corp. v. United States, 298 U.S. 131 (1936).

3. See, e.g., United Shoe Machinery Corp. v. United States, 258 U.S. 451 (1922); International Business Machines Corp. v. United States, supra; International Salt Co. v. United States, 332 U.S. 392 (1947). A patent is actually a poor proxy for monopoly power, since most patents confer too little monopoly power to be a proper object of antitrust concern. (Some patents confer no monopoly power at all. A patent may simply enable a firm to reduce the cost advantage of a competing firm; in such a case the patent might actually reduce the amount of monopoly power in the market.) Its popularity in tie-in cases may stem from the fact that the earliest such cases were not antitrust cases at all. They were patent-misuse cases (see, e.g., Motion Picture Patents Co. v. Universal Films Mfg. Co., 243 U.S. 502 [1917]), where the issue was whether the patentee had improperly extended the patent monopoly by monopolizing an unpatented product tied to the patented product.

4. For a useful review of the current law on the question see Detroit City Dairy, Inc. v. Kowalski Sausage Co., 393 F. Supp. 453, 467–70 (E. D. Mich. 1975).

5. Henry v. A. B. Dick Co., 224 U.S. 1 (1912).

try is purchased for use in mimeograph machines. At most, Dick was trying to secure control over the ink used in its machines, which is not at all the same thing as trying to monopolize the ink market. Once Dick's objective is restated in this way it becomes clear that tying is like a manufacturer's owning the retail outlets through which his product is sold and thereby "tying" retail distribution to the sale of that product. It is only when the users of the tying product are also the principal customers for the tied product—by no means the typical tie-in case—that tying can righly be described as a method of obtaining a second monopoly.

A second—and fatal—weakness of the leverage theory is its inability to explain *why* a firm with a monopoly of one product would want to monopolize complementary products as well. It may seem obvious that two monopolies are better than one, but since the products are by hypothesis used in conjunction with one another to produce the final product or service in which the consumer is interested (duplication, or computation, or whatever), it is not obvious at all. If the price of the tied product is higher than the purchaser would have had to pay on the open market, the difference will represent an increase in the price of the final product or service to him, and he will demand less of it, and will therefore buy less of the tying product. To illustrate, let a purchaser of data processing be willing to pay up to $1 per unit of computation, requiring the use of one second of machine time and 10 punch cards, each of which costs 1¢ to produce. The computer monopolist can rent the computer for 90¢ a second and allow the user to buy cards on the open market for 1¢, or, if tying is permitted, he can require the user to buy cards from him at 10¢ a card—but in that case he must reduce his machine rental charge to nothing, so what has he gained?

As this example suggests, in the absence of price discrimination a monopolist will obtain no additional profits from monopolizing a complementary product. The qualification, however, is crucial. Tying can be used as a method of price discrimination, and discrimination, as we know from an earlier discussion, enables a monopolist to earn higher profits.[6] By providing the computer at cost and selling each card at a monopoly price, the computer monopolist can vary the charge for computation according to the amount of each purchaser's use. The purchaser who uses a thou-

6. See pp. 62–63 supra.

sand cards a month pays a good deal more for the use of the business machine than the user of a hundred cards a month (though the additional *cost* imposed by his greater use, in machine wear and tear, may be slight), but he is also getting much more value out of the machine so that, assuming an absence of competitive machines, he will be willing to pay more. This method of charging for computation resembles "value-of-service" pricing in public-utility and common-carrier industries—a widely used method of price discrimination that is effective so long as the high-value users have no good alternatives.[7]

Although the replacement of leverage by price discrimination in the theory of tie-ins has been a part of the economic literature for almost twenty years,[8] it has had virtually no impact on public policy. The reasons for the lack of impact are instructive.

1. Some commentators have argued that to show that the purpose of tying is discrimination rather than exclusion misses the point—the *effect* is exclusionary and that is all that matters.[9] This argument is erroneous for two reasons. First, the exclusion of competitors that is objectionable from an antitrust standpoint is exclusion that results in an increase in the market price above the competitive level. A tie-in imposed as a means of price discrimination is neither intended nor likely to increase the price level in the market for the tied product at all, the purpose of the tie-in being, rather, to enable the monopolist to extract higher profits

---

7. In one recent case, the defendant boldly (though unavailingly) acknowledged, and indeed asserted as a defense, that it had imposed a tie-in in order to discriminate in price among its customers more effectively than it could have done by other methods. Mid-America ICEEE, Inc. v. John E. Mitchell Co., 1973 Trade Cases ¶ 74,681, at 94,982 (D. Ore.).

8. See Ward S. Bowman, Jr., "Tying Arrangements and the Leverage Problem," 67 *Yale L.J.* 19 (1957). See also M. L. Burstein, "A Theory of Full-Line Forcing," 55 *Nw. U.L. Rev.* 62 (1960). The theory was originally developed by Aaron Director. There are, incidentally, other reasons besides discrimination why sellers might impose tying arrangements, such as the avoidance of price control or a cartel price, protection of good will (which is discussed in the text below), and the joint pricing of complements (a practice related to price discrimination). See Franklin R. Edwards, "The Economics of 'Tying' Arrangements: Some Proposed Guidelines for Bank Holding-Company Regulation," 6 *Antitrust Law & Econ. Rev.* 87 (1973).

9. See Carl Kaysen & Donald F. Turner, *Antitrust Policy: An Economic and Legal Analysis* 157 (1959); Donald F. Turner, "The Validity of Tying Arrangements Under the Antitrust Laws," 72 *Harv. L. Rev.* 50, 63, n. 42 (1958).

from his monopoly in a separate market. Only in the rare case where the sale of the tied product for use with the tying product represents a substantial share of all sales of the tied product might preventing the independent producers of the tied product from selling it to the customers of the tying product substantially affect competition in the market for the tied product.

Second, if the purpose of the tie-in is price discrimination there will be no exclusion of independent producers at all. The computer monopolist in our example has no motive for driving the existing producers of punch cards out of business and producing the cards himself. He only wants the sale of cards channeled through him so that he can reprice them. Therefore, provided that the existing producers are competitive with one another and efficient, he will buy the cards from them for resale to the customers for his computers.

There will be an exclusionary effect if the purpose of the tie-in is to protect the manufacturer's good will rather than to discriminate. Our hypothetical computer manufacturer might decide to make the cards himself because he believes that another firm would not produce them to the exacting tolerances required to make them function optimally in his computers. But exclusion in this case results solely from the superior efficiency of the tied sale to a sale of the products separately in promoting customer satisfaction. The Supreme Court brushed aside the good-will argument in a real punch-card case[10] with the observation that the manufacturer had an alternative that would have restricted competition less: he could have issued specifications for any manufacturer of punch cards to try to meet. The real issue, however, is the cost rather than the existence of an alternative. If the purpose of imposing the tie-in really was to protect good will rather than to discriminate, the specifications alternative was presumably less efficient than the tie-in; otherwise the manufacturer would have promulgated specifications voluntarily. In these circumstances, to hold that the tie-in unlawfully restricts competition is tantamount to saying that any time a monopolist decides to handle a step in the production process internally rather than to invite competitive bids, he is guilty of monopolizing because he is unnecessarily restricting competition. This is not the general rule, and it makes no sense to apply it just in the tying context.

10. See note 2 supra.

It might seem that the cost savings from a tie-in imposed for the purpose of protecting the manufacturer's good will ought to be balanced against the costs in reduced competition resulting from the exclusion of the independent producers of the tied product. But, if so, the balance will almost always be in favor of upholding the good-will defense, since, as suggested earlier, the exclusion of independent sales of the tied product just for use with the tying product is unlikely to have any competitive significance in the market for the tied product. If 1 per cent of the ink sold in this country were sold to users of A. B. Dick mimeograph machines (undoubtedly an overestimate), the effect of Dick's deciding to make its own ink (an improbable decision, incidentally) would be to reduce the sales of other ink manufacturers by an average of 1 per cent.

2. Whatever its purpose, tying is widely believed to make new competition in the market for the tying product less likely. A firm wanting to enter that market must enter the market for the tied product as well—a new computer manufacturer would have to produce his own cards.[11] The premise of this argument is invalid, of course, if the existing manufacturer is buying and repricing, rather than making cards. I have argued that if he is manufacturing cards the presumption is that the tie-in has an efficiency justification. To this it might be replied that the manufacturer might decide to make his own cards precisely in order to impede entry into the computer market. But there are few if any tie-in cases where such a motive could plausibly be attributed to the manufacturer. As mentioned already, tying rarely if ever gives the producer of the tying product a monopoly position in the market for the tied product, thus making it necessary for a firm desiring to enter the market for the tying product to produce the tied product also, since there are no independent producers. A new entrant would have no difficulty in procuring in the open market the requisite cards or ink or salt[12] to supply together with its business machines, duplicating equipment, or salt machinery.

3. To identify a practice as a form of price discrimination is not to commend it in most people's eyes. Much of the hostility to price discrimination is based on erroneous premises, for ex-

11. See, e.g., Carl Kaysen & Donald F. Turner, supra note 9, at 157.
12. See International Salt Co. v. United States, 332 U.S. 392 (1947).

ample that it is an exclusionary practice.[13] Nonetheless, as we have seen, there is an economic objection to systematic (as distinct from sporadic) price discrimination. By increasing the expected gains from monopoly, it increases the social costs of monopoly. The higher expected profits of discriminating monopoly induce the expenditure of additional resources on getting and holding monopolies, and there is no presumption that these resource costs will be offset by the efficiency gains from a greater output under discriminating monopoly; there is no evidence that discrimination results, on average, in a greater output than nondiscriminating monopoly.[14]

This assumes, of course, that there is no social interest in promoting monopoly. In areas where society wants to increase the amount of monopoly—for example, in order to spur invention— the effect of higher monopoly profits in inducing more monopolizing may count as a social gain rather than as a social loss. This observation is especially relevant to the many cases in which tie-ins have been imposed by firms owning patents in order to increase their profits from the patented invention. If one thought that the patent laws tended to undercompensate inventors, resulting in a suboptimal rate of innovation, one might want to encourage price discrimination in order to increase the amount of investment in inventive activity. Unfortunately, no one has any idea whether the nondiscriminatory exploitation of patents would result in too much, too little, or just the right amount of invention.[15]

It may seem odd in light of this analysis that the earliest cases in which tie-ins were condemned were patent tie-in cases. One might try to defend the results in these cases on the legal rather than the economic ground that the patent laws were not intended to permit patentees to discriminate in price, in which event there would be a legitimate sense in which tying could be thought to

---

13. See p. 206 infra.

14. See pp. 64–65 supra, and Appendix, infra pp. 242–43. In addition, price discrimination impairs efficiency in the market in which the purchasers from the discriminating seller sell, by creating competitive cost disparities unrelated to differences in the relative efficiency of the competitors. The purchaser to whom the discriminating seller sells at a lower price may be no more efficient than the competing purchaser who is charged a higher price.

15. See Ward S. Bowman, Jr., supra note 1, at 15–31.

extend the patent monopoly beyond the scope authorized by law. The trouble with this argument is that it has generally been assumed that patentees are perfectly free to discriminate in price directly[16] (as Xerox, for example, does, by varying the charge for the use of its machines according to the amount of use, just as in a tie-in). It seems arbitrary to prohibit doing the same thing indirectly, by means of tie-ins, unless tie-ins have an exclusionary effect—and we have just seen that where the purpose of the tie-in is discrimination there is no reason to expect any such effect to be present.

My main point, which has been overlooked by the (other) antagonists of the leverage theory, is that considering tie-ins as a form of price discrimination rather than an exclusionary practice does not automatically establish that they ought to be permitted. There are serious objections to prohibiting tie-ins, but they are not based on the premise that since tie-ins are not a form of leverage they ought to be permitted. One objection is that, as mentioned, in the absence of any general prohibition against price discrimination, forbidding tie-ins is a trivial measure; the effect will simply be to deflect the monopolist to another, and lawful, method of discrimination.[17] To this it might be replied that there is, or ought to be, a general prohibition against discrimination. Discrimination has been considered evidence of a Sherman Act section 2 violation when used by a monopolist to repel competition, as we shall see a little later when we discuss the *United Shoe Machinery* case. And a distinguished Federal Trade Commissioner, Philip Elman, in a concurring opinion in the *Peelers* case[18] that was discussed approvingly by the court of appeals which reviewed the commission's decision,[19] once suggested that discrimination by a monopolist between competing customers was an unlawful act of monopolization even if the monopoly itself was a lawful one

16. But cf. discussion of *Peelers* case in text below.
17. To be sure, if all of the alternative methods were either substantially more costly or substantially less effective than tying, the amount of discrimination might be substantially reduced as a result even of the limited prohibition. But the premise is implausible. Intensity of use can be metered directly (as Xerox, for example, does with its copying machines) as well as indirectly by use of a tie-in.
18. Peelers Co., 65 F.T.C. 799, 865–69 (1964).
19. LaPeyre v. FTC, 366 F.2d 117 (5th Cir. 1966).

(e.g., a patent monopoly).[20] In that case, the patentee of the only process for cleaning shrimp by machine leased the machine at a higher price to Pacific Northwest shrimp processors than to Gulf Coast processors because the costs of cleaning by hand were higher for the former group. The result was to perpetuate a cost difference between competing segments of the industry that the development of machine cleaning, in the absence of discrimination, would have eliminated.

Commissioner Elman cited, as a precedent for his view that a monopolist has a duty to refrain from discrimination, *United States* v. *Terminal Railroad Ass'n*,[21] but that case (like *United Shoe Machinery*) is distinguishable because the targets of the discrimination were competitors of the discriminating firms rather than customers. (Although discrimination against a competitor was alleged in the *Peelers* case, and found by the commission, Commissioner Elman did not rely upon this finding in his opinion.)

A narrow interpretation of the result in *Peelers* is that it was a case in which section 5 of the Federal Trade Commission Act was used to plug a loophole in the Robinson-Patman Act; the discrimination there was effected through lease rather than sale, which placed it beyond the reach of the latter act. And since, even under Commissioner Elman's broader reading of section 5, the antitrust laws would forbid discrimination by a monopolist only where the higher-price and lower-price customers were in competition with each other, I conclude that there is not as yet a general prohibition against price discrimination and ask: should there be one?

The common argument that such a prohibition would merely treat a symptom of monopoly, rather than monopoly itself, is unpersuasive. If, as I have argued, systematic discrimination is a source of net social costs, an effective and inexpensive prohibition would increase social welfare. A more serious objection to prohibiting price discrimination is that it is often just a by-product of movement from one equilibrium to another—sometimes from a monopolistic to a competitive equilibrium—and prohibiting it

20. Peelers had a monopoly of an economically relevant market. Elman did not suggest that *no* patentee could ever discriminate, though one could of course, argue that the fact of discrimination establishes the existence of at least some economic, as well as formal legal, monopoly power.

21. 224 U.S. 383 (1912).

would impede such movements.[22] The point is well taken; one must distinguish between persistent or systematic discrimination, an unequivocal sign of monopoly, and temporary or sporadic discrimination, which might accompany a shift to a new equilibrium or indicate cheating by the members of a cartel. But it is extremely difficult in practice to make such distinctions. The Robinson-Patman Act illustrates the problems of administering a price-discrimination law sensibly. It is not an entirely apt example, however, since the framers of the act may not have been concerned just with price discrimination in the economic sense.

The question whether to forbid price discrimination (the systematic, rather than the sporadic, sort) is closely related to the question, discussed in chapter 4, whether to permit the use of (systematic) price discrimination as evidence of collusive pricing. The limitations of economic science and of the judicial process are such as to make one doubt that the antitrust laws are capable of distinguishing systematic price discrimination not only from sporadic discrimination but from cost-justified price differences. The solution that I find most appealing at this early stage in the development of our understanding is to permit experimentation with the use of evidence of price discrimination in collusion cases, meanwhile deferring decision on whether to institute (either through interpretation of sections 1 or 2 of the Sherman Act or new legislation) a general ban on persistent price discrimination. Under this approach, tie-ins would be permitted, at least for the present.

Even if banning tie-ins were thought to be an effective method of preventing price discrimination in the absence of a general prohibition of discrimination, it would be a very costly, perhaps prohibitively costly, method of dealing with discrimination, due to the difficulties of distinguishing tie-ins imposed for the purpose of discriminating in price from tie-ins designed to protect good will or to get around a cartel price, and of distinguishing tie-ins from perfectly innocuous combination or package sales (e.g., an automobile manufacturer's refusal to sell the automobile separately from the carburetor). These are serious problems in the analysis of tying which have received inadequate attention from academic lawyers and economists. Indeed, an unfortunate consequence of

22. See p. 63 supra.

the debate over leverage is that it has tended to define the issue for policy as whether tie-ins are a device for obtaining a second monopoly or a method of price discrimination, as if these were the only possibilities. They are not. In particular, in many cases it has been argued that the purpose of the tie-in was neither leverage nor price discrimination but protection of good will by assuring the compatibility of two products used together to produce the final service (computation, or whatever) that the consumer is interested in. The courts have tended to brush aside good-will arguments without really examining them, on the ground that compatibility can be assured by the issuance and enforcement of suitable specifications for producers of the complementary product. As mentioned earlier, this is an inadequate response because it ignores the possibly substantial cost differences between tying and specifications as methods of protecting good will. In principle, it remains open to the defendant in a tie-in case to prove that the specifications alternative is infeasible; but this narrow "good-will defense" is only grudgingly allowed, and rarely succeeds. Yet there is neither theoretical nor empirical basis for dismissing good-will considerations as unimportant in many tying arrangements.

An even more serious problem arises from the fact that like the concept of vertical integration[23] the concept of a tie-in is conventional rather than analytical. We think of a mimeograph machine and its paper and ink as separate products which if sold together are "tied," but we do not think of a left and right glove, or an automobile and its radiator, in the same way. Yet nothing in the traditional legal thinking about tie-ins enables one to distinguish among these cases. The tie-in doctrine furnishes no answer to the question of when a sale consists of a combination of separate products or when it is a single product made up of components. Since virtually all products have components, the potential reach of the doctrine is thus devastating. I suppose that what keeps the doctrine from expanding to its logical limits is a tacit assumption that the more obvious combination sales could readily be justified by their lower costs compared to selling the components separately. But there is something seriously wrong about a doctrine under which virtually every combination sale is prima facie an unlawful tie-in that the seller may have to convince a jury is cost justified.

23. See pp. 196–97 infra.

That the very concept of a tie-in is undefined within the terms of the traditional legal doctrine—which combines the idea of leverage with severe attenuation of the requirement of proving monopoly power in the market for the tying product—is well illustrated by the case of the "best-efforts" clause. This perfectly standard—indeed virtually implicit—provision in distribution agreements requires the distributor to promote the manufacturer's product vigorously. If the manufacturer sells more than one product to his distributor and the best-efforts provision covers his entire line, the provision may, like a tie-in agreement, induce the distributor to buy a product that he would prefer not to carry, as a condition of being permitted to buy the products in the manufacturer's line that he does want to carry. A doctrine which implies that most distribution agreements contain, unbeknown to their signatories, a provision that constitutes virtually a per se violation of the antitrust laws is radically defective. Fortunately, best-efforts provisions can be distinguished from an actionable tie-in on the ground that they promote the manufacturer's legitimate interest in obtaining effective distribution of his goods, a factor absent in conventional tie-in cases. Yet in terms of traditional tie-in doctrine the attempted distinction invites the facile response that the manufacturer should be required to devise a less restrictive method of obtaining effective distribution.

The prohibition against tie-ins ought to be radically curtailed, and in the absence of a general prohibition of systematic price discrimination eliminated. To this it may be objected, first, that while a rational profit-maximizing monopolist would not attempt to take over the manufacture of a complementary product unless the existing manufacturers were either less efficient at producing it than he or were charging a higher than competitive price, there may be some cases where a monopolist does not behave as a rational profit maximizer would. The question of providing legal sanctions for irrational behavior is a recurrent one in the analysis of exclusionary practices, and I shall discuss it at greater length in connection with predatory pricing. For now, it is sufficient to observe that, even if there were no separate prohibition of tie-ins, the general prohibitions of monopolistic behavior in sections 1 and 2 of the Sherman Act would remain available to deal with cases where a firm had imposed a tie-in with the purpose or likely effect of monopolizing the market for the tied product. A special tie-in doctrine, with (inevitably) a life of its own, is unnecessary and inappropriate to deal with aberrant behavior.

A second objection to eliminating the separate prohibition of tie-ins is based on statutory language. Section 3 of the Clayton Act, passed in 1914, forbids (with certain immaterial limitations) tie-in and exclusive-dealing contracts where the effect may be substantially to lessen competition.[24] The legislative history of this provision indicates that its framers believed in the leverage theory. Courts do not have the authority to disregard legislative policy because they think the premises of the policy mistaken. It is arguable, however, that, since Congress did not outlaw tie-ins altogether, but expressly required some evidence of anticompetitive effect, it implicitly authorized the courts to alter the scope of the prohibition in accordance with changing perceptions of the competitive effects of particular practices.

No doubt it is utopian to think that the courts will ever abolish the rule against tie-ins altogether. A moderate and perhaps even attainable reform, however, would be to limit the rule to tie-ins employed for purposes of discriminating.[25] With the leverage theory discredited, discrimination appears to be the only general basis upon which to object to tying. The prohibition should accordingly be confined to those tie-ins whose object is discrimination. This is preferable to trying to decide when a combination sale or promotion is a tie-in and when it is something else, a distinction that cannot be made on any rational basis. Of course it will not always be clear whether a tie-in is being used to discriminate or to protect the manufacturer's good will, but the suggested approach would at least get rid of the large number of potential tie-in cases in which the same amount of the "tied" product is always used with the "tying" product—one radiator per car, one left glove with every right glove, etc. These cannot be price-discrimination cases because the amount of the tied product purchased does not vary with the intensity of the use of the tying product.

Price discrimination by means of tie-ins or otherwise is the most important but not the only form of what I have infelicitously

24. 15 U.S.C. § 14.
25. The general prohibitions of the Sherman Act would as ever remain available to deal with any attempts to employ tying as a method of leverage.

termed unilateral noncoercive monopolizing. Professor Coase has argued that the lease-only policy of a monopolist of a durable good, such as United Shoe Machinery Corporation, may be designed to overcome the difficulties encountered in trying to charge a monopoly price for a durable good.[26] Perhaps the lease-only policy should have been forbidden on that ground but I shall argue later that, as with tie-ins, the lease-only policy is not exclusionary.

Predatory Pricing

Coming at last to genuinely exclusionary practices, we must distinguish between those practices that require the cooperation of a customer to be effective and those that do not. Predatory pricing depends on the purchasers' willingness to buy from the predator (or the intended victim) at the predatory price; blowing up a competitor's plant or procuring a patent from the Patent Office by fraud does not. This distinction is important to our analysis because exclusionary practices that require the buyer's cooperation will often fail because it is not in the buyers' interest to cooperate.

Suppose that the Standard Oil Trust reduces its price in one market below cost, hoping to drive out its competitors there and later raise its price to a monopoly level. Presumably it expects its eventual monopoly profits, discounted to present value, to exceed the losses from selling below cost now. This assessment assumes, however, that the average purchaser in this market will sustain a net loss by paying a lower price to Standard instead of a higher price to a competitor of Standard;[27] the lower price he pays now will be more than offset by the higher price he will pay later when Standard, with his help, has obtained a monopoly. The purchaser would be better off continuing to patronize Standard's nominally higher-priced competitor.

This analysis does not, however, completely negate the possibility of effective predatory pricing. The purchaser may not be sufficiently informed and far-sighted to realize the cost to him of

26. See Ronald H. Coase, "Durability and Monopoly," 15 *J. Law & Econ.* 143 (1972).
27. It is irrelevant how long the purchaser expects to remain in the market, provided that the purchaser is a firm: the anticipation of higher supply prices in the future will adversely affect a firm's present market value.

taking advantage of the temporarily lower price, or he may decide to act as a "free rider," taking advantage of the lower price in the hope that the refusal of other purchasers to do so will cause the predator's campaign to fail. The second possibility is especially great when there are many purchasers.

An extensive literature seeks to show on other grounds that predatory pricing is not an effective method of monopolizing.[28] That literature has been excessively influenced, however, by John McGee's pathbreaking article on the use, or rather nonuse, of predatory pricing by the Standard Oil Trust.[29] Ever since that article appeared, scholars have stated the question of predatory pricing as whether it was rational *for the Standard Oil Trust* to practice such pricing. The answer has been negative, because it is cheaper to acquire than to undersell a competitor. But this answer is convincing only if mergers are assumed to be legal, and, although this assumption was reasonable throughout most of the history of the Standard Oil Trust, the illegality of mergers to create a monopoly has been clear for a long time now. Predatory pricing is also illegal, but it is more difficult to detect than mergers. Therefore, given the legal environment, predation may in fact be a cheaper method of monopolization than acquisition. And, even if predation were a more costly method of obtaining a monopoly than acquisition, it would not follow that it was non-existent. Settlement is cheaper than litigation as a method of resolving legal disputes, yet one observes litigation occurring. The basic reason is that the parties to a dispute may have divergent expectations regarding the likely outcome of litigation which may make it impossible for them to agree on a mutually advantageous settlement price. Similarly, competing firms might fail to agree on a mutually advantageous price for the sale of one firm's assets to the other, and predation might be resorted to as a second-best way to get a monopoly.

To be sure, this analysis does not establish that predation is an *effective* method of monopolization. To impose costs on a competitor by imposing the same or greater costs on oneself does not seem a very promising method of excluding a competitor. If, however, a firm operates in a number of markets and faces actual

28. Most of this literature is cited in B. S. Yamey, "Predatory Price Cutting: Notes and Comments," 15 *J. Law & Econ.* 129 (1972).

29. John S. McGee, "Predatory Price Cutting: The Standard Oil (N.J.) Case," 1 *J. Law & Econ.* 137 (1958).

or potential competitors each of whom is limited to one of its markets, it may find it worthwhile to expend considerable resources on crushing a single competitor in order to develop a reputation (for willingness to use predatory pricing) that may enable the firm to exclude other potential competitors without any additional below-cost selling. Stated otherwise, the costs incurred by the firm in using predatory pricing in one market may generate greater deterrence benefits in other markets. Knowing that the dominant firm might act in this way, a competitor may be reluctant to enter any market in which the firm operates, and if he is already in such a market he may refrain from price competition or agree to sell out to the dominant firm at a low price.

If this analysis is correct, the threat of predatory pricing could have been effectively employed by the Standard Oil Trust because it operated in more markets than many of its actual and potential competitors. To the extent that the threat was effective actual predatory pricing would have been unnecessary; moreover, an implicit threat may have been sufficient. In either case, McGee's study of the record in the *Standard Oil* case might not have uncovered the extent to which Standard Oil owed its market position to predatory tactics. (Moreover, that a practice is not discovered by the lawyers for a party to a lawsuit is not always compelling evidence that the practice did not occur.)

My conclusion is that predatory pricing cannot be dismissed as inevitably an irrational practice. This conclusion does not assume that the predator has superior access to the capital market and is therefore able to finance a campaign of below-cost selling more cheaply than a small competitor or a new entrant could. But it does assume that the competitor has committed to the market at least some resources that are specialized to the market, in the sense that, if he tried to shift them to another use, he would incur a cost. If the resources he uses to compete with the predator are perfectly mobile, the predator cannot hurt him; at the first sign of below-cost pricing he will withdraw from the market without suffering any loss.

My analysis also implies that predatory pricing at most is likely to delay, rather than prevent, the entry of new competitors. A firm planning to enter *all* of the markets of the dominant firm would not be deterred by fear of predatory pricing. In that situation the benefits of predatory pricing are unlikely to exceed the costs— which must be incurred in every market in which the predator operates—and therefore the dominant firm will find it difficult to make a credible threat to engage in predatory pricing. Accordingly, freedom to practice predatory pricing would be expected only to increase the *scale* of new entry. This might lengthen the time that it took for entry to occur—as discussed in chapter 4, more time may be required to launch a large enterprise than a small one[30] —but it should not preclude entry entirely. Having to enter on a larger scale will not increase the costs of the new entrant relative to those of the existing firm, since the latter also operates on the larger scale and therefore also experiences any diseconomies caused by operating on such a scale or in so many markets. To be sure, anything that delays entry prolongs the period of monopoly pricing and thereby increases the social costs of monopoly, but the increase in these costs may not be large. A commonly overlooked point is that an increase in the time required for new entry may actually make entry more attractive to some firms, since they can anticipate a longer period before any profits that they obtain in the market disappear due to the competition of additional, newer entrants.

What are the implications for legal policy of a correct economic analysis of predation? I have argued that the case for relegating predatory pricing to the realm of the irrational has not been made, but even if it had been made, as some economists believe, it would not follow that predatory pricing should be freely permitted. The correct level of an activity is achieved by compelling the actors to bear the full social costs of their actions, including their mistakes, and the predator's losses may not equal those costs. This possibility arises whenever predation succeeds at least to the extent that the period of below-cost pricing is followed by a period of monopoly pricing. The misallocative effects of a firm's selling a product below cost, thus inducing inefficient substitution toward it, are not reduced by its subsequently selling the product at a monopoly price and thus inducing inefficient substitution away from it. The private costs of predatory pricing are accordingly lower than the social costs because the period of monopoly pricing compensates the seller—though if predatory pricing is invariably irrational, never fully—for the losses he incurred when he sold the product below cost. In addi-

30. See p. 58 supra.

tion, all of the costs of the inefficiently low prices will not be borne by the predator; some will be borne by other firms in the market.

That forbidding predatory pricing would be a source of some social benefits—either because predation is sometimes a rational practice or because, although always irrational, it would be practiced occasionally by firms that misconceived their self-interest and did not bear the entire costs of their mistake—does not mean that such a prohibition is warranted. That depends on the costs of the prohibition in relation to its benefits. Those costs are substantial because of the difficulty of distinguishing between predatory and efficient pricing.

There are two conventional approaches to the identification of predatory pricing, one through intent and the other through costs, and neither is adequate. To forbid pricing intended to weaken or destroy a competitor is to forbid too much. A seller may want to destroy a competitor, but if the only method used is underselling him by virtue of having lower costs there is no rational antitrust objection to the seller's conduct. But too little is forbidden also. Intent may be impossible to prove; and inadvertently pricing below cost could be as injurious as pricing below cost with intent to exclude competitors. The alternative definition of predatory pricing as pricing below "cost" is empty without specification of the concept of cost that will be used.

I believe the most useful definition of predatory pricing is the following: *pricing at a level calculated to exclude from the market an equally or more efficient competitor.* Only two practices fit this definition. The first is selling below short-run marginal cost. There is no reason consistent with an interest in efficiency for selling a good at a price lower than the cost that the seller incurs by the sale. We expect the clothing store to sell last year's fashions at a drastic discount—its price may even be lower than what it paid for the goods—but not at a price lower than the cost of making the sale, which includes any profit it might have expected to make from charging a higher price. A sale below cost in this sense can only have the purpose and (if persisted in) the likely effect of excluding an equally, or more, efficient rival. Unfortunately, measurement problems make this definition of the forbidden practice difficult to apply. A firm may be offering goods at a price below cost—perhaps even at a zero price—as a method of sales promotion. In such a case the real sales price can be calculated only by including any future revenues generated by the sale—other than anticipated revenues from monopoly pricing.[31]

The second practice that is predatory under my definition is selling below long-run marginal cost with the intent to exclude a competitor. Long-run marginal costs are those that must be recovered to stay in business for the more or less indefinite future. In a retail store they would include rent, insurance, other overhead costs, and cost of inventory. If the retailer's total revenues are not large enough to cover all of these costs, he will eventually be forced out of business. But selling below long-run marginal cost is only suggestive, and not conclusive, evidence of socially inefficient pricing. Some businesses or parts of businesses have no future. No social purpose is served by forcing a seller to include in his price a charge for the depreciation of a plant that will never be replaced. In these circumstances pricing below long-run marginal cost does not imply an exclusionary intent or effect; on the contrary, the purpose and effect are to make a graceful—a cost-minimizing—exit, leaving the field to more efficient firms. That is why pricing below long-run as distinct from short-run marginal cost cannot be presumed to be anticompetitive unless there is intent to exclude—in which event it becomes a tactic calculated to exclude an equally efficient competitor (if the "predator" were more efficient he could, and would, exclude his competitor by charging a price equal to or higher than his own long-run marginal costs).

Again, measurement problems abound; in particular, it will sometimes be difficult or even impossible to make a nonarbitrary allocation of marginal costs to an individual product or market. Moreover, the dependence of this approach on evidence of intent is a considerable limitation on its utility. It is extraordinarily difficult to ascertain the intent of a large corporation by the methods of litigation. What juries (and many judges) do not understand is that the availability of evidence of improper intent is often a function of luck and of the defendant's legal sophistication, not of the underlying reality. A firm with executives sensitized to

31. Even the qualification must be qualified. A firm might dispose of some of its output below cost in one market in order to limit its output, and thus increase its prices and profits, in another market, where it had a monopoly. Such "dumping" may be objectionable, but generally not on the ground of tending to exclude competitors in the market where the dumping occurred.

antitrust problems will not leave any documentary trail of improper intent; one whose executives lack this sensitivity will often create rich evidence of such intent simply by the clumsy choice of words to describe innocent behavior. Especially misleading here is the inveterate tendency of sales executives to brag to their superiors about their competitive prowess, often using metaphors of coercion that are compelling evidence of predatory intent to the naïve. Any doctrine that relies upon proof of intent is going to be applied erratically at best. (An alternative approach—which seems, however, of doubtful practicality given the limitations both of economic science and of the judicial process—would be to examine the full range of possible reasons for a particular pricing policy and to infer predation only after rejecting all other possible reasons for selling below long-run marginal cost, such as declining demand or obsolete plant, as implausible in the circumstances of the case.)

The above criterion of predatory pricing could be made somewhat more workable by substituting "average balance-sheet costs" for "long-run marginal costs." By average balance-sheet costs I mean the company's total costs as stated on its books divided by the number of units of output produced. Long-run marginal cost, the additional cost that the producer will incur in producing a unit of output after his existing plant has worn out and must be replaced, is conceptually quite distinct. Average balance-sheet cost is backward-looking; it is based on the historical cost experience (e.g., debt incurred in the purchase of existing plants and machinery) reflected on the company's books. Marginal cost is forward-looking; it is based on current and future replacement costs. However, in practice, average balance-sheet cost—a considerably easier figure to calculate—is sometimes a tolerable proxy for long-run marginal cost, at least in "steady-state" situations where demand and cost are stable over reasonably long periods of time.

Proof of sales below average balance-sheet cost with intent to exclude might be enough to establish a prima facie case of predatory pricing. The defendant's costs would, of course, have to be allocated between the market in which it was alleged to be pricing below cost and its other markets. This would require estimation of the additional overhead expenses (interest, rent, depreciation, cost of equity capital, and administrative expenses) incurred in operating in the market in question. The defendant could rebut the prima facie case of predatory pricing by showing that, because of changes in the conditions of demand or supply, the average costs shown on its books were different from its long-run marginal costs, or that short-run rather than long-run marginal costs were the correct guide to efficient pricing in its circumstances.

As a safeguard against abuse of the predatory-pricing concept, it might be wise to require the plaintiff to prove that the relevant market has characteristics predisposing it toward the effective use of predatory pricing. The inquiry here would be much the same as I envisage for collusive-pricing cases,[32] since in both sorts of case the defendant's conduct is unlikely to be seriously harmful unless the structure of the market is conducive to monopolization. The additional predisposing characteristics in the predatory-pricing inquiry are whether there are many purchasers[33] and whether the defendant operates in more markets than its competitors and prospective entrants.

Professors Areeda and Turner have argued that only sales below short-run marginal cost should ever be regarded as predatory.[34] They reject the use of any average-cost concept for purposes of determining predation. They reason that for short-run marginal cost to be lower than average cost implies that the market has excess capacity, in which event market price should be set equal to short-run marginal cost in order to discourage the replacement of productive capacity as it wears out, and so eventually eliminate the excess. This reasoning ignores the fact that short-run marginal cost is lower than long-run marginal cost (for which I have argued that average accounting or balance-sheet cost is sometimes a tolerable proxy) even when there is no excess capacity. In the short run, marginal cost does not include interest, rent, depreciation, and other overhead items, because they do not vary in the short run with the amount of output produced; but they are part of the long-run marginal cost of production, which is why a firm's short-run marginal cost is normally lower than its long-run marginal

32. See chapter 4 supra.

33. See p. 185 supra.

34. Phillip Areeda & Donald F. Turner, "Predatory Pricing and Related Practices Under Section 2 of the Sherman Act," 88 *Harv. L. Rev.* 697 (1975). Their position was accepted in a recent court of appeals opinion. M. C. Mfg. Co. v. Texas Foundries, Inc., 1975-2 CCH Trade Cas., ¶ 60,466 (C.A. 5th Cir. 1975); petition for cert. filed, CCH Trade Reg. Rep., ¶ 75-1083 (Jan. 30, 1976).

cost. This means, however, that a price equal to seller A's short-run marginal cost might enable A to drive from the market his competitor, B, who was more efficient than A because his long-run marginal cost was lower than A's, but who was unwilling to remain in the market if forced to meet a price lower than his long-run marginal cost. For this reason,

> Long-run marginal costs are likely to be the preferred criterion [of legality] also in competitive situations. Permitting rate reductions to a lower level of SRMC [short-run marginal cost], which would prove to be unremunerative if the business thus attracted were to continue over time, might constitute predatory competition—driving out of business rivals whose *long-run* costs of production might well be lower than those of the price-cutter.[35]

A numerical illustration of this point may be helpful. Widgets are produced by Firm A in a plant that cost $1 million to build and has a useful life of 10 years and a capacity of producing 100,000 widgets per year. The average fixed costs of production are therefore $1 at full capacity. Suppose the average variable cost (labor and materials) is also $1 per widget. Then average total cost is $2, composed of $1 average fixed costs (I am ignoring interest costs) and $1 average variable costs, the latter also being the short-run marginal cost of producing widgets. Assume further that the various factors that determine costs and demands are expected to remain constant for the indefinite future. For example, A's plant is expected to be replaced when it wears out at the end of 10 years, and at the same cost as the current plant. In these circumstances the average total costs of production are also the long-run marginal costs of production.

Let there be another firm in the industry, B, which is just like A except that B's plant has a 20-year life, so that B's long-run marginal cost is only $1.50. Although its short-run marginal cost, $1, is the same as A's, B is clearly the more efficient firm, and if A reduced its price to $1 in an effort to induce B to merge with it on favorable terms, we would have a clear case of a pricing policy that if persisted in would eliminate a more efficient competitor. Nor can the policy be justified by reference to the existence of excess capacity. There is no excess capacity in the

35. 1 Alfred E. Kahn, *The Economics of Regulation: Principles and Institutions* 85 (1970) (emphasis in original).

example. It is true that since A's reduction in price to $1, even if matched by B, will increase the demand for A's output (people will substitute widgets for other products at its new, lower price), A will have to produce beyond its (optimal) capacity. But the fact that a plant can, and if demand conditions justify will, produce beyond its cost-minimizing output does not imply the existence of excess capacity at its normal output.

Production beyond optimal capacity will, to be sure, increase A's short-run marginal costs and therefore—assuming, as do Areeda and Turner, that pricing below short-run marginal cost is unlawful—force A to increase its price above $1 to cover its short-run marginal costs at its new output. But the higher price may still be below B's long-run marginal cost, and hence exclusionary in the sense that it is calculated to exclude from the market an equally or (as in the example) a more efficient competitor, in circumstances where a price below long-run marginal cost cannot be justified by reference to the existence of excess capacity or any other legitimate economic reason for such pricing.

If the demand for widgets collapsed, and it was clear that neither A's nor B's plant was ever going to be replaced, then pricing according to short-run marginal cost would be entirely appropriate. It would, of course, discourage any further investment in widget plants, but in doing so it would be serving the socially valuable function of equilibrating the long-run supply to the changed long-run demand. But where pricing below long-run (even if above short-run) marginal cost is not in response to changes in demand or supply, but is merely a device for intimidating or destroying an equally or more efficient competitor, it is —contrary to what I understand to be the position of Areeda and Turner—inefficient.

The courts have frequently applied incorrect tests of predatory pricing. For example, a common judicial approach has been to infer predation from proof of price discrimination plus exclusionary intent. However, if the alleged predator's price is above his long-run marginal costs in the relevant market, it is irrelevant that he is charging a higher price elsewhere, where he faces less competition. His lower price in the relevant market can exclude only a less efficient competitor—one whose long-run marginal costs are higher than the defendant's. By linking exclusionary intent and geographical price discrimination, while ignoring the relationship between price and long-run marginal cost in the relevant market, the Supreme Court reached an anticompetitive result in *Utah Pie Co.* v. *Continental Baking Co.*[36] The defendants were charging lower prices in markets in which the plaintiff competed than in other markets, but the Court cited no evidence of sales at a price below long-run marginal cost.[37] Intent to weaken Utah Pie was shown but this was neither surprising nor disreputable—especially since Utah Pie, rather than any of the defendants, was the dominant firm in the markets involved.

Another example of judicial ineptitude in this area is the celebrated district-court decision in *Telex Corp.* v. *International Bus. Mach. Corp.*[38] IBM had made drastic price reductions in equipment that was "plug-compatible" with its main-frame computer equipment in order to repel the competitive inroads made by Telex, another producer of equipment plug-compatible with IBM computers. In holding that the price reductions were evidence of unlawful monopoly, the district court emphasized that (1) IBM was the dominant firm in the relevant market (oddly and inaccurately defined as the sale of equipment plug-compatible with *IBM* computers); (2) the price reductions reduced IBM's net revenue from sales of the products in question; (3) the reductions were not cost justified; and (4) IBM's purpose was to weaken Telex.

All of this evidence, however, is entirely consistent with the hypothesis—neither mentioned by the court nor argued by either party but one that fairly leaps to the eye—that IBM was adjusting in a natural and socially appropriate manner to the erosion of its monopoly position caused by Telex's entry into the market. IBM began with 100 percent of the relevant market, and even though the court incorrectly defined the market we may assume that IBM had *some* monopoly power and that its price exceeded its cost. Telex's advent provided competitive alternatives to IBM's customers, and as a result the demand curve facing IBM became more elastic, the profit-maximizing monopoly price fell, and IBM lowered its price. The price reduction was not cost justified; it

36. 386 U.S. 685 (1967).

37. The Court did state that one of the defendants was not recouping its "full overhead," id. at 698–99, but did not suggest that the amount of overhead forgone was a long-run marginal cost of selling in Utah Pie's markets.

38. 367 F. Supp. 258 (N.D. Okla. 1973), rev'd, 510 F.2d 894 (10th Cir. 1975).

was a reaction to a change in demand rather than to a change in cost, and the final price may still have exceeded IBM's long-run marginal cost. IBM's net revenues in the relevant market fell, because Telex's entry was an adverse development to which IBM reacted by attempting to limit its losses—and they would have fallen even further had IBM permitted Telex to take over the entire market. IBM could not hope to *increase* its net revenues above what they would have been had Telex not entered the market; a monopolist's profits must fall if the demand for his product becomes more elastic as a result of new entry.[39]

The thrust of the district court's approach in *Telex* is to force a dominant firm to operate at a price higher than the monopoly price; the firm is prohibited from closing the umbrella of high, monopoly prices that encouraged firms like Telex to enter its markets. This result is perverse and would have been avoided if the court had used the two-part test of predatory pricing suggested

39. This analysis is questioned in Comment, *"Telex v. IBM*: Monopoly Pricing Under Section 2 of the Sherman Act," 84 *Yale L.J.* 558, 571–75 (1975). The author of the Comment argues that IBM was not simply re-computing the monopoly price on the basis of the higher elasticity of demand consequent on the entry of Telex and other competitors; it was engaged in "limit pricing." This term describes the practice whereby a monopolist establishes a price just below the cost of the potential entrants in order to prevent any entry from occurring. It is a dubious strategy of monopolistic profit maximization since, in general, the long-run marginal costs of potential entrants will be the same as the long-run marginal cost of the monopoly seller. Thus charging a price below a new entrant's long-run marginal cost will yield *negative* profits. If the monopolist does have lower costs than potential entrants, and does decide that he can make more money by forestalling entry than by charging a higher price which will eventually result in an erosion of his profits through new entry, the results of the entry-forestalling price are still preferable from a social standpoint to what they would be if the monopolist were forced to hold an umbrella over new entrants by having his price frozen at the preentry level. The author of the *Yale Law Journal* Comment is well aware of this and agrees that the district court decided the *Telex* case incorrectly; IBM's limit pricing should have been permitted. Thus it appears to make no difference to policy whether the monopolist's response is described as reducing price because the elasticity of demand has increased or as limit pricing—i.e., as closing the umbrella a little less or a little more—so long as the resulting price is not below the monopolist's long-run marginal costs. I both fail to see what purpose is served by attempting to distinguish between "limit" and "dominant firm" pricing and doubt the feasibility of distinguishing between them by the methods of litigation.

above. Fortunately, the court of appeals reversed the district court's decision, correctly holding that since IBM's price reductions were plainly not below its costs in any sense (it continued to earn a 20-percent rate of return on sales made at the allegedly predatory prices), it could not be guilty of violating the Sherman Act even if its purpose was to destroy Telex.

Vertical Integration

If a firm purchases a customer or a supplier and directs the newly acquired division to deal only with it, the market for its competitors' goods (if the acquired firm is a customer), or its competitors' access to inputs (if the acquired firm is a supplier), will be curtailed. The same effect can be achieved, without any acquisition, by the firm's opening a new outlet, or a new source of supply, and channeling all sales (or all purchases) through the new division. The withdrawal of patronage from the independent outlets or suppliers will lead to a shrinkage of the independent sector similar to what would have occurred if the firm had purchased enough outlets or suppliers to make it self-sufficient.[40] There is, however, a compelling practical reason why vertical integration through internal expansion as distinct from acquisition has rarely been challenged under the antitrust laws. Any time a firm decides to perform internally a part of the productive process that it could have contracted out, it has opted for vertical integration. Consequently, if vertical integration were deemed a suspect activity under the antitrust laws because of its possible exclusionary effect, all commercial activity would be placed under an enormous cloud of potential antitrust liability. It would be like saying that since a firm's decision to enlarge its productive capacity might result in an increase in concentration and so facilitate collusion, every such decision (at least by a firm having a substantial market share) should be carefully scrutinized by the antitrust enforcers. It is perhaps arbitrary as a matter of substantive doctrine, but it is inevitable and on the whole desirable, that the law's focus has been on vertical integration accomplished by means of mergers.

The exclusionary effect of a vertical merger is similar to that of a contract between a firm and one of its customers or suppliers

40. See Sam Peltzman, "Issues in Vertical Integration Policy," in *Public Policy Toward Mergers* 167, 175–76 (J. Fred Weston & Sam Peltzman eds. 1969).

whereby the latter agrees to deal exclusively in the firm's goods. However, there are enough differences between the contract and merger methods of exclusive dealing to warrant separate treatment; exclusive dealing by contract is accordingly discussed in the next section of this chapter.

I have said that any time a firm performs internally an economic function that it could have contracted out, it is vertically integrated (indeed, the idea of vertical integration is implicit in the concept of the firm). In conventional antitrust analysis, however, the term "vertical integration" is reserved for the joinder of two levels or phases of production that are usually performed by different firms. This conventional albeit nonanalytical definition has the advantage of focusing attention on the sorts of vertical integration that might in some circumstances have significant effects on competition; in contrast, it is hard to imagine how, for example, the decision of a firm to perform its legal services in-house could affect competition in any market.

Imagine an industry with two levels, production and distribution: if production is monopolized and distribution is competitive, can the monopolist increase his profits by buying out the distributors? The analysis is parallel to that of tying. If the producer acquires the distributors and increases the retail markup he will have to decrease the producer markup by the same amount. He cannot maximize his profits by charging a price above the monopoly price determined with reference to all relevant costs, including the cost of distribution. It is also necessary, however, to consider the possibility that the acquisition of the distributors will delay new entry at the production level by making it necessary for a new entrant to enter at two levels.[41] We brushed aside a similar argument with respect to tying arrangements by observing that the tied product is usually a trivial adjunct to the tying product. The argument has greater force in the present context. As explained earlier, a firm's cost of production is inversely related to the time interval between the decision to produce and the delivery to the purchaser of the output; the optimum delay will depend in part on the rate at which cost falls with delay; and the rate is likely to be higher for more

41. Delay, not prevent, because a new entrant's costs will be no higher than the existing firm's; each will have costs of distribution as well as of production.

complicated activities, such as operating at two distinct levels in the chain of distribution.[42]

One can quarrel with the assumption that where the existing producer owns all of the distribution outlets a new entrant into production must open its own distribution outlets: if entry into production is anticipated, new firms will enter at the distribution level in order to provide a market for the new producers. But this anticipation merely converts explicit coordination into implicit coordination. A new firm will not enter at the production level until it is reasonably confident that it will have distribution outlets, and new firms will not enter into distribution until they are reasonably confident that there will be producers to supply them. The parallel entry of the new producer and the new distributors could take longer than entry at one level.

In sum, the monopoly producer's acquisition of the existing distribution outlets could delay new entry into production, and the delay would tend to increase the optimum monopoly price. It is also possible, as suggested in chapter 5, that having to enter at the distribution level might increase the costs of the new producer relative to those of the existing firm by increasing the risk premium charged by the suppliers of capital to the new entrant. This factor is independent of the new entrant's choice between creating his own distribution outlets and awaiting the entry of new distributors, since any risk premium charged the latter is an indirect cost of production.

Although the monopoly producer thus might derive benefits from acquiring all of his distributors, there would be costs as well:[43]

1. Acquisition will delay entry rather than prevent it, and when entry does occur the producer who owns all of the existing distribution outlets and refuses to carry his competitors' goods will find himself with excess distributive capacity because he will lose some business to the new entrant. This loss will increase his average costs and decrease his profits compared to what they would have been with a smaller investment in distribution. If the market is growing, the monopolist can avoid this result by opening new distribution outlets at a slower rate than necessary to provide distribution for the entire market, but if this is his policy there will

---

42. See p. 58 supra.
43. As stressed in Sam Peltzman, supra note 40, at 169–70.

be independent distributors for the new entrant's goods when the entrant appears.

2. The firm that attempts to delay the entry of new competitors by precluding the development of an independent distribution system is likely to experience diseconomies of vertical integration. Integration for purposes of exclusion implies that there are no economies of integration (if there were such economies, that would be an independent and socially acceptable reason for integration). And if there are no economies of integration there are probably diseconomies.

3. Finally, a firm's known policy of monopolizing distribution might induce people to start distribution outlets for the sole purpose of being bought out by the firm—a form of lawful extortion. To deter such extortion the acquiring firm might have to resort to predatory pricing, a costly as well as illegal response.

The next question I want to consider is whether vertical integration can be used not just to delay entry but to exclude an existing competitor. Imagine that there are two producers, each with 50 percent of the market, and one decides to eliminate the other by buying all of the distribution outlets and then terminating their purchase of competing products. The other producer will respond by opening his own outlets, or independent firms will open them. In the end, the first producer will own twice as many outlets as he needs to distribute his output and his average costs of distribution will be about twice those of his competitor. This is not an appealing recipe for monopolization.

If for some unlikely reason it is impossible to create new distribution outlets, the analysis resembles that of predatory pricing. The existing distributors are the producers' only customers, and the only possible response by the second producer to the first producer's offer to acquire the distributors is to match the offer. If the first producer can somehow succeed in obtaining control of distribution, and with it a monopoly of production, the price of control will be high. The minimum price for the distributors' assets will be the cost to the second producer of being forced out of business, since the second producer will pay any price up to that cost in order not to be forced out.

Consider finally the case in which all or most of the firms in a competitive industry are acquiring distributors or other customers, a situation in which if the trend is not checked the industry will eventually become completely integrated. New entry might be hindered as a result, but there are two powerful objections to a rule forbidding further vertical acquisition in these circumstances. First, delaying new entry will have no effect if, as assumed, the industry is competitive; price will be at the competitive level regardless of the condition of entry. (To be sure, delaying entry may increase the gains from cartelization, making it more likely that the industry will be cartelized, and vertical integration may reduce the problem of cheating by cartel members;[44] but these effects seem too remote to support a prohibition.) Second, the simultaneous movement of a number of independent producers to acquire customers or suppliers is more likely to reflect the existence of economies of integration than a purpose of hindering entry. At least in an industry of more than a very few firms, it is unlikely that each would act on the belief that if it acquired its distributors, and its competitors happened to do the same (so that no independent distributors remained), collusion would be more profitable because new entry would take longer. Since there are motives for mergers unrelated to either monopolistic intent or economies of integration, one cannot be certain that a series of vertical mergers reflects the existence of substantial economies of vertical integration; but it is more likely to reflect economies than exclusionary motives.

If my analysis is correct, the case for prohibiting vertical mergers is very weak, except possibly where one of the parties to the merger has a monopoly. Even there, the effect of vertical integration in delaying entry seems a tenuous basis for prohibition, especially when it is considered that vertical integration may often be a source of cost savings. To be sure, horizontal mergers may also create cost savings, as we saw in chapter 6, but the difference is that the affirmative case for prohibiting mergers that substantially increase the level of concentration in a market is much stronger. It seems doubtful, therefore, whether vertical mergers should be forbidden save in the unusual case where actually made with an exclusionary or otherwise improper (e.g., to shore up a cartel) intent.

One class of vertical mergers deserves separate discussion. These are mergers between the producer of a final product and the monopoly producer of an input which (unlike distribution) is used in variable proportions with other inputs to produce the final prod-

44. See p. 60 supra.

uct. If the monopoly producer of the input charges a monopoly price to the producer of the final product, the latter will substitute away from that input by using more of some other input. If, however, the input monopolist acquires the final-product producer, this substitution possibility is eliminated. Such a merger should perhaps be viewed as basically horizontal in character, since it is equivalent to the input producer's acquiring the producers of the input that is substituted against his. However, the effect on the output of the final product is complex, since there is not only the elimination of a substitute, which tends to reduce output, but a more efficient combination of inputs (monopoly pricing of the input would lead an independent producer of the final product to use more of other inputs than is optimal, just as monopoly pricing always induces inefficient substitutions), which tends to increase it. Which effect dominates is an empirical question in each case,[45] and probably an unanswerable one in the present state of economic science. There is accordingly no basis, as yet at least, for prohibiting these vertical mergers either. Notice, also, that so long as the monopolized input is indispensable to the production of the final product, the monopolist need not acquire the producer of the latter in order to maximize profits. He need only price the input without regard to the amount used, as by levying a royalty proportioned to the final-product producer's sales for the right to use the input rather than by charging for the input directly.[46]

Exclusive Dealing and the Shoe-Machinery Case

In our original vertical-merger example, the monopoly producer, instead of buying distributors and forbidding them to sell to any newcomer, could have entered into contracts with the (independent) distributors whereby they would agree not to handle the goods of a competing producer. Whether such a contract will have any exclusionary effect depends on its duration. If the contract is terminable on short notice, as in the *Standard Stations* case,[47] the exclusionary effect will normally be zero, since the distributor is free to take on a new supplier at any time. The only exception to

45. See John S. McGee and Lowell R. Bassett, "Vertical Integration Revisited," *J. Law & Econ.* (April 1976), and references cited therein.
46. But end-product royalties have been held to constitute patent misuse. See Zenith Radio Corp. v. Hazeltine Research, Inc., 395 U.S. 100 (1969).
47. Standard Oil Co. v. United States, 337 U.S. 293 (1949).

this general rule is where there are such economies of scale in distribution, or efficiencies in distributing a variety of products at the same outlet, that a distributor forced to choose between handling only the goods of his present supplier and only the goods of other suppliers—the choice forced upon him by the exclusive-dealing contract—will choose the former.[48] The effect is merely to increase the scale necessary for new entry, but by our earlier analysis this may very well increase the time required for entry and hence the opportunity for monopoly pricing.

The exception was inapplicable in the *Standard Stations* case itself, the leading precedent on exclusive dealing. The distributors in that case were retail gasoline dealers. A new entrant into the production of gasoline would have had no trouble obtaining retail outlets, because service stations find it uneconomical to handle more than one brand of gasoline.[49] Nevertheless, the Court invalidated the exclusive-dealing contracts between one of the gasoline suppliers and its retail dealers.

Even an exclusive-dealing contract of indefinite or very long duration is unlikely to be an effective method of monopolization, any more than a vertical merger is. To be sure, compared to a vertical merger, exclusive dealing has the advantage of avoiding possible diseconomies of vertical integration. But in another respect it is distinctly inferior to merger. The distributor who sells his business is indifferent to the amount of competition that remains in the market; he is out of it. But the distributor who agrees to carry the goods of only one producer as part of a scheme to give that producer a monopoly assumes a big risk. Once the producer achieves a monopoly, the distributor will be at his mercy, unless the contractual terms prevent the producer from later charging him a monopoly price or compensate him for the future exactions. But if the distributor obtains such terms, it means the producer will gain nothing from having excluded his competitors.

The shortcomings of exclusive dealing as a method of monopolization are illustrated by the second *United Shoe Machinery* monop-

---

48. Standard Fashions Co. v. Magrane-Houston Co., 258 U.S. 346 (1922), may have been such a case. See Aaron Director & Edward H. Levi, "Law and the Future: Trade Regulation," 51 *Nw. U.L. Rev.* 281, 293 (1956).

49. Thus, despite the Court's invalidation of exclusive-dealing contracts in the gasoline industry, multibrand stations remain extremely rare.

olization case,[50] although the case did not involve exclusive dealing in the strict sense. United, which had a virtual monopoly of
the production of shoe machinery, refused to sell its machines to
customers (shoe manufacturers); it would only lease them, and
for a minimum term of 10 years. The district court found that this
policy impaired the prospects of competing producers by preventing them from entering during the terms of the leases the large
market consisting of United's customers. There are several objections to the court's analysis. One is that competing shoe-machinery
firms would not be foreclosed since they could always buy a shoe
manufacturer. However, this might take a long time to arrange and
could involve diseconomies of integration not borne by United.[51]
A more forceful objection is that the competing producers could
line up United customers in advance of the expiration date of the
leases. Every year about 10 percent of the market would be free
to contract. And since the useful life of shoe machinery is longer
than 10 years, a shoe manufacturer that bought rather than leased
its machinery would rarely be in the market for a new machine
less than 10 years after having purchased one anyway, in which
event a 10-year lease may not be substantially more restrictive
than an unconditional sale.

The point I particularly want to emphasize is that the customers
of United would be unlikely to participate in a campaign to
strengthen United's monopoly position without insisting on being
compensated for the loss of alternative, and less costly (because
competitive), sources of supply. Firms often allocate their purchases among competing suppliers in order to preserve competition in their supply markets. They do this though there is a free-
rider problem. Suppose that a competing shoe-machinery manufacturer offers to lease a machine for $10,000 a year under a lease
terminable at will, while United offers to lease a similar machine
for $9,000 a year but insists on a 10-year lease designed to de-
stroy competing producers and enable United to raise its price to

50. United States v. United Shoe Machinery Corp., 110 F. Supp. 295
(D. Mass.), aff'd per curiam, 347 U.S. 521 (1953). Much of the responsibility for the court's deficient economic analysis appears to lie with the
distinguished economist who served as the court's "law clerk" on the case.
See, e.g., Carl Kaysen, *United States v. United Shoe Machinery Corporation: An Economic Analysis of an Anti-trust Case* 64–72 (1956).

51. Those diseconomies would be avoided, however, if the shoe-machinery manufacturer could count on independent shoe manufacturers entering the market to provide him with customers for his machinery.

$20,000 at the end of the term. The $9,000 price is no bargain to the shoe manufacturers since the deal offered by United imposes an additional cost on the purchaser measured by the present value of the higher price in the future. If that value is, say, $2,000 a year, United's offer is tantamount to charging the lessee $11,000. Each shoe manufacturer might still accept United's offer, figuring either (1) that other shoe manufacturers would lease from the second producer at $10,000, thereby keeping that firm in business and so protecting himself from a United monopoly, or (2) that other manufacturers would lease from United at $9,000, leaving him with higher costs if he paid $10,000 to the second producer but no protection for the future unless the second producer could survive on his patronage alone. However, although each shoe manufacturer *might* reason either way, there is no certainty that he would. If people always thought in such ways, no cartel, other than one that was legally enforceable, would be even partially effective. Each member of the cartel would undersell the cartel price, figuring that everyone else was doing so or that everyone else was selling at the cartel price; under either assumption, cheating pays.

Moreover, the second producer can overcome the free-rider problem by offering to lease the machine for $10,000 on the condition that a specified minimum number of shoe manufacturers lease machines from him. Each lessee would find it advantageous to enter into such a contract rather than pay $9,000 and accept an exclusivity condition from United, since the annual cost of the United lease is actually $11,000.

The record of the *United Shoe Machinery* case indicates that United in fact offered extensive financial concessions to induce shoe manufacturers to lease its machinery. My analysis suggests that if United's purpose was exclusion, these concessions may have dissipated all or most of the potential monopoly profits to be gained by excluding competition. The alternative, nonexclusionary motive for the lease-only policy, mentioned earlier,[52] thus seems a more plausible explanation than exclusion. The fact that the court's injunction against the lease-only policy did not in fact lead to a significant erosion of United's monopoly[53] is some corroboration of the lack of exclusionary effect.

52. See p. 184 supra.
53. See United States v. United Shoe Machinery Corp., 391 U.S. 244 (1968).

To summarize, it is unlikely that a rational profit-maximizing firm will use exclusive dealing as a method of excluding a competitor. But one cannot be sure that it will never do so. Once again, it is necessary in formulating the correct legal rule to relax the assumption that firms invariably adopt profit-maximizing policies. United might have decided, deliberately or through ignorance, to exclude competition at the price of forgoing all or most of its monopoly profits. Even if so, the implications for policy are unclear. It would be odd to punish the monopolist who charged the competitive price, albeit in order to retain his monopoly market share. Surely punishment could not be justified on the theory that the competitors of a monopolist have a right to insist that he facilitate entry by maintaining high prices—the curious, probably inadvertent, theory of the district-court decision in the *Telex* case.

As noted earlier, some exclusionary practices that reduce a monopolist's profits also reduce efficiency. This would be the case if a period of below-cost pricing—the effects of which are parallel to, and no less inefficient than, monopoly pricing—were succeeded by a period of higher monopoly prices than if the monopolist had followed the dominant-firm approach of IBM, before the entry of Telex, or of U.S. Steel in the old *U.S. Steel* monopolization case,[54] where price is set at a level that both generates monopoly profits and attracts new entrants. There is no comparable source of inefficiency, however, in the lease-only case. If United was charging the competitive lease rate because it was for some reason willing to trade monopoly profits for monopoly market share, the efficiency of resource use was enhanced.

This conclusion assumes, of course, that the only social costs of monopoly arise from monopoly pricing. If monopoly led to other sorts of social cost, such as suboptimum innovation or failure to minimize input costs, the conclusion would have to be modified. I have, however, rejected these other grounds as a basis for antitrust policy.[55]

Another exclusionary practice alleged in the *United Shoe Machinery* case was the charging of a single price for machinery and its repair. The court found that this "bundling" had retarded the emergence of an independent shoe-machinery repair industry and so made it more difficult for other manufacturers of shoe ma-

54. See p. 29 supra.
55. See chapter 2 supra.

chinery to compete with United. The theory was that since United was charging its customers for repair service whether or not they utilized it, the customer was discouraged from looking elsewhere for repair service for his United machines.

According to the court, bundling made it difficult for other manufacturers of shoe machinery to compete with United. But only if there were economies of scale in repair would forcing other shoe-machinery producers to arrange for repair services increase their costs relative to those of United. In the absence of such economies the only possible effect of the bundling would be to delay, probably trivially, the entry of new firms into shoe-machinery production. Bundling is simply a form of vertical integration—of manufacture and repair—too minor to be likely to affect entry.

The court also failed to analyze correctly the allegation that United had practiced price discrimination as an exclusionary tactic. The ratio of United's price to its marginal cost was found to be lower in leases of those types of United machinery for which competing producers offered close substitutes than in United's other leases. This relationship is not at all surprising. Competition would increase the elasticity of demand for United's machinery and thereby reduce the profit-maximizing price. It is true that the market would become less attractive to other producers as the price of United's machinery decreased. But it is distinctly odd to characterize this consequence of price discrimination as exclusionary in a pejorative sense. There was no allegation of below-cost pricing; there was merely variance across markets in the proportion of monopoly profit in United's prices. As in *Telex,* the court was telling a monopolist to hold the umbrella of monopoly prices over its competitors. As suggested earlier in this chapter, it might be possible to base a general prohibition of systematic price discrimination on its effect on the amount of resources expended (wastefully) in monopolizing. It is indefensible, however, to try to justify such a prohibition on the ground that it makes entry less attractive. The effect of the discriminating firm's charging lower prices in markets in which demand is more elastic is to increase output in those markets—a good effect of discrimination.

If we place the old *U.S. Steel* case alongside *United Shoe Machinery* and *Alcoa*,[56] the leading monopolization decisions of the mod-

56. United States v. Aluminum Co. of America, 148 F.2d 416 (2d Cir. 1945).

ern period, we discover that the antitrust laws treat the firm that charges low, but not inefficiently low, prices in order to retain a monopoly position more harshly than the firm that seeks to maximize its monopoly profits by charging a high price. Judge Hand criticized Alcoa for expanding its productive capacity in anticipation of increases in the demand for aluminum. U.S. Steel had followed the opposite strategy of limiting output in order to maintain price above the competitive level and had been exonerated. These results are perverse. A monopolist should be encouraged to expand rather than to restrict its output, to reduce prices to meet competition (unless the price reduction is below long-run marginal cost and made with intent to exclude), and to trade high prices and monopoly profits for continued possession of a large market share. The thrust of monopolization law has been to encourage the charging of monopoly prices.

Boycotts

A "boycott," or group refusal to deal, is typically described as a per se violation of section 1 of the Sherman Act, like price fixing. Yet it is distinctly odd to treat boycotts as a substantive antitrust practice comparable to tying, collusive pricing, vertical integration, and the others. A boycott is simply a method of self-help enforcement. It can be used by firms to enforce a cartel, in which event it is bad because cartels are bad; but it can equally well be used, and often is, by firms or individuals to enforce a code of truthful advertising, to minimize credit risk, or to express opposition to communism, or racial discrimination, or the use of nonunion labor. It is therefore no surprise that the antitrust boycott cases involve an extraordinarily heterogenous body of practices, many of which are not exclusionary, at least in any sense relevant to the subject matter of this chapter.

Kiefer-Stewart Co. v. *Joseph E. Seagram & Sons, Inc.*[57] illustrates the nonexclusionary boycott. Two producers had stopped selling to a wholesaler who refused to comply with their resale price ceilings. The only victim of the producers' refusal to deal, the wholesaler, was a customer of the producers; there was no exclusion of a competitor. The Supreme Court, however, treated the refusal to deal as an illegal boycott, thereby implying—unwittingly one assumes—that every price-fixing case is also a boy-

57. 340 U.S. 211 (1951).

cott case since the members of a cartel will naturally refuse to sell to a customer unwilling to pay the cartel price.

Another questionable use of the boycott concept is illustrated by *Silver* v. *New York Stock Exchange*,[58] which held that the New York Stock Exchange had violated the Sherman Act by excluding a broker from access to its facilities without giving him a hearing. The Court seemed to consider the reason for exclusion irrelevant. It did not ask for any evidence that the exclusion of Silver was intended or likely to limit competition, say because he was a price cutter. At the time of the *Silver* case the stock exchange was a cartel,[59] and thus *Silver* can be read as supporting the curious proposition that a cartel has a legal duty—imposed by antitrust law—to accord due process to its members! The *Terminal* case, discussed earlier in this chapter,[60] is in the same vein. The defendants in that case were railroads that controlled the only terminal facilities in St. Louis. These facilities were found to constitute a natural monopoly and the court therefore declined to order them divested. But the court was worried about the access of defendants' competitors to the facilities and accordingly its decree required the defendants to grant competing railroads access on nondiscriminatory terms. It is difficult to understand how such a decree protects the public; its purpose and effect are, rather, to let the defendants' competitors share in the monopoly position enjoyed by the defendants. Again we see a duty to divide monopoly profits equitably derived mysteriously from antitrust principles.

A boycott is a proper object of concern under the antitrust laws, it seems to me, when, and only when, it is used to enforce an anticompetitive practice, as in the *Eastern States*[61] and *Fashion Originators' Guild*[62] cases. The former involved a blacklist by retail lumber dealers of any wholesaler who sold directly to a retail purchaser, that is, to a customer of one of the dealers. The success of the blacklist did not depend on enlisting the customers' cooperation; this distinguishes the case from an exclusive-dealing case.

58. 373 U.S. 341 (1963).

59. See William F. Baxter, "NYSE Fixed Commission Rates: A Private Cartel Goes Public," 22 *Stan. L. Rev.* 675 (1970).

60. United States v. Terminal R.R. Ass'n, 224 U.S. 383 (1912); see p. 179 supra.

61. Eastern States Retail Lumber Dealers' Ass'n v. United States, 234 U.S. 600 (1914).

62. Fashion Originators' Guild of America v. FTC, 312 U.S. 457 (1941).

Success depended on just two things: (1) that the retail dealers possess monopsony power vis-à-vis any single wholesaler (otherwise the threat of refusing to buy from him would not induce him to forgo presumably profitable sales to retail customers); and (2) that the wholesalers not be sufficiently well organized to be able to make a credible threat of cutting off a boycotting retailer from alternative sources of supply.

To be sure, by refusing to deal with direct-selling wholesalers, the retailers lost the profits that they would have obtained by charging wholesalers for the privilege of selling directly to consumers. In other words, the monopsony price might have been lower without the blacklist, which imposed an additional cost on the wholesalers in the form of the lost profits from direct selling. But refusing to deal may have made better sense than depressing the purchase price if either one of two conditions existed: (1) the wholesalers' direct sales to consumers hurt the retailers more than they helped the wholesalers (perhaps because the wholesalers were less efficient at direct selling than the retailers and were able to do so at a profit only because the retailers were charging monopoly prices); or (2) the retail dealers found it easier (cheaper) to agree to cut off direct-selling wholesalers than to agree on an optimum monopsony price.

In *Fashion Originators' Guild*, an association of dress manufacturers threatened to stop selling to any retailer who carried the dresses of competing manufacturers, which the guild called "style pirates." Thus, the guild was trying to force the retailers to buy exclusively from its members. Our earlier discussion indicates that the guild may have had to pay a high price to prevent the "style pirates" from opening retail outlets, but if efficient distribution requires that a variety of clothing styles be made available in each retail store, as it probably does, the costs of opening retail outlets may have been prohibitive for the "style pirates."[63] As further support for the conjecture that this was the rare case where exclusive dealing is an effective exclusionary tactic, I point out that no one suggested any nonexclusionary reason for the boycott.

The guild's main argument was that the exclusion was justified because the style pirates were guilty of a tort. The Supreme Court rejected this contention as unsupported by the facts, but went on to say that the attempted justification was irrelevant. Actually the

63. See pp. 201–2 supra.

justification is decisive, since the antitrust laws were never intended to protect unfair competition.[64]

The *Eastern States* and *Fashion Originators' Guild* decisions are correct because in each case the boycott was designed to enforce an anticompetitive practice, collusion in the first case and exclusive dealing—in one of the rare instances where exclusive dealing can be an effective method of excluding competitors—in the second. Boycotts are properly attacked under the antitrust laws when, and only when, they are employed to enforce a practice that is objectionable on the basis of substantive antitrust policy. Any broader principle would extend the antitrust laws beyond their proper domain.

Although the suggested principle is inconsistent with the Supreme Court's treatment of the tort issue in *Fashion Originators' Guild*, and with much else besides, it seems to be gaining some support at the court-of-appeals level.[65] Furthermore, it has an honorable precedent in the famous and mysterious *Chicago Board of Trade* case.[66] That case involved the legality of a rule adopted by the Board of Trade, a commodities exchange, that forbade members to trade certain grain contracts after the board closed for the day at any price different from the closing price on the board. Apparently the purpose of the rule was to reduce the amount of trading done after hours by members having their own warehouses, and thus to increase the business of the smaller members. In effect, the board was threatening to expel members who tried to exploit a perfectly lawful competitive advantage. Thus the case presented a classic antitrust boycott situation. The Supreme Court held, however, that the board's rule was to be tested by the Rule of Reason. *Chicago Board of Trade* has never been overruled, and its basic (albeit implicit) principle is surely a sensible one: the test of a boycott challenged under the antitrust laws is whether it is being used to enforce a practice that is contrary to the policy of those laws.

---

64. One might argue that allowing the use of boycotts to enforce tort law or other sources of legal rights might be objectionable as interfering with a more or less carefully calibrated or proportioned system of legal remedies, but this would not be an objection founded on the policy of the antitrust laws. Its premise is also questionable.

65. See, e.g., Joseph E. Seagram & Sons, Inc. v. Hawaiian Oke & Liquors, Ltd., 416 F.2d 71 (9th Cir. 1969).

66. Chicago Board of Trade v. United States, 246 U.S. 231 (1918).

For the sake of completeness, I will discuss briefly the unilateral refusal to deal. The reader will recall from chapter 7 the principle of the *Colgate* case, that a seller is free to refuse to deal for reasons sufficient unto himself, unless his refusal is monopolistic. The qualification is important, and unsound. It is an example of the substitution of the syllogism for good sense. The syllogism runs as follows: a unilateral refusal to deal is not actionable under section 1 of the Sherman Act because there is no agreement; but section 2 of the Act does not require agreement; therefore a unilateral refusal to deal, if monopolistic in its likely effect, is actionable under section 2. This syllogism has been used to decide a few cases,[67] but is unwise and should be abandoned. The problem is remedy. A decision holding a group refusal to deal (a boycott in the proper sense of the term) unlawful does not require anyone to deal with anyone else. An *agreement* among a group of firms not to deal is dissolved, leaving the individual firms comprising the group perfectly free to deal or not to deal with the boycotted firm, as they wish; no one is ordered to do business with anyone else. In a unilateral refusal-to-deal case, in contrast, the only effective remedy is an order that the defendant do business with the victim of the refusal to deal. The antitrust court becomes charged with the detailed and continuous supervision of an ongoing commercial relationship, a function that courts are ill equipped to perform effectively.

This analysis suggests another reason why the *Terminal* case was decided incorrectly. Because the district court was unwilling to order the terminal association dissolved, for remedial purposes it had to treat the case as if it involved a unilateral refusal to deal, and thus had to order the association to deal with the competing railroads on nondiscriminatory terms. The decree reads remarkably like the Interstate Commerce Act (not surprisingly since the court borrowed some of the express language of that act). But it cannot be sound antitrust law that, when Congress refuses or omits to regulate some aspect of a natural monopolist's behavior, the antitrust court will step in and, by decree, supply the missing regulatory regime.

---

67. Such as Eastman Kodak Co. v. Southern Photo Materials Co., 273 U.S. 359 (1927), and Otter Tail Power Co. v. United States, 410 U.S. 366 (1973).

9 Toward the Simplification of Antitrust Doctrine

Having completed my examination of substantive antitrust policy, I would like now to develop some of the implications of this examination for the overall structure of antitrust law. There are six major federal antitrust statutes: sections 1 and 2 of the Sherman Act, sections 2, 3, and 7 of the Clayton Act, and section 5 of the Federal Trade Commission Act; and section 2 of the Sherman Act, with its separate prohibitions of monopolizing, attempting to monopolize, and conspiracy to monopolize, is really three statutes in one. If the analysis in the preceding chapters is sound, this elaborate statutory edifice is almost entirely superfluous. Section 1 of the Sherman Act, which forbids contracts, combinations, and conspiracies in restraint of trade, is sufficiently broad to encompass any anticompetitive practice worth worrying about that involves the cooperation of two or more firms, and virtually all of the practices discussed in this book, including all of the exclusionary practices discussed in the last chapter, involve such cooperation. The only truly unilateral acts by which firms can get or keep monopoly power are practices like committing fraud on the Patent Office or blowing up a competitor's plant, and fraud and force are in general adequately punished under other statutes.

I would like to see the antitrust laws other than section 1 of the Sherman Act repealed. My purpose in advancing so academic and impractical a suggestion is not, however, merely to increase the law's elegance. The problem of the redundant antitrust statutes is that they have stimulated an uncritical and unwise expansion in the prohibitory scope of antitrust. The courts have tended to reason that, since section 1 of the Sherman Act is itself so encompassing in its prohibition of anticompetitive practices, any supplementary prohibitions, whether contained in section 2 of the Sherman Act or in the Clayton or Federal Trade Commission Acts, must have been intended to attenuate the requirements in section 1 for proving anticompetitive effect—which were never that demanding—still further. The *Standard Stations* case, discussed in the last chapter, illustrates this tendency. Since, the Court reasoned, section 1 of the Sherman Act would forbid exclusive dealing in any case where a substantial adverse effect on competition was demonstrated, section 3 of the Clayton Act must have been meant to forbid exclusive dealing without proof of such an effect; otherwise it would have been a superfluous addition to the statute books.

But the Court was reasoning unhistorically and unrealistically. The Clayton Act was passed in a climate of concern that the Supreme Court's opinion in the *Standard Oil* case, although it upheld the trial judge's decision ordering the dissolution of the Rockefeller trust, was insufficiently clear-cut in its condemnation of trusts and their tactics.[1] Congress responded by singling out several practices, including exclusive dealing, for condemnation in any case where the possibility of a substantial anticompetitive effect was shown, whatever might be the result under the vague "Rule of Reason" announced in the *Standard Oil* decision. Now it has long been clear, as it may not have been in 1914 when the Clayton Act was enacted in the wake of the cloudy *Standard Oil* opinion, that section 1 of the Sherman Act forbids the use of exclusive dealing as an anticompetitive tactic. The implicit rationale of *Standard Stations*—that whatever the current scope and meaning of section 1, section 3 of the Clayton Act must forbid more than section 1 of the Sherman Act because otherwise section 3 would have no independent significance for antitrust policy—thus ignores completely the circumstances in which the Clayton Act was passed. Congress did not provide in that act that, whatever the Supreme Court might in the future decide was forbidden by the Sherman Act, some attenuated version of the forbidden practice would have to be deemed to violate the Clayton Act in order to maintain a fixed proportion between Sherman and Clayton Act prohibitions.

The 1950 amendments to section 7 of the Clayton Act present a similar interpretive problem. As mentioned in chapter 6, these amendments were responsive in part to the Supreme Court's *Columbia Steel* opinion. The legislative history of the 1950 amendments indicates that Congress did not like the standard announced

---

1. See chapter 3 supra. Justice Harlan's demagogic dissenting opinion in the *Standard Oil* case accused the majority of having emasculated the Sherman Act by interpreting it in light of the "Rule of Reason" announced in the majority opinion.

in *Columbia Steel*, which, as we saw in Chapter 6, was both excessively vague and strongly suggestive of judicial inability to grasp how a merger that did not create an actual monopoly could still be anticompetitive. What cannot fairly be inferred from the legislative history is that, since the Sherman Act, *properly* interpreted, forbids any substantially anticompetitive practice, section 7 of the Clayton Act must forbid a class of mergers that cannot fairly be described as being substantially anticompetitive, so as to remain a more stringent provision than section 1.

Among the most serious consequences of statutory redundancy in the antitrust field are those resulting from attempts to give a separate meaning to section 2 of the Sherman Act and distinguish among the three violations specified in that section. An example of the mischief to which section 2 has given rise is Judge Learned Hand's famous opinion in the *Alcoa* case, alluded to in the last chapter. Were it not for section 2, the only issue in *Alcoa* would have been whether the defendant had committed any anticompetitive practices, such as mergers or predatory pricing, and the answer to this question—"no"—would have been the end of the case. But on this view the offense of monopolization is simply the commission of section 1 violations by a monopolist, a view which, while not inconsistent with what little we know of the framers' intentions in making monopolization a separate offense, hardly gives the concept of monopolization an important place in the statutory scheme. Perhaps that is why Judge Hand read section 2 to forbid any active efforts to obtain or maintain monopoly power even if the efforts did not violate section 1, so that Alcoa was guilty of monopolization because it had tried to satisfy as much of the growth in demand for aluminum as possible by expanding its own capacity, instead of sitting back and letting its competitors, or new entrants, provide for the growth of the market.

This theory of monopolization is a bad one because it encourages inefficient conduct. If a firm enjoys a monopoly position for many years, as did Alcoa, without engaging in any anticompetitive practices, there is a strong presumption that either a monopolistic organization of the market is the most efficient or that the monopolist is selling at the competitive price (perhaps because he really doesn't have any monopoly power). If in these circumstances the monopolist is told to let his market share decline or be punished under section 2, he will raise his price and thereby encourage the expansion or entry of firms that may be less efficient; thus the consequences of his monopoly will be aggravated.

The *Alcoa* approach, which had never attracted much judicial support, was rejected in the Tenth Circuit's *Telex* decision, discussed in the last chapter. IBM's action in reducing price to hold on to a market share assumed to be of monopolistic proportions[2] was a clear case of "monopolizing" in the *Alcoa* sense, even if the price reduction was in no sense predatory; IBM was a monopolist actively endeavoring to maintain its market share. The logic of *Alcoa* would have required IBM to continue charging a monopoly price so as to foster the growth of its competitors and accelerate the decline in its market share. I suspect that if the plaintiff in *Alcoa* had been a competing aluminum producer which was claiming that the Sherman Act required Alcoa to maintain a monopoly price so as to foster and protect the plaintiff's expansion, Judge Hand would have perceived the perversity of a doctrine that forbids a monopolist to compete for new business in his market.

The opinion in the *United Shoe Machinery* case discussed in the last chapter represents an uneasy compromise between Judge Hand's position and the view that monopolization is simply a violation of section 1 committed by a monopolist or resulting in monopoly. The *United Shoe* opinion, unlike *Alcoa,* requires proof of exclusionary practices. They need not, however, be violations of section 1; they may be "honestly industrial."[3] It is extremely difficult, however, to conceive of practices midway, as it were, between building plants, cutting prices (but not below cost), and otherwise using "honestly industrial"[4] practices to limit a competitor's expansion, on the one hand, and committing violations of section 1 to the same end, on the other. Consider for example the ten-year leases in the case. If the court's analysis of the leases was correct, their effect was exclusionary and was not justified by any showing that a shorter term would have imposed additional costs on United or its customers. In other words, the leases were unreasonably

---

2. The Tenth Circuit found that the district court had incorrectly defined the market; but, in discussing the contention that IBM's price cuts were evidence of monopolization, it assumed for purposes of that discussion that IBM did have a monopolistic market share.

3. See 110 F. Supp. at 341, 344–345.

4. Indeed, the expression, which Judge Wyzanski picked up in the *United Shoe Machinery* case, had been used by Hand in *Alcoa* to describe Alcoa's lawful efforts to maintain its monopoly. See 148 F.2d at 431.

anticompetitive in the circumstances of the case—and hence unlawful under section 1.

There is no place in a rational system of antitrust law for a
separate doctrine of monopolization. There are unreasonably anticompetitive practices, and whether or not a practice is unreasonably anticompetitive sometimes depends on the market share of
the firm or firms employing it (an example being the exchange of
price information, discussed in chapter 7). The task of antitrust
policy is to identify such practices and forbid them, and it is a
task to which section 1 of the Sherman Act is fully adequate. The
only nonconsensual practices by which a firm can restrict competition involve fraud or force for which normally adequate sanctions are provided in other statutes; in any event, I can think of
no important examples of monopolies founded exclusively on such
practices.

There is equally little reason for having separate offenses of
attempting, and of conspiring, to monopolize. If a firm has engaged in a practice unreasonably restrictive of competition, it has
violated section 1 regardles of whether monopoly has been achieved.
The main practical consequence of the separate doctrine of attempted monopolization has been to promote the erroneous view
that *wanting* to have a monopoly, coupled with efforts to obtain
it, whether by methods anticompetitive (mergers, predatory pricing, or whatever) or competitive (better product, lower costs, better service), is unlawful.[5] This was the idea behind the district
court's opinion in the *Telex* case. As for conspiracy to monopolize, any such conspiracy is also a conspiracy in restraint of trade,
which violates section 1.

If one could write on a completely clean slate, it would be best,
I believe, to substitute for the numerous substantive provisions of
antitrust law a simple prohibition against agreements, explicit or
tacit, that unreasonably restrict competition. The courts would of

5. For an articulate refutation of this idea see Union Leader Corp. v.
Newspapers of New England, Inc., 180 F. Supp. 125, 140 (D. Mass. 1959),
modified on other grounds, 284 F.2d 582 (1st Cir. 1960), and for good
recent discussions of the attempt offense see Edward H. Cooper, "Attempts
and Monopolization: A Mildly Expansionary Answer to the Prophylactic
Riddle of Section Two," 72 *Mich. L. Rev.* 373 (1974); Donald F. Turner,
"The Scope of 'Attempt to Monopolize,' " 30 *The Record of the Assn. of
the Bar of the City of N.Y.* 487 (1975).

course develop specific rules of illegality, as they have done with section 1 of the Sherman Act. But they would not be distracted from what is the sufficiently difficult task of appraising the competitive effects and possible efficiency justifications of business practices by having to worry about the meaning to be assigned to amendatory provisions typically added in reaction to recent and often transitory expressions of judicial antitrust policy, and without consideration of how the new provision fits together with the existing ones.

IV Administering the Antitrust Laws

10   The Problem of Enforcement

      The previous chapters of this book presented a number of suggestions for the reform of antitrust doctrine. If all of these suggestions were adopted, antitrust policy would still remain in a highly unsatisfactory state. It is not enough to have good doctrine; it is also necessary to have enforcement mechanisms that assure, at reasonable cost, a reasonable degree of compliance with the law. Antitrust is seriously deficient in such mechanisms.

Remedies

      The question of enforcement has three major aspects: remedies, enforcers, and procedures. The basic objective of a remedial system is to deter people from violating the law. Another is to compensate the victims of the violators, but I regard this as subsidiary because a well-designed system of deterrence would reduce the incidence of antitrust violations to a low level and because, as we shall see, such a system would, as a by-product, assure adequate compensation except in those instances where the costs of administering compensation were prohibitive.

      The way in which we deter an activity is by making it costly to engage in, and a key question is: how costly? We could fine antitrust violators $1, or hang them. How do we decide what the proper punishment is? The answer depends in the first instance on the gravity of the offense. As a first approximation, the penalty for an antitrust violation should be such as to impose on the violator a cost, whether in pecuniary or nonpecuniary terms, equal to the cost that his violation imposed on society. This criterion is not derived from notions of symmetry or from the biblical notion of "an eye for an eye." It is a criterion of efficiency—and hence an especially appropriate one to use in designing remedies for antitrust violations. If the penalty for violating the antitrust laws were less than the cost of the violation to society, the potential violator, in deciding whether to commit a violation, would reckon the cost to him (the punishment cost, since he presumably cares nothing about the consequences of his conduct for the society at large) at a figure lower than the social cost. This would result in an excessive amount of unlawful activity, just as a divergence between private and social cost will lead to an excessive amount of pollution. If, on the other hand, the penalty for a violation is set at a level higher than the social cost of the violation, we may have too little unlawful activity: some illegal acts will be deterred that confer benefits on society greater than the costs they impose.[1] A good example would be a monopolistic merger that imposed costs of $1 million on society but that conferred benefits, as a result of the lower costs of a monopolistic organization of the market in question, of $2 million. If, as I have argued throughout this book, the purpose of the antitrust laws is to promote efficiency, such a merger should be permitted, yet it may be deterred if the penalty is set substantially above the social cost of the violation.

The problem of the excessive penalty could be solved, in principle at least, by limiting the prohibitions of antitrust to practices that impose a net social loss on society. This would mean that it would be open to the defendant in every case to show that his conduct produced a benefit in excess of the harm caused. But this approach would impose a heavy burden on the courts and the parties, and mistakes would be frequent. The alternative is to set a penalty equal to the social costs of the practice and let the defendant decide for himself whether the benefits exceed those costs. This is the preferable approach in general but it will not work well in cases where the social costs of a violation are very difficult to quantify. An example is a merger that increases concentration. In principle, the social costs of such a merger could be quantified by measuring the increase in market price brought about by the merger. But in practice this would be extremely difficult to do, if only because the firm resulting from the merger might decide to hold down its price until, through passage of time, it became impossible to disentangle the effect of the merger from that of other determinants of the current price level. In such a case the only feasible remedy is to stop the merger by an injunction or undo it by divestiture.

1. On the economic theory of punishment see Gary S. Becker, "Crime and Punishment: An Economic Approach," 76 *J. Pol. Econ.* 169 (1968), and for a nontechnical presentation Richard A. Posner, *Economic Analysis of Law* ch. 25 (1973).

Structural remedies such as divestiture are slow, costly, frequently ineffectual, and sometimes anticompetitive.[2] That we are sometimes compelled to utilize them instead of monetary penalties is another example of the heavy price that is paid for the failure to have developed an economic approach to proving collusive pricing. If we knew how to identify collusive pricing in markets where the sellers did not commit detectable acts of collusion, there would be no need to punish horizontal mergers (save mergers that created a monopoly);[3] we would only need to punish collusive pricing. Exclusionary practices, since they impose costs on competing firms that are ordinarily quantifiable without too much difficulty, can readily be controlled by penalties designed to bring the costs of unlawful conduct home to the actor. Clearly, the monetary penalty should be the normal remedy in antitrust cases; nonmonetary remedies should be reserved for cases where a monetary penalty would be infeasible.

I have said that the penalty should be designed to place the social costs of the violation on the violator. It is easy to jump to the conclusion that the penalty should be equal to those costs, but this conclusion would be incorrect in those cases where the violation was concealable. If, because of concealability, the probability of being punished for a particular antitrust violation is less than unity, the prospective violator will discount (i.e., multiply) the punishment cost by that probability in determining the expected punishment cost for the violation. The result will be to drive a wedge between the social cost of the violation and the private cost to the violator, unless the punishment cost is appropriately higher than the social cost. For example, suppose that the social cost of a particular price-fixing conspiracy is $1 million, but the probability of the conspirators' being apprehended and punished is only .25. If the fine is set at $1 million the conspirators, assuming they are risk neutral,[4] will discount the fine by .25, which yields an ex-

2. See chapter 5 supra.
3. See p. 26 supra.
4. An individual is risk neutral if he is indifferent as between an expected cost (or value) and its certain equivalent. Thus, a risk-neutral individual would be indifferent as between a 1 percent chance of having to pay $100 and the certainty of having to pay $1. A risk-averse individual would consider himself worse off if forced to accept the expected choice rather than its certain equivalent, while a risk preferrer would react the opposite way. Corporations are generally assumed to be risk neutral since any riskiness involved in the corporation's business can be eliminated or

pected punishment cost of only $250,000—far below the social cost of the conspiracy. The correct fine is calculated by *dividing* the social cost of the violation by the probability of apprehension and punishment. In the last example this would yield $4 million, the optimal fine.[5]

I have spoken thus far as though the social costs of price fixing (or any other violation, other than a horizontal merger) could be determined without difficulty. This is of course not the case. In price-fixing cases the courts have used as their measure of cost the difference between the competitive and collusive price, multiplied by the number of units sold at the collusive price during the relevant time period. This is an incorrect measure because it leaves out the cost resulting from the reduced output of the monopolist.[6] It would not be insuperably difficult to measure this additional cost; the only additional information that is necessary is the elasticity of demand at the collusive price. The appendix to this book contains some simple formulas that can be used for estimating the total social costs of collusion.[7]

The determination of the costs of most exclusionary practices is even more straightforward. The method by which the exclusionary practice operates is to impose costs on a competitor and thus discourage him from competing with the firm utilizing the practice. If that firm is made liable for the costs imposed on his victim, the exclusionary practice will be ineffective; the victim will not be deterred by a practice that costs his predator very heavily, and

minimized by the individual shareholder; he can combine his shares in the corporation with other shares or other assets so as to create a portfolio that will be as risky or as risk-free as he desires, and therefore the corporation needn't worry about its shareholders' attitude toward risk. Of course, if the corporation's managers are not running the firm in the shareholders' interest—a popular, though unverified, theory—their personal attitudes toward risk may become relevant in determining the impact of antitrust sanctions containing various amounts of risk. However, nothing essential in my analysis would be affected by modifying the assumption of risk neutrality utilized in the text.

5. That is, since $E(C_p) = pf = C_s$ (where $E(C_p)$ is the expected punishment cost, f the fine, p the probability that it will be imposed, and C_s the social cost of the violation), $f = C_s/p$. I ignore, as inessential to my main point, the costs of apprehending and punishing the violator, which ought properly to be added to the social cost of the violation before division by p.

6. See pp. 10–11 supra.

7. See pp. 250–55 infra.

himself not at all since his losses are compensated. Accordingly, the appropriate measure of damages in an exclusionary-practice case is the cost of the practice to the intended victims. It may be argued that this measure is inadequate where the exclusionary practice assumes the form of a threat rather than actual exclusion. But the essence of a successful threat is that it be credible.[8] A threat to exclude would not be credible if carrying out the threat would require the threatener to compensate the victim fully for the costs of the exclusionary conduct.

Compared to the scheme of antitrust remedies described above, the actual remedial scheme found in the antitrust statutes leaves much to be desired. There is, to begin with, the unnecessary and therefore inappropriate reliance on the criminal sanction, including imprisonment (now for as long as three years). Imprisonment should be regarded as a sanction of last resort, in general and with particular reference to antitrust. First, it is difficult to translate a monetary sum (the costs of a particular price-fixing conspiracy, say) into a nonpecuniary cost—so many days in prison. The effort to do so is almost certain to lead to excessive leniency. Second, imprisonment is a much costlier sanction for society to administer than the collection of a fine. Imprisonment consumes real resources, not the least of which is the legitimate production of the imprisoned individual, which is lost during his term of imprisonment. Fines involve no such waste. Apart from (ordinarily slight) collection costs, the entire loss to the defendant who is fined is offset by an equal benefit to the taxpayers (or whoever else receives the fine). A fine is a transfer payment that only negligibly reduces the aggregate wealth of the society. Not so with imprisonment: the cost to the defendant of being imprisoned is a deadweight loss to society.

Where violators are judgment-proof, society is compelled to resort to imprisonment or some other method of nonpecuniary sanction despite the advantages of the fine. But inability to pay judgments is not a problem in the antitrust field. True, individuals are frequently joined as defendants in antitrust suits—the individuals who participated actively in whatever violation the corporate defendant is accused of having committed—and, although they are a good deal more affluent than the common criminal, they might

8. See pp. 186–87 supra.

sometimes be unable to pay judgments measured by the social costs of their violations. But I consider this a detail, for it is in general unimportant whether the individual corporate employees are joined as defendants in antitrust cases. A corporation has effective methods of preventing its employees from commiting acts that impose huge liabilities on it. A sales manager whose unauthorized participation in a price-fixing scheme resulted in the imposition of a $1-million fine on his employer would thereafter, I predict, have great difficulty finding responsible employment, and this prospect would appear to be sufficient to exert a substantial deterrent effect, one at least comparable to the generally light individual fines and very short prison sentences of existing law.[9]

Merely to abolish imprisonment in antitrust cases would not constitute a sufficient reform of the antitrust penalty structure. It would leave in effect a fine remedy and a damages remedy which, considered either separately or in combination, are inadequate. The maximum antitrust fine is only $1 million, which is plainly too little. The social costs of a particular price-fixing conspiracy or other antitrust violation may greatly exceed $1 million, and, as explained earlier, the penalty for a concealable offense such as price fixing should be greater than the social costs imposed by the particular conspiracy in suit. To be sure, damages are awarded in private antitrust suits and are automatically trebled, but that is not the correct way to handle the problem of concealment. This multiple was set (back in 1890) and it has been maintained without any effort to determine whether the probability (determined with reference either to all antitrust violators or to specific classes of violators such as price fixers) that a violator will be caught is anywhere near .33. Admittedly, the estimation of such probabilities presents a formidable, perhaps impossible, task since we do not know how many antitrust violations escape detection. But it is clear that many antitrust violations are so difficult to conceal that the probability of detection is much greater than one-third. Mergers and most exclusionary practices, such as tying agreements

9. On the infrequency of the imposition of prison sentences in antitrust cases, especially where no extraneous element such as violence or labor racketeering is involved, see table 3 in chapter 3 supra. I do not know what the average fine for an individual in an antitrust case is, but I do know that it is much below the (until very recently) statutory maximum of $50,000 (now $100,000).

(and even most cases of predatory pricing), fall into this category. The provision of treble damages in such cases serves simply to draw excessive enforcement resources into attempts to discover and prosecute such violations and to expand the prohibitions of the law. Only single damages should be available in such cases.

Enforcers

Once it is agreed that the distinctive sanctions of the criminal process have little role to play in the antitrust field, the question arises why it is necessary to have any public remedy for antitrust violations. Why not rely entirely on private damage actions? It would of course be necessary to build into the damage remedy some appropriate multiple to reflect the concealability of many antitrust violations, but this is already a feature of the private damage remedy in antitrust. There are several reasons for nonetheless retaining the public action, although I own to some uncertainty as to how compelling these reasons are. The first is our inability (at least currently) to quantify the effects of many antitrust violations, such as mergers that increase concentration. This problem could perhaps be overcome, however, by the device of the "private attorney general" (I postpone for a moment the question whether this much privatization of the antitrust enforcement process would be desirable). The second reason for retaining a public remedy is the difficulty of administering the private damage action in situations in which the victims of the antitrust violation are so numerous that the individual injury is small although the aggregate injury may be very substantial as in the tetracycline price-fixing conspiracy. The ingenious answer of the private plaintiff's antitrust bar has been the antitrust class action. This is not the place to discuss the intricacies of the class action and the substantial problems, about which I and others have written,[10] that it raises. I am not persuaded that these problems are insurmountable.[11] The class action appears to be a workable method of aggregating a multitude of small claims, and while it is possible to imagine alternatives ranging from middlemen's suits to state *parens patriae* actions to

10. See Kenneth W. Dam, "Class Actions: Efficiency, Compensation, Deterrence, and Conflict of Interest," 4 *J. Leg. Studies* 47 (1975), and references cited therein.
11. See Richard A. Posner, "An Economic Approach to Legal Procedure and Judicial Administration," 2 *J. Leg. Studies* 399, 439–41 (1973).

a preemptive federal damage suit, it is not at all clear that any of them is superior to—or even markedly different from—the class action.

The third and most substantial objection to exclusive reliance on the private damage action to provide the sole remedy for antitrust violations is that the private plaintiff's bar cannot be relied upon to exercise appropriate self-restraint. Students of the antitrust laws have been appalled by the wild and woolly antitrust suits that the private bar has brought—and won. It is felt that many of these would not have been brought by a public agency and that, in short, the influence of the private action on the development of antitrust doctrine has been on the whole a pernicious one.

There is some basis for concern that the growth of the private antitrust action has resulted in an overexpansion of antitrust liability. The resources of the public agencies—the Justice Department and the Federal Trade Commission—are limited to what the Congress appropriates each year, and traditionally the appropriations for antitrust enforcement have been quite parsimonious in relation to the universe of potential antitrust suits. The tight budget constraint has forced the agencies to be selective in their choice of cases. Although they might select the silliest cases to bring, there is no reason in theory why they should[12] and no evidence that they do. The Justice Department's Merger Guidelines are a good example of how an antitrust enforcement agency subject to a budget constraint that forces the agency to bring far fewer cases than it could win under current interpretations of the antitrust statutes will generally try to define a class of more serious violations and limit its enforcement activities to them.[13] The private plaintiff and bar labor under no budget constraint. They have an incentive to bring any case where the expected judgment is greater than the expected cost of litigating the case.

---

12. See Richard A. Posner, "The Behavior of Administrative Agencies," 1 *J. Leg. Studies* 305 (1972), reprinted in *Essays in the Economics of Crime and Punishment* 215 (Gary S. Becker & William M. Landes eds. 1974).

13. Compare Department of Justice Merger Guidelines, 1 CCH Trade Reg. Rep. ¶ 4510 (1968), with United States v. Pabst Brewing Co., 384 U.S. 546 (1966), and United States v. Von's Grocery Co., 384 U.S. 270 (1966).

It is possible, however, that this problem is largely a transitional one. In the 1960s, when most of the important antitrust cases were still government cases and the typical private plaintiff was (or at least was believed to be) a "free rider" on some earlier government suit,[14] the Supreme Court—in part I believe in order to lighten its own antitrust docket—wrote the enforcement agencies virtually a blank check,[15] perhaps trusting to the continued exercise by the agencies of a sober self-restraint in filling in the blanks. At just about this time the private suit was gathering its astonishing momentum,[16] greatly assisted by the Court's blank check, which the private bar now began busily to fill in. The private action caught the courts off guard. Previously, as I have said, most important antitrust cases were government cases, and there were few of these, the Justice Department rarely bringing more than fifty a year.[17] Moreover, these cases were appealed directly to the Supreme Court. As a result few district judges and fewer circuit judges were experienced in the antitrust field. Now they were hit by thousands of private antitrust suits and the only guidance to deciding them consisted of the Supreme Court's sweeping and uncritical declarations of antitrust liability.

With the more careful, or at any rate more conservative, Supreme Court in antitrust matters that we now seem to have,[18] and with evidence in some recent court-of-appeals opinions of a reaction to the excesses of a plaintiff-oriented antitrust law,[19] there is some basis for hope that the field may be calming down a little and that the ultimate impact of the private action on antitrust doctrine may not be so pernicious as currently appears. Perhaps it will eventually be possible to rely even more heavily than we do today on the damage remedy in the enforcement of the antitrust law. And it would be a serious mistake to regard the impact of

14. Taking advantage of the provision in section 5(a) of the Clayton Act that makes certain judgments in government suits prima facie evidence of illegality in a subsequent private suit.

15. As in the *Von's* case; see pp. 106–8 supra.

16. See p. 34 supra (table 4).

17. See p. 25 supra (table 1).

18. See pp. 109–10 supra.

19. See, e.g., Telex Corp. v. International Business Mach. Corp., 510 F.2d 894 (10th Cir. 1975); ITT Corp. v. GT&E, 518 F.2d 913 (9th Cir. 1975).

the private suit as entirely negative. Private actions have made an enormous contribution to the effective enforcement of the antitrust laws against collusive pricing.[20]

Moreover, it is easy to exaggerate the degree of self-restraint exercised by public antitrust enforcers. For example, the Justice Department's Antitrust Division, the most distinguished component of the public antitrust enforcement system, several years ago brought a monopolization suit against IBM which at this writing is in trial. Shortly before the commencement of trial the division's lawyers incorporated as a part of the government's case the allegations made by Telex in its groundless suit against IBM, discussed in the last chapter. As this example suggests, while in principle the division's limited resources force it to concentrate on the most serious violations, the practice is often different. The Antitrust Division is made up of several hundred trial lawyers (many of them engaged at any given time in investigation and other activities preparatory or incidental to trial), under a tiny staff of supervisors. The supervisors exercise little in the way of supervision, review, control, or direction. The reasons appear to be several. There are very few supervisors; most of them are trial lawyers who have been rewarded for their long and faithful service by being elevated to supervisory jobs; and they have little effective control over their nominal subordinates, who enjoy de facto tenure partly because of the regulations governing federal-government employment and partly because of the friendly relations that these lawyers sometimes develop with influential members of Congress or of congressional staffs. Above all, there appear to be few if any rewards for exercising effective control over the division. The most distinguished head of the Antitrust Division since Thurman Arnold, Donald Turner, who was responsible for the Merger Guidelines, the increased attention paid by the division to competition in the regulated industries, the upgrading of the status of economists within the division, and the first attempt to exercise a critical review over the trial lawyers' initiatives, was rewarded for his achievements with widespread hostility not only within the division but among congressional supporters of antitrust, other "liberals," and the members of the antitrust defendants' as well as plaintiffs' bar. (The antitrust defense bar likes the government to bring many antitrust cases; if it did not, the demand for antitrust defense

20. See pp. 73–74 and nn. 51–52 supra.

specialists would decline. Turner's unwillingness to rubber-stamp the cases proposed by the division's trial lawyers resulted in a diminution in the number of complaints issued by the division during his term of office.)

The initiative in the division lies with the trial lawyers—along with the execution, the theorizing, the design of remedies, and virtually every other aspect of the enforcement process.[21] Trial lawyers tend to be combative rather than reflective, and the division's trial lawyers, because they are relatively poorly paid, tend to be young or mediocre, or to be zealots. They are not the right people to be the custodians of the government's antitrust policy, but that is what they are. In these circumstances, while limiting private enforcement would reduce the total amount of antitrust enforcement, it might not greatly increase its quality.

Two reforms would do much to cure the remaining excesses of the private action. First, as explained in this chapter, the trebling of damages in cases where the alleged violation is not the kind that can normally be concealed is wholly unjustified in terms of the theory of sanctions; it merely attracts excessive resources into private antitrust enforcement and should be discontinued. The practical implementation of this reform is not without difficulty, however. Any attempt to compile a list of practices judged insufficiently concealable to warrant a trebling of damages would be tedious, incomplete, and controversial. A much cruder, but also much simpler, alternative would be to treble damages only in a suit brought by a customer or supplier of the defendant, and never in a suit brought by a competitor. The justification for this distinction is that a firm is likely to be well aware of misconduct directed against it by a competing firm, whereas a customer may find it very difficult to discover whether the price it pays is a competitive or a cartel price, and a supplier may find it almost impossible to discover whether the price it is receiving is competitive or monopolistic.

Second, while the plaintiff who prevails in an antitrust damage action is entitled under the law to an award of reasonable attorneys' fees, there is no similar provision for the case where the

21. One result is that contradictory theories of antitrust liability frequently coexist within the division, their resolution being left to the courts. See, e.g., United States v. Citizens & Southern National Bank, 422 U.S. 86 (1975).

defendant wins. There is no basis for such asymmetrical treatment. If the plaintiff puts the defendant to the expense of defending against charges that prove to be unfounded, the plaintiff ought to be required to reimburse the reasonable cost of the defense. Amending the law to this effect would significantly reduce the number of frivolous private antitrust actions that are brought.

Procedures

Even if the foregoing administrative reforms were adopted, one would still be concerned about the enormous cost of antitrust proceedings, and about the substantial probability of error that is inherent in the unwieldy and archaic procedures that are responsible, at least in part, for that cost. The monstrous, indeed grotesque, proportions of the modern antitrust suit are difficult to convey to the uninitiated. At this writing, the government's suit against IBM has been in trial for six months and completion of the government's case in chief is expected to take another year; it is estimated that the trial record will exceed a *million* pages in length. In the government's suit, also pending, against AT&T, the defendants have estimated that the government's request for the production of documents would require them to examine more than seven *billion* documents and that compliance with the request would cost several hundred million dollars. These are unusual cases. In a typical antitrust case, trial might take "only" two or three months and the trial record might run to "only" 10–15,000 pages. But has the reader any idea what it costs to try an antitrust case for several months? Or how much of the trial will be taken up with the presentation of facts not seriously in dispute? Or how difficult it is for the human mind to assimilate a 10,000-page trial record? The ordinary antitrust case is unmanageable, cases like the IBM and AT&T suits being in the nature of malignant growths on the judicial system.

The basic problem, I believe, is that the traditional sequence and format of the Anglo-American court trial are ill-adapted to the litigation of complex economic issues. First the plaintiff puts in his evidence, much of it merely the raw data of his case and all of it subject to cross-examination designed to undermine the trier's confidence in the plaintiff and his witnesses; then there is plaintiff's redirect examination designed to restore that confidence; then defendant does the same, subject of course to cross-examination and redirect and recross, etc.; and finally the plaintiff puts on his rebuttal case, again subject to cross-examination, redirect, and recross. As a result of this sequencing, the evidence bearing on a particular issue is not presented all at once. Weeks or even months may elapse between the presentation of the plaintiff's version of an event, in his case in chief, and the defendant's version, presented after the plaintiff has completed his case; and weeks later there may be still more evidence on the same issue, presented in the plaintiff's rebuttal. Not only does evidence on an issue get introduced piecemeal, at different stages of the trial, but much of the trial is taken up with evidence not addressed to any issue in dispute but introduced simply in order to create a favorable atmosphere. And there are constant interruptions in the presentation of evidence, for cross-examination, objections, and procedural motions.

This is an inefficient, and ineffective, process for getting the relevant facts before the trier of facts in a comprehensible form, and I would like to suggest a different process. (I put to one side to what extent the suggested reform could be implemented within the framework of the existing Federal Rules of Civil Procedure or would require an amendment to the rules or perhaps new legislation.) The process I propose is the following: At the completion of pretrial discovery, each party would prepare a chronological narrative of the facts relevant to his case, including defenses and replies thereto. The parties would then sit down together and, to the extent possible, hammer out an agreed-upon narrative of the relevant facts. Sanctions would be imposed for the unreasonable refusal of one party to agree to inclusions or exclusions requested by the other. The narrative might be incomplete, for to the extent that there were facts in genuine dispute the parties would not be able to reconcile their differing versions.

At trial, the agreed-upon narrative would be presented to the trier of the facts in a writing that would constitute the basic trial record. The introduction of other documents and of testimony would be limited to those facts not covered by the narrative, i.e., the facts to which the parties had been unable—bargaining as it were in good faith and reasonably—to agree upon. The "live" portions of the trial would constitute, together with the agreed-upon narrative, the record upon which the trier of facts, whether judge or jury, would base its decision.

The success of this scheme in reducing the length and compressing the record of the antitrust trial would of course depend upon the willingness of the lawyers for the parties to negotiate a comprehensive narrative of the undisputed facts. That willingness would in turn be a function of the rewards for such negotiation and the penalties for arbitrary refusals to agree. Purely as an example of the kind of reward-penalty that might be effective in inducing lawyers to forgo the luxury of trying issues not actually in dispute, a party whose attorney had refused to agree to the inclusion in the agreed-upon narrative of a fact later found by the trier of facts at the trial to be true might be required to pay the opposing party $1,000 plus the costs of establishing the fact at trial. If negotiations over the agreed-upon narrative broke down over wording, length, form, sequence, etc., the matter would be referred to arbitration, and, if the arbitrator found that the party refusing to accept language proposed by his opponent had acted unreasonably, he would order him to pay $1,000 to the opposing party plus the costs of the arbitration.

I have not attempted to work out the details of the suggested reform. It is not the details that are important, but the principle that the basic record of an antitrust trial should consist not of the raw data of testimony and documents but of a factual narrative introduced without any backup materials, and binding on the trier of facts. The presentation of documents and testimony should be confined to the few issues that are genuinely in dispute.

I shall offer a concrete example of how the suggested procedure would differ from the present practice. Suppose that the only contested issue in a merger case was whether the acquired firm was failing at the time of the merger.[22] Under the present trial system the executives of the acquired firm would be called by the defendant to testify about the financial position of the company prior to the merger, the efforts they made to find alternative purchasers, the consequences of failure, etc. Probably defendant would also introduce supporting documents—financial statements, correspondence with prospective purchasers, etc. And there would be cross-examination, redirect examination, and introduction of testimony and documents by the plaintiff (subject of course to cross-examination), rebuttal testimony, and so forth. Under the procedure I have proposed, in contrast, the parties would get together before the trial and prepare a narrative that would describe, step by step, the changes in the acquired company's finan-

22. See pp. 20–22 supra.

cial position and the measures taken by the firm to identify and approach prospective purchasers, the prospects' responses, and the negotiations with the acquiring firm. The narrative would resemble the findings of fact that a trial judge prepares on the basis of the trial record, and would be introduced in trial in lieu of testimony or documents concerning any of the facts recited in the narrative. There would be a "live" hearing only to the extent that the narrative omitted facts because they were irreconcilably in dispute— e.g., whether on a given date the acquired company in fact had a deficit of $1 million, whether the first prospective purchaser approached said "yes" or "no," whether another prospect was rejected because he offered a low price or because he was not thought seriously interested in purchasing the company.

No factual dispute would be submitted for hearing until it was clear that it could not be decomposed into more basic facts that were undisputed. For example, if the dispute over the size of the acquired firm's deficit turned on the inference to be drawn from a particular write-off of a debt as uncollectible, the write-off and its surrounding circumstances would be set forth in the narrative, leaving the size of the deficit to be inferred from these undisputed facts by the trier of facts. Thus, there would be no live hearing at all in the case if no basic facts, but only the inferences to be drawn from them, were in dispute. For example, the only dispute might be over whether the agreed-upon facts showed that the acquired company was "failing" in the legal sense. This would be an issue of ultimate fact for the trier of facts to decide, but on the basis of the agreed-upon narrative rather than of live testimony or documentary evidence.

It may be objected that juries, at least, are too unsophisticated to be able to grasp the facts of a case from a written narrative. I agree that most jurors are insufficiently sophisticated in matters of business and economics to be able to decide antitrust cases intelligently, but I do not agree that their ability to decide such cases is enhanced by their being made to sit through a trial lasting months at which they are forbidden to take notes, or even to discuss the case among themselves until its conclusion. The parade of live witnesses and the introduction of raw documents (which jurors I believe almost never read, although excerpts may be read to them by counsel or witnesses) create a spurious immediacy that may convince the juror that he really understands the case— but what he is seeing is theater, not business reality.

The procedural reformation that I have suggested is worth making for its own sake, and regardless of any changes which might be made in the substantive doctrines of antitrust. Needless to say, however, it would also facilitate the introduction into antitrust trial procedure of the kind of flexible inquiry into the economic consequences of challenged practices advocated in earlier chapters of this book.

In closing, I would like to recapitulate very briefly the main theme of the book. As a result of neglect of economic principles, the judges, lawyers, and enforcement personnel who are responsible for giving meaning to the vague language of the antitrust statutes have fashioned a body of substantive doctrine and a system of sanctions and procedures that are poorly suited to carrying out the fundamental objectives of antitrust policy—the promotion of competition and efficiency. The per se rule against price fixing, the merger rules, the rules governing competition in the distribution of goods, the tie-in rule, the use of structural remedies, the trial of antitrust cases according to methods of proof developed hundreds of years ago—these and the other features of the antitrust system examined in this book reflect above all an endeavor, sometimes ingenious and sometimes pathetic, to set antitrust free from any dependence on economic principles. The endeavor has failed; the system is in disarray. The time has come to rethink antitrust with the aid of economics. This book is offered as a contribution to the process of rethinking.

Appendix: An Introduction to the Formal Analysis of Monopoly

The main purpose of this appendix is to introduce the reader to some of the simpler geometrical and mathematical methods by which the monopoly problem can be analyzed, in the hope that lawyers, law students, and other noneconomists can be helped to read the economic literature relating to antitrust. A subsidiary purpose of the appendix is to establish a little (but only a little) more rigorously some of the propositions asserted in previous chapters.

The first question we consider is how the monopolist decides at what price to sell his product. His decision process is illustrated in figure 2. Three curves are drawn in Figure 2. The first is the demand curve, *dd*. A demand curve shows the different prices at which the monopolist's product will sell, depending on how much he produces. The negative (downward) slope of the demand curve

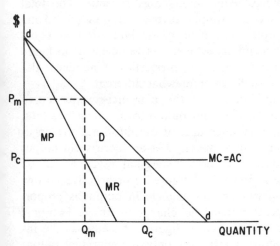

Fig. 2

as one moves from left to right reflects the fact that lower prices are associated with larger quantities demanded and higher prices with smaller quantities demanded. The higher the price of the product relative to other products, the greater is the incentive of the consumer to substitute other, and now cheaper, products. Conversely, the lower the price of the product relative to substitutes, the greater is the incentive of the consumer to switch to the product from the now dearer substitutes. The relationship between price and quantity operates in both directions. A reduction in quantity supplied will lead to an increase in price in order to ration the smaller quantity among consumers, while an increase in the quantity supplied will lead to a reduction in the price in order to attract the marginal consumer.

Several further points should be noted about the demand curve. First, it is a schedule of relative, not absolute, prices. A rise in the average price level in the economy (i.e., inflation) will not cause a movement up the demand curve for particular products; the relative prices of products are not affected by inflation. Second, the negative relationship between price and quantity assumes that other things which might affect the demand for the good are being held constant. For example, if the demand for a particular product rises as people's incomes rise, one might well observe a simultaneous increase in both the price and the quantity sold. Third, while the demand curve is to the consumer a schedule of prices, to the producers it is a schedule of average revenue. The total revenues of the industry are simply prices times output. Total revenue divided by output—i.e., average revenue—is thus equal to price. Fourth, the demand curve need not be linear as in figure 2. The mathematical (and economic) properties of nonlinear demand curves are, as we shall see, somewhat different.

The second curve in figure 2 is the marginal-revenue curve (MR). Marginal revenue is the contribution to the industry's total revenues made by selling another unit of output. Since the negative slope of the demand curve means that an increase in output is associated with a decline in price, marginal revenue will be positive (above the horizontal axis in figure 2) or negative (below the axis) depending on whether the change in output is proportionately smaller or greater than the change in price. Marginal revenue is everywhere below price in figure 2 because as the industry increases its output it sells not only the marginal output at a lower price but *all* of its output at that price. This assumes, of course, that the industry cannot sell the marginal output at the price that the marginal purchaser will pay and the rest of its output at the former, and higher, price. We discuss a bit later the consequences of relaxing this assumption; for now, our analysis focuses on the monopolist who is constrained either by law (or more precisely by the costs of violating the law) or by the (other) costs of preventing arbitrage from selling at more than one price.

The third curve in figure 2 is the industry's marginal cost (*MC*) at various levels of output. Marginal cost is the increase in total cost if output is expanded by one unit. There are also fixed costs, that is, costs that are independent of output. Even if the industry stopped producing, the fixed costs (e.g., the cost of servicing the industry's long-term debt) would remain. We are not especially interested in the fixed costs, however. By definition they do not enter into the producer's decision as to what quantity to sell, and therefore what price to charge, for he cannot alter these costs by his decision on quantity or price; they are independent of the scale of his activity. So we shall assume for convenience that all of the costs of our industry are variable costs reflected in the marginal-cost curve.

Another way of justifying the exclusion of fixed costs is to observe that, in the long run, *all* costs are marginal; all, that is, depend ultimately on what decisions are made with regard to the output of the product. When a plant wears out, it will be replaced only if the expected revenues from the plant are greater than its total costs. From this perspective, the cost of building the plant is a variable rather than a fixed cost (and will enter into marginal cost) since it will determine how much (if anything) will be produced. We can therefore think of *MC* as the industry long-run marginal-cost curve.[1]

In figure 2, *MC* is a horizontal line. This implies that the cost of producing a unit of output is the same regardless of the number of units produced. Although the principal reason for assuming a constant-costs supply curve is expository convenience—and nothing vital to the analysis would be altered by dropping the assumption—it probably approximates the cost conditions facing many, or even most, industries within a broad range of possible

1. On the difference between short-run and long-run marginal costs see also pp. 191–92 supra.

outputs. But this is *not* because individual firms typically have constant costs. That would imply that firm size was indeterminate —a firm that produced one automobile a year would have the same long-run marginal costs as a firm that produced 250,000 automobiles, or for that matter 10,000,000.

To reconcile a constant-costs industry curve with a U-shaped firm-cost curve, it is necessary to introduce the concept of average cost, i.e., total cost divided by output. With a horizontal marginal-cost curve and no fixed costs, average cost is identical to marginal cost at all outputs. But if marginal cost (say) rises with output, average cost will rise too (though more slowly, just as price, i.e., average revenue, falls more slowly than marginal revenue).

In an industry that has many firms, all facing identical cost conditions and therefore having identical average-cost curves, each firm will produce the output at which its average costs are minimized, for at any other level of output its average costs would be higher than those of other firms and it would be in danger of being underpriced. Thus the industry marginal-cost curve will be a horizontal line lying along the locus of the minimum points of the firms' (identical) average-cost curves. This is the industry's marginal-cost curve because, were it necessary to expand the output of the industry, this would be accomplished by the entry of one or more firms which would produce at the point of their lowest average costs, the same point at which the existing firms are producing. Thus the cost of the additional units would be the same as those of the existing units, and the industry's marginal costs are constant.[2]

2. If there are only a few firms in the industry, the analysis becomes a bit more complicated. Unless the total demand for the industry's output can be divided by the cost-minimizing output of each firm to yield a whole number, it will be impossible to satisfy that demand at a cost equal to the minimum average cost of each firm. If, for example, the total demand for the industry's output is 100,000 units but the cost-minimizing output of each firm in the industry is 15,000 units, there is no way in which the total demand can be satisfied by production at the lowest average cost of each firm. One firm will have to produce at a level of output at which its average costs are not minimized. Moreover, even if the current output of the industry is being produced at an average cost equal to the lowest average cost of each of the (identical) firms comprising the industry, should it become necessary to expand the output of the industry to satisfy a growth in demand it may be impossible to do so without incurring higher costs. The increase in demand may not be great enough to justify the entry of a new

The optimal monopoly price in figure 2 is given by the intersection of *MR* and *MC*. Profit is simply the difference between total revenues and total costs and is maximized by carrying production to the point where the last unit produced contributes just as much to total revenues as to total costs—that is, where marginal revenue and marginal cost are equal. At any output to the left of Q_m (the output corresponding to the profit-maximizing price, P_m) the monopolist could increase his profits by expanding output, for at such points marginal revenue lies above marginal cost, meaning that additional output adds more to total revenue than to total cost and thus generates additional profit. To the right of Q_m the relationship is reversed. Producing quantity Q_m thus maximizes the difference between the area under the marginal-revenue curve and the area under the marginal-cost curve—i.e., maximizes profits.

If the industry were organized competitively and its marginal-cost curve were identical to that of the monopolist, output would be carried to point Q_c in figure 2, the point at which price (P_c) is just equal to marginal cost. Assume that the market contains many firms of roughly equal size so that the output of any single firm is small relative to the total output of the market, and that the firms do not coordinate their price and output decisions. To a firm whose decisions to increase or reduce output do not (measurably) affect the market price because the firm's output is very small relative to that of the market as a whole, the demand curve appears as a horizontal line at the market price and the firm's marginal-revenue curve is identical to its demand curve. That is, the firm assumes that every additional sale is made at the same price as the existing sale (which is why the demand curve appears to the firm as a horizontal rather than as a downward-sloping line) and increases its total revenues by the full amount of the sales price (which is why its marginal-revenue curve is a horizontal line identical to the demand curve). Each seller in a market of many sellers that are not colluding will continue expanding his output along what he perceives to be his horizontal demand curve

firm that would produce the level of output at which its average costs would be minimized. Rather, it may be necessary to satisfy the increase in demand by an expansion in the output of one or more of the existing firms in the market, resulting in an increase in the average and marginal costs of the industry.

until the combined effect of all of the sellers' actions in increasing the supply of the industry's product depresses price to the point at which it is equal to the industry's marginal-cost curve. At this point, the sellers will cease to expand their output, since if they produced more units they would have to sell below their costs.

It is plain from figure 2 that monopoly results in a lower output than competition, as well as generating monopoly profits which are equal to the rectangle denoted *MP*. The reduction in output generates a subtle form of social loss measured by the triangle labeled *D*. This represents the loss in value to those consumers who at the competitive price would buy the product, but at the monopoly price are deflected to substitutes. The fact that the demand curve lies above the marginal-cost curve in this region indicates that the value of the product to consumers who no longer purchase it exceeds the opportunity costs of producing it. This extra value is lost when the product is monopolized, and it is not recouped by the monopolist (or anyone else), for the monopolist obtains no revenues from output that he does not produce.

Thus far we have assumed that the monopolist is constrained to sell at a single price. He would, of course, prefer to vary his price with the intensity of the consumer desire for his product, charging more to those who have poor substitutes for it and less to those who have good substitutes. Suppose that the monopolist can discriminate in price perfectly and costlessly: every sale is made at a price equal to the value that the consumer places on the purchase and no costs are incurred in ascertaining those values or in dealing separately with each consumer over each unit of output purchased. Then the monopolist will proceed down the demand curve from its intersection with the vertical axis to its intersection with the marginal-cost curve, and the demand curve in that interval will become a schedule of different prices for each unit of output. The results of perfect price discrimination are compared with those of single-price monopoly in figure 3.

Observe that the output of the perfectly discriminating monopolist is identical to that of the competitive industry. Thus, perfect price discrimination eliminates the social loss of monopoly that we earlier denoted by *D*. However, *MP*, monopoly profits, are greater under perfect price discrimination than under single-price monopoly. Indeed *MP* in figure 3(b) is larger than *MP* + *D* in figure 3(a), implying, according to our assumption that ex-

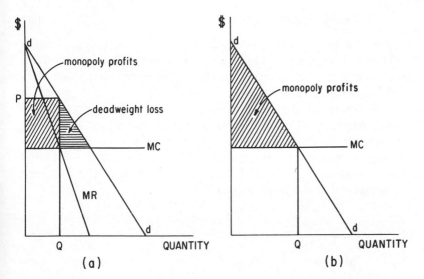

Fig. 3

pected monopoly profits are transformed into social costs,[3] that the social costs of perfect price discrimination are actually greater than those of single-price monopoly even though the output of the perfectly price-discriminating monopolist is identical to that under competition.

Let us now derive the major results of the analysis of monopoly pricing algebraically, beginning with the simple case in which the demand curve can, as in figures 2 and 3, be approximated by a straight rather than a curved line. The algebraic form of a negatively sloped straight line such as *dd* in figure 2 is $a - bQ$, where a is the intercept on the vertical axis, $-b$ is the slope of the curve (and is negative because the slope of a downward-curving line is negative), and Q is the independent variable. Since the demand curve is a price schedule we can write $P = a - bQ$. The marginal-cost curve is simply C, by our assumption of constant costs. Since total revenue equals price times quantity, since total cost (under our assumption that there are no fixed costs) equals marginal cost times quantity, and since profit is simply the difference between total revenue and total cost, we can write

3. See pp. 11–13 supra.

$$\pi = (a - bQ)Q - CQ, \tag{1}$$

where π is profit. The monopolist's goal is to sell that quantity (Q) of the product at which his profits (π) will be maximized, and we can use elementary calculus to determine what value of Q will maximize π. Since π is a function of Q (i.e., our choice of Q will determine the value of π), we set the first derivative of π with respect to Q equal to zero. The geometric equivalent of this is shown in figure 4. The point where the function π of Q attains its highest point (i.e., maximum profits) is the point where the first derivative (i.e., slope) of the profit function is equal to zero (a horizontal line has no slope).[4]

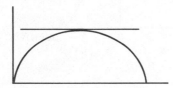

Fig. 4

Using a standard formula which can be found in any elementary calculus text,[5] we differentiate π with respect to Q to obtain the first derivative, yielding

$$\frac{d\pi}{dQ} = a - 2bQ - C. \tag{2}$$

Setting this equal to zero and adding C to each side of the resulting equation we obtain

$$a - 2bQ = C. \tag{3}$$

4. As a detail, but an important one, note that merely knowing that the slope of a function is equal to zero doesn't tell you whether the function is at a maximum or minimum point. For a maximum, the second derivative of the function must be negative (i.e., changing from positive to negative at its extreme point). That is, the slope of the slope must be negative. (One's upward movement slows as one approaches the top of a hill and turns negative as one begins to descend the hill on the other side.) This means that, in the area of the putative maximum, profits as a function of quantity produced must be increasing at a decreasing rate. Since the second derivative of our profit function (equation [1]) is negative ($-2b$), the "second order" condition for a maximum is indeed satisfied.

5. Particularly good for people interested in economics is Alpha C. Chiang, *Fundamental Methods of Mathematical Economics* (2d ed. 1974).

The left-hand side of equation (3) is the first derivative of total revenue, or marginal revenue; the right-hand side is the first derivative of total cost, or marginal cost (this can be verified by applying the formula for obtaining a first derivative directly to our expressions for total revenue and total cost, $(a - bQ)Q$ and CQ). In short, profits are maximized when $MR = MC$. Observe that the slope of the marginal-revenue curve, $-2b$, is exactly twice the slope of the demand curve $(-b)$. At a price of zero, Q is equal to a/b, while at a marginal revenue of zero Q is equal to $a/2b$. That is, when the demand curve is linear, the marginal-revenue curve intersects the horizontal axis exactly midway between the origin and the intersection of the demand curve with that axis—as shown in figure 2.

It will be useful to have a more general expression for the optimal price and quantity under monopoly, one that does not depend on the assumption that the demand curve has a particular shape (other than that it be negatively sloped and differentiable at all relevant points). The more general expression for the monopolist's profit function is

$$\pi = P(Q)Q - CQ, \tag{4}$$

where $P(Q)$ (or P for short) is the demand curve (i.e., price is written as a function of the quantity demanded). Taking the first derivative of π with respect to Q and setting the result equal to zero, we have

$$\frac{d\pi}{dQ} = \frac{dP}{dQ}Q + P - C = 0, \tag{5}$$

or

$$\frac{dp}{dQ}Q + P = C. \tag{6}$$

The left-hand side of the equation again denotes marginal revenue and the right-hand side marginal cost.[6]

6. Now let us check the second-order condition. The second derivative of (4) with respect to Q is

$$\frac{d^2\pi}{dQ^2} = \frac{d^2P}{dQ^2}Q + 2\frac{dP}{dQ}. \tag{i}$$

How are we to know whether this expression is negative? To begin with, we know that the second term is negative since the slope of the demand curve (dP/dQ) is negative. To be sure that the entire expression is negative,

Let us now introduce a new symbol, ϵ, signifying the elasticity of demand for the monopolist's product with respect to price. As we know from Chapter 1, ϵ represents the proportional impact on Q of a small change in P, and is thus, strictly speaking, negative; but for the sake of simplicity we will express ϵ as a positive number. The mathematical formula for ϵ (expressed as a positive number) is

$$\epsilon = -\frac{dQ}{dP} \cdot \frac{P}{Q}. \tag{7}$$

Substituting this into (6) we obtain

$$P(1 - \frac{1}{\epsilon}) = C. \tag{8}$$

Since if the market were competitive, price would equal marginal cost, C can be relabeled P_c, the competitive price. And since P in

---

however, we must assume that the second derivative of the demand curve (d^2P/dQ^2) is negative, i.e., that demand falls at a diminishing rate with greater output. This assumption makes the first term in (i) negative, and thus assures that (6) states the conditions for profit maximization.

The analysis becomes somewhat more complicated if we relax the assumption of constant costs. Then (4) becomes

$$\pi = P(Q)Q - C(Q)Q \tag{4'}$$

and (6)

$$\frac{dP}{dQ} Q + P = C + \frac{dC}{dQ} Q \tag{6'}$$

and (i)

$$\frac{d^2\pi}{dQ^2} = \frac{d^2P}{dQ^2} Q + 2\frac{dp}{dQ} - \frac{d^2C}{dP^2} - 2\frac{dC}{dQ}. \tag{ii}$$

To assure that (ii) is negative and thus that the second-order condition for a maximum is satisfied, we must make the additional assumption that marginal cost is increasing at an increasing rate. This assumption will make the third and fourth terms in the expression negative.

Incidentally, the analysis is unchanged if we treat quantity as a function of price rather than price as a function of quantity. Rewriting (4) as

$$\pi = Q(P)P - CQ(P), \tag{4''}$$

differentiating with respect to P, setting the result equal to zero, and rearranging terms, we obtain

$$\frac{dQ}{dP} P + Q = \frac{dQ}{dP} C. \tag{6''}$$

If we then multiply both sides of the equation by dP/dQ, we are back to (6).

equation (8) is of course the monopoly price, we shall relabel it P_m and now rewrite (8) as

$$P_c = P_m \left(1 - \frac{1}{\epsilon}\right), \tag{9}$$

or equivalently,

$$\frac{P_m}{P_c} = \frac{\epsilon}{\epsilon - 1}. \tag{10}$$

From (10) it is clear that, the more elastic the demand for the monopolist's product, the closer together the monopoly and competitive prices will be. If demand were infinitely elastic, the right-hand side of (10) would be equal to 1 and the monopoly price would be no higher than the monopoly price. If instead $\epsilon = 2$, the monopoly price would be twice as high as the competitive price.

Observe that ϵ *must* be greater than 1 in the monopoly case.[7] The reason is that marginal revenue in (8) is given by $P(1 - 1/\epsilon)$, and would be zero if $\epsilon = 1$ and negative if $\epsilon < 1$. Since marginal cost is bound to be positive, the optimal monopoly price cannot be one that yields zero or negative marginal revenue. Put differently, a monopolist will never operate in a region of the demand curve in which the elasticity of demand is less than or equal to 1.

We have thus far been considering the elasticity of demand at the monopoly price. Suppose that the elasticity of demand varies along the demand curve. This is quite possible. Indeed, where the demand curve is linear, the elasticity of demand is different at every point on the demand curve. For example, demand at all points on the demand curve in figure 2 to the right of the intersection of MR with the horizontal axis is inelastic, for at all of these points an increase in output would yield negative marginal revenue. At all points to the left of this point demand is elastic (i.e., greater than 1), because in this region increases in output generate positive marginal revenues. The formulas that we have been using do not tell us which markets are likely to be monopo-

---

7. If $\epsilon < 1$ the right-hand side of (10) would become negative, which would make the equation fail, since the left-hand side cannot be negative—firms do not charge negative prices. If $\epsilon = 1$ we have division by zero in (10), which is undefined, or if we use equation (9), a monopoly price of zero.

lized because that depends on the shape of the demand curve above the competitive price.

We can use equation (10) to answer questions about how the monopolist will react to changes in his environment. It can easily be shown that, if the elasticity of demand increases, and other things remain unchanged, he will reduce his price; if the elasticity decreases, he will raise his price.[8] Equally clearly, if the monopolist's marginal cost declines (other things being the same), he will reduce his price, for MC is equal to P_c in (10), and if P_c falls while nothing else changes, P_m must fall by the same proportion to maintain the equality between the left-hand and right-hand sides of (10). Conversely, if his marginal cost increases he will make a proportionately equal price increase. The amounts but not the directions of these price changes will be different if we relax the assumption of constant marginal costs.

The assumption that the elasticity of demand is unchanged by the monopolist's price adjustments implies, of course, that the demand curve in the relevant region has a constant elasticity. Assume instead that the demand curve is linear. As mentioned, the elasticity of demand is different at every point along a linear demand curve—higher as one moves up the curve and lower as one moves down it. Accordingly, the monopolist's initial attempt to adjust to a reduction in his marginal cost by reducing his price will bring him into a region of the demand curve in which the demand for his product is less elastic than it was at his former price. The ϵ in equation (10) will be lower, and this will cause him to readjust his price upward. Thus, the monopolist confronting a linear demand will respond to a reduction in his marginal costs by reducing his price by a smaller percentage than the cost reduction; conversely, if his costs rise, he will raise his price by a smaller percentage than the cost increase. Accordingly, unless we

8. $\dfrac{dP_m/P_c}{d\epsilon} = \dfrac{\epsilon^2 - \epsilon}{(\epsilon - 1)^2}.$ (iii)

This expression, which denotes the effect on the ratio of the monopoly to the competitive price of a small change in ϵ, is greater than zero for all $\epsilon > 1$ (meaning that an increase in the elasticity of demand at the monopoly price will increase the ratio of that price to the competitive price, and hence, if the competitive price ($=MC$) is unchanged, will cause the monopoly price to be increased), because the denominator is positive (being the square of some number) and the numerator is positive so long as $\epsilon > 1$.

(implausibly) posit a demand curve in which elasticity decreases as price increases, a monopolized industry will never make a proportionately greater price change in response to a cost change than a competitive industry responding to the identical change would make; and it will sometimes make a proportionately smaller change than the competitive industry, in which $P = MC$ so that an increase in MC will always lead to an identical increase in P, assuming constant marginal costs. This analysis provides some support for the proposition mentioned in chapter 4 that the price fluctuations of a monopolized industry will have a smaller amplitude than those of a competitive industry.

Now let us ask what happens to the monopoly price if demand declines with the elasticity of demand unchanged, meaning that at any price the quantity demanded is less by a proportionately equal amount. The answer turns on the shape of the marginal-cost curve. If the monopolist has constant costs his price will not change. Remember that the only determinants of the monopoly price in equation (10) are P_c (i.e., marginal cost) and elasticity of demand. If both the elasticity of demand and the marginal cost are unchanged by the shift of the demand curve, the monopoly price must be unchanged too; the monopolist simply sells fewer units of output under the new conditions of demand. Suppose, however, that his marginal costs rise with output; then a decline in demand will lead to a reduction in the monopoly price. Clearly, the monopolist cannot sell the same output at the same price as he did before demand declined, and his first reaction, as in the preceding case, will be to reduce his output. But since marginal costs rise with output, the reduction in output will result in a lower marginal cost, so he will reduce his price. If his marginal costs fall with output, then when the monopolist reduces his output to adjust to the fall in demand he will find that his marginal costs are higher, and so by (10) he will raise his price. These reactions are shown geometrically in figure 5, where, for the sake of simplicity, linear demand curves are used and a 50 per cent decline in demand is assumed.

We are interested not only in the relationship between the monopoly and the competitive price but also, and more, in the social costs of monopoly, both the loss that results from the lower output under monopoly (a loss we denote by D) and the additional loss that results from the transformation of the expected profits of monopoly into social costs of obtaining (or maintaining, or pre-

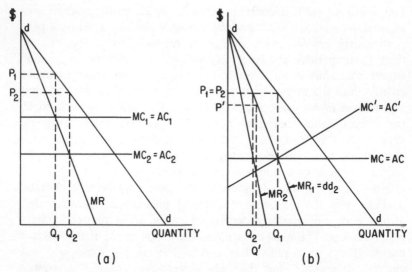

Fig. 5

venting) monopoly. Moreover, in computing these costs, we do not want to continue to assume that the price charged by the monopolist or cartel is the optimum monopoly price determined with reference to the elasticity of demand for the industry's product. The elasticity of demand facing the monopolist or the cartel may well be greater than the elasticity of the industry demand curve, for example because the monopolist or cartel does not have 100 per cent of the market. There are also the costs of monopolizing to be considered—these may rise with the price charged (e.g., the danger of punishment may be greater at higher prices) and thereby induce the monopolist or cartel to charge less than the optimum price computed without reference to these costs. It is therefore useful to have formulas for the social cost of monopoly in which the monopolistic price increase is not treated as determined automatically by the elasticity of demand for the industry's product, although, as we shall see, that elasticity remains important in gauging the social cost.

By the assumption that monopoly profits equal social costs of monopoly, the total social costs of monopoly (C) in figure 6 are simply $D + MP$, and since $D \cong \frac{1}{2} \Delta P \Delta Q$ and $MP = \Delta P(Q_c - \Delta Q)$, the relative sizes of D and MP are given by

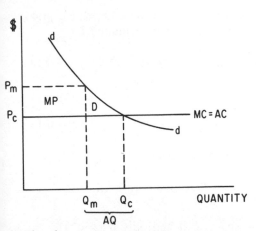

Fig. 6

$$\frac{D}{MP} \cong \frac{\Delta Q}{2(Q_c - \Delta Q)}. \tag{11}$$

The ratio can also be expressed in terms of the elasticity of demand for the product in question at the competitive price and the percentage increase in price brought about by monopolization (p). Since $\epsilon = \frac{\Delta Q}{\Delta P} \cdot \frac{P_c}{Q_c}$ and $p = \frac{\Delta P}{P_c}$ (which can be rewritten $P_c = \frac{\Delta P}{p}$), $\epsilon = \frac{\Delta Q}{pQ_c}$. Therefore, $\Delta Q = \epsilon p Q_c$ and $Q_c = \frac{\Delta Q}{\epsilon p}$, and (11) can be rewritten as

$$\frac{D}{MP} \cong \frac{p}{2(1/\epsilon - p)}. \tag{12}$$

The partial derivatives of this expression are

$$\frac{\partial(D/MP)}{\partial \epsilon} \cong \frac{2p}{(2 - 2p\epsilon)^2} > 0; \tag{13}$$

$$\frac{\partial(D/MP)}{\partial p} \cong \frac{2\epsilon}{(2 - 2p\epsilon)^2} > 0.$$

In words, the ratio of D to MP is smaller, the less elastic the demand for the industry's product at the competitive price and the smaller the percentage price increase over the competitive level. At moderate elasticities and percentage price increases, D is only a small fraction of MP (and hence of the total costs of monopoly). For example, at an elasticity of 1 and a price increase over the competitive level of 10 percent, D is only .056 MP.

Using R_c to denote total sales revenues at the competitive price, C, the total social costs of monopoly, is approximated by

$$C = D + MP = pR_c - \frac{1}{2}\Delta P\Delta Q \qquad (14)$$

or equivalently

$$C = D + MP = R_c(p - \frac{1}{2}\epsilon p^2). \qquad (15)$$

The partial derivates of C are (approximately)

$$\frac{\partial C}{\partial R_c} = p - \frac{1}{2}\epsilon p^2 > 0 \text{ if and only if } \epsilon p < 2;$$

$$\frac{\partial C}{\partial p} = R_c(1 - \epsilon p) > 0 \text{ if and only if } \epsilon p < 1;$$

$$\frac{\partial C}{\partial \epsilon} = \frac{-R_c p^2}{2} < 0.$$

In words, the social costs of monopoly will usually—not always —be higher, the larger the industry's sales revenues at the competitive price and output and the greater the percentage price increase over the competitive level. They will always be higher, the less elastic the demand for the product at the competitive price —the costs of monopoly being greatest when demand is totally inelastic at the competitive price.

Formulas (12) and (15) are accurate only for small changes in the price level, and since monopolization might result in large price increases (11) and (14) remain useful. For purposes of empirical estimation, it is helpful to have two additional formulas: one for the case where data on the deadweight loss, the elasticity of demand, and the monopoly price increase are available and the elasticity of demand is assumed to be constant, and the other for the case where data on the monopoly price increase, the monopoly output, and the elasticity of demand at the monopoly price are available and the demand curve is assumed to be linear.

To derive the formula for the second case,[9] we begin with the slope of the demand curve at the monopoly price, which can be written (from the formula for ϵ) as

9. The formula for the first case may be found in Richard A. Posner, "The Social Costs of Monopoly and Regulation," 83 *J. Pol. Econ.* 807, 814 (1975).

$$\frac{\Delta Q}{\Delta P} = \frac{\epsilon Q_m}{P_m}.$$
(16)

Since the slope of a linear demand curve is constant, (16) can be used to find ΔQ and hence C and D/MP:

$$C = R_m(1 - \frac{P_c}{P_m})[1 + \frac{1}{2}\epsilon\,(1 - \frac{P_c}{P_m})];^{10}$$
(17)

$$\frac{D}{MP} = \frac{\epsilon(1 - \frac{P_c}{P_m})}{2}.$$
(18)

In the special case where the firm is able to charge the optimum monopoly price,

$$C = \frac{3}{2}\frac{R_m}{\epsilon};^{11}$$
(19)

$$\frac{D}{MP} = \frac{1}{2}.$$
(20)

10. R_m is total sales revenue at the monopoly price and output. The intermediate steps are as follows:

From Figure A1 it is obvious that

$$C = D + MP = \Delta P(Q_m + \frac{1}{2}\Delta Q).$$
(i)

Using (16), we can rewrite (i) as

$$C = \Delta P(Q_m + \frac{\frac{1}{2}\epsilon\Delta P}{P_m}).$$
(ii)

Since R_m is simply P_mQ_m, (ii) can be rewritten as

$$C = \Delta P\frac{R_m}{P_m}(1 + \frac{\frac{1}{2}\epsilon\Delta P}{P_m}).$$
(iii)

The final step is to note that

$$\frac{\Delta P}{P_m} = \frac{P_m - P_c}{P_m} = 1 - \frac{P_c}{P_m},$$
(iv)

which can be substituted into (iii) to yield (17).

11. This is obtained simply by substituting the formula for the optimal monopoly price, $P_c = P_m(1 - \frac{1}{\epsilon})$, into (17). I am grateful to Göran Skogh for having pointed out the mathematical error in the version of (19) that appears in my article, "The Social Costs of Monopoly and Regulation," supra note 9, at 815 n.8. The figures in tables 7 and 8, infra in text, have been corrected in accordance with the corrected version of (19).

In tables 7 and 8, I have used equations (17) and (19) to derive estimates of the social costs of monopoly. Table 7 presents estimates of those costs in industries where government regulation has forced prices above competitive levels, and table 8 presents similar estimates for several well-organized (mainly international) private cartels. Such estimates enable us to derive some crude idea of the potential benefits of antitrust policy.

Table 7   Social Costs of Regulation

Industry	Regulatory Price Increase (%)	Elasticity ϵ_1	ϵ_2	Costs (as % of Industry's Sales) C_1	C_2
Physician's services	.40	3.500	0.575	.42	.31
Eyeglasses	.34	0.394	0.450	.39	.24
Milk	.11	10.000	0.339	.15	.10
Motor carriers	.62	2.630	1.140	.57	.30
Oil	.65	2.500	0.900	.60	.32
Airlines	.66	2.500	2.360	.60	.19

Source: Richard A. Posner, "The Social Costs of Monopoly and Regulation," 83 *J. Pol. Econ.* 807, 818 (1975).

Table 8   Social Costs of Cartelization

Industry	Cartel Price Increase (%)	Elasticity ϵ_1	ϵ_2	Costs (as % of Industry's Sales) C_1	C_2
Nitrogen	0.75	2.3256	1.4493	.62	.30
Sugar	0.30	4.3276	0.3390	.36	.22
Aluminum	1.00	2.000	..	.75	...
Aluminum	0.38	3.6311	..	.42	...
Rubber	1.00	2.000	..	.75	...
Electric bulbs	0.37	3.7023	..	.42	...
Copper	0.31	4.2499	..	.36	...
Cast-iron pipe	0.39	3.5641	..	.42	...

Source: Richard A. Posner, "The Social Costs of Monopoly and Regulation," 83 *J. Pol. Econ.* 807, 820 (1975).

Two estimates of elasticity are used in these calculations. One (ϵ_1) is derived from the price-increase data themselves, on the assumption that the industry is charging the optimum monopoly price; the other (ϵ_2) is an independent estimate of elasticity. The estimates of the total social costs of the regulation in question (C_1, where ϵ_1 is the estimate of elasticity used, and C_2, where ϵ_2 is used) are based on the assumption that the industry's demand curve is linear in the relevant region and are expressed as a percentage of the total revenues of the industry.

Plainly, the estimates presented in these two tables, crude as they are, indicate that monopolization can impose on society costs that are very substantial in relation to the output of the monopolized markets. These costs are the economic basis of antitrust policy.

Index